MW00780516

Mar 3, 2023

INTO THE DRAGON'S MOUTH

STORIES FROM AN AMERICAN ARCHITECT WHO CHANGED CHINA

BENJAMIN WOOD

Into The Dragon's Mouth

By Benjamin Wood

ISBN-13: 978-988-8769-62-9

© 2022 Benjamin Wood

BIOGRAPHY & AUTOBIOGRAPHY

EB171

All rights reserved. No part of this book may be reproduced in material form, by any means, whether graphic, electronic, mechanical or other, including photocopying or information storage, in whole or in part. May not be used to prepare other publications without written permission from the publisher except in the case of brief quotations embodied in critical articles or reviews. For information contact info@earnshawbooks.com

Published by Earnshaw Books Ltd. (Hong Kong)

I dedicate this book
to
my children Amy Elizabeth and Travis Roy.

And to
their mother, Sarah.

And to my mentor, Benjamin Casper Thompson,
whose contribution to my life's work is immeasurable.

Forever rest-in-peace, Daniel Ng, Jane Thompson,
Michael McCaskey, and Paul Duffly.
All passed in the past decade. All had hearts of gold,
precious minds, and lifting spirits.

Mothers Day, 2022

Precious Boo boo Amy
and well drawn boy Travis
On the second Sunday
In May
Mothers Day
have you some fun
bathe in rainbow jungles
tap dance Bojangles
My birth angels

Listen not with ears
To an aging Mouseketeer
Why wait for history
not yet here

Teach your dogs to point
Juke the nearest joint
Keep an open mind
Stay outside the lines
Nothing happens for a reason
everything else is out of season
Stay the course but not the date
the On-time Ferry is never late

Sarah's love for you
Forever will endure
And mine
Has no cure

Contents

A single thought can grow into a forest of ideas …
Painting by my son, Travis.

Preamble

My last name is Wood and one of my father's nicknames was Splinter. I am in many ways a chip off the old block. I have spent a lot of time looking up at the sky through the canopies of trees and dreaming of the future. My life, I believe, proves that a single thought can grow into a forest of ideas.

This book chronicles the long journey that delivered a Southerner from America's Deep South onto a great world stage in the mouth of the dragon, the Yangtze River delta. It combines anecdotes describing real incidents with the true confessions of a Deep South transplant. I am an American who played a major part in making the remarkable, world city of Shanghai leap to a new reality. In 1998 a bold visionary from Hong Kong invited a former supersonic Phantom Jet pilot to come to "join up" and fly "tight formation" with him, and together we made history, creating Shanghai's Xintiandi, China's first world-class landmark urban entertainment and cultural destination. That project and others I have designed during over two decades of architectural practice in post-Cultural Revolution China, have changed the lives of hundreds of millions of ordinary, middle-class people.

I considered using a ghost writer to put this book together, but then remembered a line from a Leonard Cohen song, "Like a drunk in a midnight choir, I have tried in my way to be free." Come hell or high water I am always going to sing my own solo.

The way I have structured this book is not chronological, it's both vertical and horizontal with lateral detours into other times and places wherever appropriate. Rigid hierarchical structures have always been the bane of my life, and I prefer to have stories and topics ricocheting off each other. To prevent readers from getting motion sickness, let me give you a brief run-through of the extraordinary life I have had to date.

I was born in 1947 in Roswell, a small town north of Atlanta, Georgia, the eldest son and second of three children. We attended public, racially segregated, schools, then in 1961, at age fourteen, we moved to Alexandria, Virginia as my father, Roy Wood, had been appointed by President John F. Kennedy to serve as Special Assistant to the Secretary of the Department of Interior. In 1968, I was studying at North Carolina State University majoring in Civil Engineering, and enrolled the following year at the University of Colorado Law School in Boulder, Colorado. Midway through the second semester, with at best six months before induction into the US Army, I was granted a "leave of absence" and moved to Durango, Colorado for a long summer with two former high school friends. We borrowed enough money to purchase and renovate an abandoned Victorian House, and for a short while that was home. But by September, a decision had to be made, and rather than be drafted and shipped to Vietnam, I volunteered to serve in the United States Air Force. In 1971, I graduated from USAF Officer's School and became one of the youngest pilots ever to fly an RF4 Phantom fighter jet. Before leaving for a USAF base in Germany, I married my high school sweetheart, Sarah.

I left active duty in 1976 after volunteering for an "early out" program for Air Force pilots following the end of the Vietnam War, but we stayed on in Europe for nine months and established an Outdoor Adventure School for young airmen in Hitler's alpine retreat, the Eagle's Nest. Back in the US, we moved into the house in Durango, and bought and renovated an historic Victorian building in the nearby former goldmining town of Silverton. It had been the French Bakery, and we turned it into a restaurant and mountaineering store. In 1978, on a trip back east to visit relatives, I was inspired by a visit to IM Pei's East Wing of the National Gallery of Art in Washington DC to become an architect.

In 1980, soon after the birth of our first child, we sold the Silverton property and moved to Cambridge, Massachusetts so I could I attend the MIT Graduate School of Architecture. I graduated in 1984 and went to work for my first and only employer in the field of architecture, Benjamin Thompson. Ben retired in 1994, and I formed a new practice in partnership with his wife, Jane, then left that partnership to form a new firm with Carlos Zapata in 1998. In that year, together, we won two important commissions: we began plans to renovate Soldier Field, the home of the Chicago Bears, and also started the planning for the Xintiandi cultural entertainment district in Shanghai. Construction began the following year and that is when I moved to Shanghai. I have lived and worked in Shanghai ever since, and what a ride it's been.

A warning to readers, if there are any other than family and friends: I am a non-recovering, incorrigible reprobate; a hopelessly romantic, aging relic, guilty of every sin in the book. A few stories herein include untoward profane admonishments of politicians, other architects, and assorted progenitors of inhumane passion plays. I use unsophisticated, crude, and coarse language when the shoe fits. My childhood friends used the N-word to describe Brazil nut "toes." Pancake mix came in a box with a picture on the front of a plump, aproned, Aunt Jemimah with a blue bandana scarf.

I confess to rubbing too many words together when writing this memoir. I write like I design, tripping over memory logs, and bumping into life-drawn trees, while navigating a forest of ideas. To stay on point and remain motivated, I draw on literary, cinematic, artistic, musical, and governance paradigm sources. This is not a book about architecture. It is a memoir. A life of cultivating serendipity led me to the dragon's mouth, determined what happened next, and has kept me here for twenty-four years and counting. One day, it may cause me to leave.

I once visited Cuba and went to every bar in Old Havana that claimed to have been a Hemingway favorite. All had one thing in common, they were places full of characters with great stories to tell about the people and the places they love. Life has given me many adventures, only some of which are to be found in this book. If I am still to be found, please visit my small martini bar in Shanghai and I will share even more tall tales with you. But only if you share some with me too. Without you, there would be no new ideas. So kids, *le bon ton ru lon*. Let the good times roll.

The Nellans and Wood kids, muddy all.

1

Waiting on a Yellow Bus

My family home was a pre-Depression Era farmhouse renovated by my father. Mother cooked on a white enamel range, frying chicken and okra, my father's favorite combination, in a deep, cast-iron skillet. My mother cooked nothing exotic. Spaghetti and meat balls was the only Italian dish she knew how to make. Her cupboard did not include any imported products, and cheese was processed Kraft cheddar or real Wisconsin. No bottle of virgin olive oil was present. Lard made from animal fat greased her frying pans. I never once saw a stick of real butter in our Westinghouse fridge. We did have real cream, however, that floated on the top of local unpasteurized buttermilk. We spread artificially bright yellow margarine across white toast and homemade buttermilk biscuits. When we were toddlers, my brother and I used to spend hours playing in a sandbox visible from the window over the kitchen sink. My mother always had a big smile on her face when she came out of the kitchen to tell us that if we dug a hole deep enough we would end up in China. She was right.

The farmhouse was built atop a gentle rise, and on a clear day we could see downtown Atlanta, nineteen miles to the south. Tangible artifacts of a pre-Civil War plantation culture, and a postwar independent farming society, were scattered over thousands of acres that surrounded our 26-acre homestead. Second-growth timber, active and fallow, tillable land, briar patches, washed-out gullies, rotting sawdust and pine bark piles, and abandoned garbage dumps encircled us. All were waiting to be explored by a skinny, tan, blond, blue-eyed, and barefooted boy, along with his sister and brother. A seemingly endless patchwork of fields, forests, rich fodder for hand-hewn outdoor playrooms, lured us. We retrieved lumber to build tree houses from abandoned barns folded over flat, hidden by thick brambles. We waded naked into old stock ponds on the bare backs of unbridled Shetland ponies. We found quartz Cherokee arrowheads sitting atop red sand, tiny, ridges, carved by the runoff of heavy rains. We followed bubbling brooks upstream, slipping on smooth rock ledges, to track down source springs. We detoured around old hand-dug water well-heads, buried under poison ivy and vicious wire briar. I lost a best friend, a hunting dog, in one of these booby traps. We tipped over plunk-plumbed outhouses next to burned-out ruins of tar paper shacks. We marveled at the stately grandeur of abandoned two-story, doric-columned, floor-less and roof-less plantation palaces. The *Gone with the Wind* days were over, but not forgotten. The KKK had replaced marauding Yankees as most-feared in the Deep South.

I was five, waiting with my mother by the side of a gravel rural road. A yellow school bus would soon come to take me to my first day at Roswell Elementary. My mother leaned down, telling me that not all the kids I played with would be on the bus. A different bus had already picked them up, as the Negro elementary school was many miles away, a county over. Only white children were allowed to go to Roswell Elementary. One day, she said, I'd understand.

Before entering the county's segregated public school system, my brother, sister, and I had all attended private kindergarten. And like the public school system, it was for whites only—not because the owners of the school believed in segregation, but because they had to live with threats of violence from those who did. One of the two owners was my mother, the other was close family friend Katherine Singletary. Both women were strong-willed and well-educated. Both cared deeply about early child development.

Originally the kindergarten was in the home of a family friend, Heath Russian. Heath and her husband lived in Great Oaks, a late-19th Century, stately, red-brick mansion on historic Roswell's Magnolia Street. The grounds surrounding Great Oaks were magnificent. The kindergarten rented the oak-paneled library room. The wealthiest family in Roswell, the Russians owned the town's first television set: a six-inch screen that produced a black and white image. The RCA television had two knobs: power and volume. The TV was built into a custom cabinet, and in a hidden compartment were an array of differently shaped vacuum tubes and high voltage transformers. A single channel of TV signal came from a huge, guy-wired, rooftop aerial.

The TV cabinet was located in the darkest corner of the library. Heath's husband sat there in a big black stuffed leather arm chair, watching television or reading books every evening. He smoked a pipe. I remember he always gave extra boxes of twisted-wire pipe cleaners to the kindergarten. We used them to make stick people and other small figures, sometimes leaving them on his desk alongside our colorful paper cut-outs.

After Heath's husband died young, of heart attack, Great Oaks was put up for sale and the kindergarten had to find a new home. The new location was in the lower level of the County Public Health Clinic, on Alpharetta Highway. Opposite the highway from the clinic there was a small neighborhood sadly

Abandoned Roswell Police Cruiser in Crimson Clover

known as "Nigger Town." Tucked into a sparsely wooded area near the bottom of a badly eroded gully, around forty rusty tin-roofed shacks with tiny rocking chair-porches clustered together under a canopy of red oak crowns. The houses had running water and electricity but no indoor bathrooms, only outhouses.

At the back of the clinic, my mother and her partner built a fenced-in playground with a few swings, a slide, and some climbing equipment. The chain link fence was eight feet high and had a padlocked gate. But soon after the new kindergarten opened, my mother and her partner began leaving the gate open after they went home, so the Black children from across the street could use the playground after the kindergarten closed. They paid a worker at the clinic to lock the gate at the end of the workday. A few months later, both my mother and her friend received anonymous phone calls warning them not to leave the gate open. "Keep the gate locked, or else." They knew the calls were from the KKK.

After reporting the threat to the police, my mother and her partner continued to leave the playground gate open. Three weeks went by. On one Friday night, just before sunset, around sixty cars and pickup trucks drove up onto our front lawn, which stretched down Woodstock Road for 250 or so yards. One of the pickups carried a large wooden cross wrapped in cotton rags. Another carried several barrels of kerosene. As the KKK members walked from their vehicles to greet each other, my mother ran to get my father. Dad told mother to stay in the house with the children, where we stood crowded together behind the thick front door. My mother left a small crack in the doorjamb open, and we could hear our father talking with the Grand Dragon. Hooded, masked, and robed, he told my father the Klansmen were on the way to the Singletary farm, a few miles further down Woodstock Road. He said the cross would be burned—not in our yard, but in the Singletary's.

My father looked down at the Dragon's shoes and uttered: "I know those shoes. They belong to my sons' little league baseball coach." The Grand Dragon, who knew my father worked for the federal government, brought out a tin of chewing tobacco. He reached under his hood to stuff a jowl, turned, and walked away. The sun had set. In darkness, the mob fired up their trucks and were on their way. A few minutes later, we got a call from Katherine. She was watching the Klan fire ritual from her living room window. Her husband, in a wheelchair and wearing an oxygen mask, was holding her hand. The Klansmen left as the flames rose.

The Klan's actions got the playground gate closed. Gravely concerned about their children's safety, retreat seemed like the only option. Four years later, after their children were in public school, my mother and Katherine closed the kindergarten permanently. Their next project was the founding of Roswell's first women's club. There was no explicit manifesto in the club's charter, but the club was founded on the belief that all of humankind was created equal, no matter what. The club flourished, sponsoring activities that benefited the poor and the sick. Meanwhile grown men, many of them pillars of our community, continued to put on their ridiculous Klan bedsheets, and continued to burn crosses.

When we were growing up, we had two mothers. We had a birth mother, of course, but our other mother was a Black woman, Aunt V. She worked for our family, helping my mother with domestic chores and childcare. Just before I became a teenager, Aunt V was accused of resisting arrest and causing bodily injury to a male police officer. The officer was a high-ranking member of our local police force. Like many of his fellow police officers, he was reputed to be a Klansman.

My father hired an attorney to represent Aunt V. who refused compensation and, like Scout's father in *To Kill a Mockingbird*, chose to provide his legal services pro bono. Also like Scout's father, my father too received death threats. At the trial, the attorney called several character witnesses chosen from a long list of white people who knew Aunt V. He advised his defendant to testify in her own defense. Aunt V told her story to a packed court room, every row filled with white people. The Blacks-only section was behind sliding wood panels at the rear of the court. Access to it was through a windowless corridor. Armed guards controlled who was allowed to enter the courthouse using this corridor, and the few Blacks that showed up for the trial were denied entrance.

After being sworn in, Aunt V recounted the events of a recent, late Saturday afternoon in "Nigger Town." Two squad cars pulled up in front of Aunt V's house. Four uniformed policemen got out, three went inside. Aunt V came out immediately, running up to the fourth officer, crying out for help. The fourth officer was the oldest, and the highest-ranking officer. He drew his gun and told Aunt V to bend over the hood of his squad car and put her hands behind her back. When she was face-down on the hood, he holstered his gun and held her there. He accused her of running a brothel in her home, using her daughters as prostitutes. Fifteen minutes later the three policemen appeared on the front porch, dragging Aunt V's three daughters. The daughters were ordered to line-up, facing away from the squad cars, heads up and their legs spread. The three deputies stood on the porch, lewdly imitating sex acts. Aunt V watched in horror.

And then it happened.

Managing to break one arm free, she reached down and grabbed the senior cop by the balls—and twisted. The deputies jumped off the porch and rushed to pull her off. They handcuffed her, forcing her into the back of a squad car, then sped away, sirens wailing and lights flashing. They locked Aunt V in a jailhouse cell with three other Black women. Allowed no visitors except her lawyer, she spent the first of many sleepless, pre-trial days and nights. My mother tried in vain to bring Aunt V a change of clothes. With her daughters under a police order to stay home, my mother reached out, providing them with money to live on.

Knowing that she faced a long sentence and possibly life imprisonment, she sat up straight in the courtroom that day and told the truth. It almost set her free. The white judge mercifully sentenced her to one year in prison and ten years of probation. But justice was not done that day.

I have haunting memories of sitting in the back seat of our family sedan and watching the three daughters come out onto the porch of their "Nigger Town" house to say hello whenever we drove up to fetch or return their mother.

This story may not be as literary as Harper Lee's, but there is some common ground: a deeply emotional account by an innocent person charged with a crime they did not commit. Bo and Aunt V were hapless victims of hate in quiet, tidy communities full of vulgar, racist, white cowards. They were vigilantes on a dark mission: to hunt down and silence a mockingbird's song.

But the story doesn't end there. My sister, Mary Jo, tells of how she was with our mother one summer afternoon when she got a call from a friend to say that a Black man had been hit by a truck and was lying on the side of the Atlanta Highway in the middle of town, with a fractured femur. The town's only medical transportation was the Roswell Funeral Home hearse which doubled as an ambulance. Asked to transport the Black man to Grady Hospital, Sonny refused. He chose to ignore the pleas and offers of money from my mother and three other socially prominent white women. He insisted that if he carried a Black man in the back of his hearse-ambulance, he would be blacklisted by his entire white clientele. Years later, in his old age, our father would often joke: "I'm glad to be cremated just so Sonny can't get his hands on my dead body."

Mother's women's group managed to contract a Negro ambulance service in Atlanta, but were informed it would take hours before an ambulance would be available. Mother and friends were still searching for emergency medical transport when word arrived that the Black man had died on the side of the road. Our mother put down the phone and burst into tears. Over the next few weeks, they raised the money to buy a secondhand station wagon which was re-purposed as Roswell's first Negro Ambulance.

Sky Pilot Phantom Jet

2

Sky Pilot

Whenever I am asked about my success as an architect, the answer is always the same: If you want your clients to choose you to do incredible projects, make sure you can spend hours talking with them about something other than architecture. Telling a story about flying the fastest jet aircraft in the world when you were twenty-two, or living large during the Summer of Love, is a good start. That leaves room for frivolity and humor. I went to Berlin less than a year after the Wall came down in 1989 and at the crack of dawn, I got on a Hotel Berliner courtesy bicycle and pedaled across Potsdamer Platz. When I got to Brandenburg Gate, I stripped naked and walked a few yards into former East Berlin. I repeated this symbolic act of defiance three times before returning to the hotel. Hundreds of stories of this kind have nothing to do with my work in architecture, and I am damn sure that Leonardo da Vinci did not waste time with his patrons telling them he was the world's greatest living painter.

I'm no da Vinci, but I can also "paint." Images and sketches of visible transformations, based on life-drawn adventures and visions of the future, help my patrons imagine and build a better world. Very few architects do that now, but it works because it helps people to transcend the mundane and to conceive of the unexpected.

Some of the stories I tell concern my years as a US Air Force jet fighter pilot during the Cold War in Europe. My father before me had joined the Army and while training to become an Army Artillery Officer, his left eardrum was permanently ruptured when an improperly breached cannon blew up a yard from where he was standing. That bad ear prevented him from joining his Arkansas college classmates on the battlefields of the Second Great War.

My personal American hero was my Uncle Ben. He lied about his age when he volunteered for that war. After serving in seven different theaters of battle, Benjamin H. King retired as the Inspector General of the Air Force. In 1970, a week before my birthday in the depths of the Vietnam War era, an Army sergeant accompanied by a Durango policeman, knocked on my door to serve me my draft notice. They had tracked me down. I was, at least in theory, guilty of draft evasion and my choices were to go to jail or board a bus for Army Basic Training. Not ready to die, lie, or run, I called my mother and got her brother Ben's telephone number.

I was sent to San Antonio, Texas for six weeks of USAF Airman Basic Training. On the last day of Basic, my Uncle picked me up in an Air Force Blue sedan with a one star license plate, drove me to the other side of San Antonio, handed me a sealed folder as I exited his car at the entry to the USAF Officers School admissions center. I exchanged my fatigues for a cadet uniform. Graduating near the top of my class three months later, I received orders to go to Williams Air Force Base in Arizona. I was going to be a pilot. Nineteen months later, I was a Phantom jet aircraft commander.

My first and last operational assignment as a jet pilot with the USAF was with the 38th Tactical Aerial Renaissance Squadron, the primary mission of which was surveillance of NATO's borders with Eastern Europe and the USSR. When not performing this mission, we flew training sorties to remain proficient and combat-ready. Like actual border patrols, these training sorties involved extremely low-level, high-speed flying. Flying a Phantom RF4C was my passport to over one thousand hours of three-dimensional, situationally aware, exact spatial maneuvering, in nature's thinnest of liquids, air. Flying at tree-top level, at speeds of more than 600 mph, through castle-studded hills, great river valleys, and rolling vineyards, was goddam amazing. Not bad experience for a future architect.

At very low levels, the electronic aids that existed during the time of the Cold War were useless. GPS was not widely available for military use until the Gulf War (1990-1991), and my navigation was almost as crude as a map and a compass. Phantom "Recce" pilots called it cut-and-paste reckoning. The best analogy would be the use of a hand sketch versus a computer-generated image to explore architectural design options. Before every mission my navigator and I spent hours cutting and pasting detailed topographic maps, with delineated field and forest ground-cover expanses, building footprints, road, rail, and trail routes, into long strips. These strips were then made into a deck of sequential cards which, when flipped through, charted our course to an intelligence "target of interest." A Velcro-strapped knee-board held this flip chart in place.

Crewed with an experienced instructor, it only took a few cut-and-paste target runs, and post-flight reviews of camera film and other intelligence gathering devices to discover that every NATO country's landscape had a unique aerial view signature. When you're moving across the landscape at speeds just below supersonic and altitudes often below high-voltage power lines, accurately reading this unique signature can be challenging. Formula-1 race car drivers consistently score victories if they are able choose the best line around each corner. They rely on dynamic depth perception, afforded by peripheral vision to enhance relative positional awareness. For exact location verification, they focus on site-specific—static—identifiers. I combined both these Formula-1 skills to become one of NATO's and the US Air Force's best low-level reconnaissance pilots. Many of my competitors favored tactical navigation using more prominent features like communication towers, power lines, river bends and bridges, and prominent works of architecture. But by doing that, they ran the risk of not being able to see the forest for the trees. Using variations in the quilt-like patterns of fields and forests, and other natural topologic features as macro references, I was able avoid the hunt-and-peck typewriting tracks of my competitors. It was only in the final leadup to the target that I visually dialed-in the line to the intelligence target using micro points. Sometimes the final feature that pinpointed my proximity to the target, either in daylight or moonlight, was as small as a footbridge across a tiny brook. By the end of my Phantom career, I could look at a photograph of two hectares of agricultural or forested land and identify the NATO country of origin—as, at the time, German farmers tilled their land and cleared their forests differently from those in France, the Italians differently from the Greeks, and so on. This ability to quickly visualize in my mind's eye three-dimensional landscapes, defined by an assemblage of natural and man-made forms, proved to be an invaluable skill when I became an architect.

Down on the ground, things were less spectacular. My disdain for military methodology soon became apparent to my squadron commander. I was standing at attention during a formal Air Base inspection when a general told me I needed a haircut. My commander was standing next to the general. The expression on his face let me know he was pissed, and the next day he called me into his office and demanded that I go immediately to the base barbershop.

"If I don't, what are you going to do, fire me?"

He puckered his jaws, chomping on a big cigar. Ash dropped on his desk. I bit my tongue and refrained from reminding him that the Air Force had spent over a million dollars on my flight training. Instead, I decided to make peace and promised to get a damn haircut. But before leaving, I asked him if he would consider designating me "Officer-in-Charge of Special Projects." I wanted to use this extra duty to devise ways to boost morale among my fellow aviators. As front-line pilots and navigators, we stood ready, on 24-hour alert. On flight duty, we spent twelve hours each day or night in a large, underground bunker. Our meals were trucked in from the Base's Commissary Kitchen. The food was served, cafeteria style, on paper plates with plastic utensils. The coffee tasted awful; the food worse.

For my first project as "Officer-in-Charge of Special Projects," I decided to explore the possibility of building a diner-style snack bar in our flight squadron's bunker. It had to be an honest-to-goodness diner, replete with hamburger grill, ice cream freezer, waffle maker, hot dog and bun steamer, and deep fat fryers. I needed money for kitchen equipment but was told the commissary had no budget for constructing flight line snack bars. They sent a chief sergeant with a copy of an Air Force citation prohibiting the on-base consumption of food not prepared in the base commissary or the NCO or Officer's Club kitchens. I decided to ignore the citation. Again, what were they going to do, fire me?

I raised money for restaurant equipment by selling stocks, in ME Inc, to fellow Phantom aviators. ME Inc hired two civilian German women to grill red and white bratwurst, hamburgers, and bacon, egg, and cheese sandwiches. The women hand-cut local potatoes for French fries. The bunker diner was an instant success. ME sold bucket loads of pommes frites, several kilograms of brats, and burgers every day. Most profits I funneled into community activities. ME purchased new uniforms for the Little League and donated hundreds of books to the base library. We bought new foosball and pool tables, and pinball machines for the Airman's Dormitory lounge. ME also hosted a charity fundraiser, dinner and dance party four times a year at the Officer's Club. These dinners were very popular with spouses: a good reason for them to go to the beauty salon, dress in evening gowns, and dance the night away.

Not long after the snack bar opened, a pilot's spouse came across her husband's ME Stock Certificate. There it was, across the entire length of the certificate, in big bold letters, MAMMOTH ERECTIONS Incorporated. Word got around. One pilot confessed to his wife that some of ME Inc's profits paid for a monthly, after-hours burlesque show in the Officer's Club bar. The strippers were local German women. The discovery of the stock certificate was ultimately ME Inc's "showstopper."

My squadron mates got fat from fries and beer-battered onion rings. Even the base commander had his chauffeur wait outside the bunker's entrance while he enjoyed a chili, grilled onion, and sauerkraut fat dog, or a "drag it through the garden" double cheeseburger. Everyone was happy, or almost everyone. Word of the culinary exploit eventually filtered out and reached the civilian-in-charge of the Base Exchange Service, a branch of GSA, the Government Services Agency. Mr Civil Servant issued an order, signed by the Director of the GSA, for ME Inc to cease and desist all operations. He included a copy of a GSA-approved and signed contract with a private, food truck concessionaire. The food truck would offer front-line aviators take-out prefabricated sandwiches and microwaved snacks. In lieu of "cafeteria" gruel, we would enjoy coach class airline food. ME stood its ground. We witnessed as a grown man fought for a measly food truck, stumbling through three years of his own red tape before enlisting the aid of the German legal system. The local government's threat to levy heavy fines on ME Inc's butcher and baker supply lines was the final blow, a sulking victory for the bad guys. We bid *auf weidersehen* to ME Inc, and passed the hat for our two German cooks.

I have no regrets about organizing the ME Inc stripper shows. My efforts helped build esprit de corps and camaraderie among a group of men serving in the Cold War, the longest military deployment in the history of the USA. We did our duty, and served our country, under threat of nuclear warfare. Today, recognizing the need for proactive course corrections leading to gender equality is crucial to the future of unwavering support for service to our country. Nowadays, brave women routinely fly combat missions in supersonic jet fighters, defending the sovereignty of nations across the world. And with mixed-gender flight squadrons, why not mixed-gender stripper nights as well?

My Mother, Baby Ben, Sister Mary.

3

A Famous Backyard

When the Second World War ended, not all the native sons and daughters who had served their country returned to their hometowns to settle down and have families. Many of the soldiers from farming communities decided to find work making a steady wage in northern factories. Our community had lost some pre-War residents to the battlefield and to postwar migration, but still we had many hardy descendants, from multi-generational farming families. There were also newcomers: G.I.'s who wanted to own their own piece of God's green earth. Every one of them was hardworking and honest, but the infertility of the Piedmont iron-red clay subsoil, with only a scant layer of organic topsoil, made it a challenge to farm for a living. Children worked the fields alongside their parents. The poorest among us had never even been to downtown Atlanta, though it wasn't far by today's standards. Roswell, nearest town to our house, was three-and-a-half miles away.

When my father went looking for a new bird dog, he chose the runt. He believed the runt puppy would make the best hunter, hungry for love. He and my mom's litter did not have a runt. They had a middle child separated in age from two siblings. Thirteen months later, my mother came home with a baby boy wrapped in a blue blanket. Weaned, I sucked dairy milk from a straw while my mother breast-fed her second son. I cried for three months. Being a middle child builds character.

My siblings and I came into this world long before the age of Mom's taxi service and PlayStation baby sitters, so we were left to our own devices. We had to find our own ways to entertain ourselves on the long lazy days of the hot summer, in the shorter sunshine of mild winters, and through the equinoxes of the changing seasons. We had enough neighbors for a weekend softball game, if the girls wanted to play; baseball if they didn't. When I was twelve, my younger brother and I decided to add a new venue for summer games: a track and field patch.

My father let us commandeer a large patch of crabgrass and red clay behind the barn, between the woods and the cow pasture. To prepare the ground for a two-lane oval, we dragged a railroad tie studded with sixteen penny nails behind an orange, Allis Chalmers, tractor. My brother acted as ballast, standing on the railroad tie, holding a rope, leaning backwards. I drove the tractor around and around and the nails broke up the sunbaked clay. The heavy squared-edge tie smoothed the surface. Crude lane lines were marked with agricultural lime. Top-raking in some fine stone dust, we had a near-perfect running surface for bare feet.

The homes of the poorest white kids that lived within a couple of miles of our house, were rusty-tin roofed, unpainted wooden shacks. Hardscrabble to the core, these girls and boys came from families only one or two generation removed from sharecroppers. If they owned shoes, they were hand-me-downs used only for going to church on Sunday. My brother and I had tennis shoes, but we weren't about to put them on when no one around us had them.

Next to the track we constructed a pit deep in sawdust for the high jump, long jump, and pole vault. We cut pole-vault poles from a bamboo forest next to a livestock wallow and water hole. After some experiments, we determined the ideal bamboo diameter for a pole. We cut up an old tire to make a scratch board for the long jump. We built a pole box for the vault with scrap lumber using some tin metal from an old gutter to line the bottom. A discarded surveyor's rod was attached to one side of the high jump so we could set the bar at the proper height. For shot-put, disk, and javelin throw, we mowed a pitch in the hay and cow pasture. For the shot we had a genuine Civil War cannonball given to us by my grandfather. A real javelin and a starting gun were donated by the father of a kid who lived on the farm across the road. Danny's father had been on his college track team, and had kept his aluminum javelin. I never asked Danny's father how he got the gun. For a disk we used a brake drum cover.

To beat the heat, the Wood Brothers Track Meets began early and were over by lunch. Danny, my brother, and I, the Track Meet's hosts, reserved afternoons for softball or baseball. The exception to this schedule was the once-a-month Roy and Tillie BBQ party, always held on a Saturday.

Fast Forward to 2007 and Chicago was preparing its bid for the 2016 Summer Olympics with the theme "Stir the Soul." Mayor Daley's Bid City Committee invited my firm in Shanghai to bid to design an Olympic Stadium and Aquatic Center. The *Chicago Tribune* published a rendering of our Olympic Stadium design on the front page of a special Sunday Arts and Entertainment section with this headline: Chicago 2016 Made in China. My design was accepted both by the City of Chicago and the US Olympic Committee, but unfortunately Brazil won the games. I had done it all pro bono, and made fourteen trips from Shanghai to Chicago over a period of eighteen months to get it right. It was the biggest disappointment of my life.

Our backyard's most prominent landmark was a large stand of century-old red oaks. Under the great canopy of this living roof of spreading limbs and branches, my father hand-dug a large Southern-style, in-ground, BBQ pit. A dozen bench-seat wooden picnic tables and small clusters of folding aluminum chairs with sawed-log coffee tables formed a large outdoor. At noon, following the Track Meet, my mother would bring to this outdoor dining room a big pitcher of hand-squeezed, ice-cold lemonade. In the South, summer drinks have to be ice-cold—almost freezing. Lunch was Hellman's mayo, tomato and baloney or Jiffy peanut butter and store-bought strawberry jelly sandwiches made with white bread and a side of Oreo cookies.

After lunch, my sister, brother, and I spent the rest of the afternoon helping our parents prepare for one of their famous supper parties under the oaks. First task: build a split oak wood fire that would produce enough hot coals to fill a trench sixteen feet long and three feet wide. Lay a fire under an iron tripod that would later be used for boiled corn-on-the-cob. At three o'clock the local grocer delivered sixty freshly plucked "fryers" and a couple of bushels of fresh sweet corn. While we shucked enough corn to fill a heavy cast iron pot to hang by a chain from the tripod, the grocer took the chickens out of thick cardboard boxes. Packed in dry ice, the grocer would hand the fryers to my father, who would cut them in half using a very sharp hatchet on a counter-high log chopping block. The half-chickens were put in the BBQ pit, where they'd slowly cook through the afternoon while my father paraded up and down bare-chested, in denim overalls and a red bandana.

Two hours before dusk, our front lawn would start to fill with cars, and my father would swap his straw hat for a white chef's hat, donning a full-length apron. Buicks, Chevys, Chryslers, Fords and the occasional Lincoln or Cadillac would line up one-by-one. My favorite was the 1959 Country Squire, Ford station wagon, with faux wood panels, real leather interior, automatic transmission, a roll-down rear window, and a push-button, Motorola radio. After the kids scrambled out of the back seats would come the mothers, carrying bowls of potato salad, cole slaw, baked beans, fresh-baked dinner rolls, string beans, fried okra and eggplant, and a great many desserts including chocolate cake, pecan and peach pies, brownies, cookies, and cherry cobbler. Vest pockets bulged with Camels, Lucky Strikes, and the odd cigar.

My brother, sister and I organized volleyball, dodge ball, and badminton games for anyone interested, kids and adults. Some of the younger kids took turns pushing each other higher and higher on the tree swing. Men played horseshoes while drinking, telling jokes we pretended not to overhear. Women went inside the house to say hello and offer to help. Most wore long Bermuda shorts with short sleeve blouses. Older daughters came in fancy, hand-sewn square dancing dresses, with white lace trim. A folding card table served as the bar, men leaving their spirits there to share with all. There was no wine unless it came in a jug. On the ground, three large tubs full of ice-cold cans of RC Cola, Coke, ginger ale, and Seven-Up. Drinks of choice for both men and women were the Kentucky bourbon highball, Bacardi rum and coke, mint julep, and Seagrams 7 and 7. No one ever brought a fine French Chardonnay or Beaujolais or a highland single malt to drink neat on a hot summer night in Georgia.

Dinner was served buffet-style in a line ending with my father. He'd keep the fire from flaming up too high with a garden hose, used a chemical sprayer to baste the slow-cooking birds, and turned them over once with a small pitchfork—letting fire do the heavy lifting. For kids who were too small to take on a whole half-chicken there were hot dogs drowned in ketchup.

And the Atlanta-made Lays "too salty" potato chips were heaped on every tot's paper plate. It would be another ten years before I tasted my first Cheeto or Dorito, twenty-five years before opening a bag of small batch Cape Cod Sea Salts or Pepperidge Farm Extra Cheesy Goldfish.

No one touched the food until after we had gathered in a circle, holding hands, for a blessing from my father or our Presbyterian minister. Definitely not a teetotaler, our reverend's drink of choice was a Julep made with fresh mint. A pipe smoker, he saved his empty Prince Albert tobacco tins to give to me and my brother. I used my tins to store miniature metal soldiers, Indian arrowheads, and marbles.

Dinner lasted until large serving spoons and forks had no place to go. Only then did my mother and sister tell all the kids to form a line for paper cups of homemade vanilla ice cream, the kind made in a wooden bucket. Topped off with homemade hot fudge syrup, it was heaven right in our backyard.

After dessert came the music. My father would get out his Gibson six-string guitar, inviting my sister, who sang like a star, to join him. Everyone would sing along to country crowd pleasers like "Red River Valley," "Oh Shenandoah," "Amazing Grace," "Home on the Range," and "Way Down South In Dixieland." After ordering a 45 record player, Elvis hits were added to his play list. On a starry night, "Love Me Tender" could bring the house down. Ironically, the 1956 song was an adaptation of a favorite Union Army refrain. I doubt anyone under the trees, bellies full of Southern cooking, were aware they were singing about love just like a Yankee soldier.

When the embers died down and the mosquitoes got thick, the people who had not already said their goodbyes would follow my father to the screened-in porch off the back of the house. Inside were some rockers, some wickers, and one long sofa. He and his best friends would spar over who had the best yarn. My father's best friend, hunting and camping buddy Charlie Nellans, was always the last to leave.

Those backyard parties were legendary. They taught me a lot about how people interact with each other, crucial information for an architect. With the Xintiandi entertainment district project in Shanghai forty years later, I knew what to do because I grew up with a father and mother who threw the best parties in the South.

A Daffodil In Spring

At first sign of warmer weather
The daffodil blooms
Spring's first blush of color
Ushers in
the year's first pony ride
Our distant neighbor Danny
Leads the rodeo
On bareback saddles
No bridle, no bit
Holding on to long manes
We gallop full speed
To a livestock pond
Still on our ponies
We strip naked
Riding into the water
In Baptismal bliss
Girl, boy, sister, brother
Five in all
The ponies are brave
we are turning blue
Back on dry land
we dismount
To lay down innocently
In a splendor of clover and grass
Pre-pubescent breasts and behinds
Spring had Sprung
Beckoned by the daffodil

Vincent Lo in Xintiandi

4

New Sky and Earth

I am an American architect and while I remain at heart a Southerner, I have spent the last quarter century helping to change China. In 2003, three years after arriving in Shanghai, my architectural debut in the Middle Kingdom, Xintiandi, opened its doors to the public. A two-city block collection of restaurants, bars, night clubs, cinemas, and shops, New Sky and Earth is widely acknowledged as "the sea change blueprint" for conserving culture and creating commerce in a myriad historic neighborhoods across China's urban communities.

Xintiandi was no fluke. The phenomenal success of this entertainment and cultural destination in China's greatest city is a reflection of my own unmitigated zest for life, quest for adventure, and relentless pursuit of cultivated serendipity. None of the ideas that helped my Hong Kong developer reap fame and fortune should be attributed to higher education, intellectual superiority, or architectural genius. The basics of how to make an ordinary place in Shanghai extraordinary were learned on the other side of the world, eight thousand miles away, in the backyard of a renovated Deep South rural farmhouse. Preordained by boyhood destiny, I did not choose China, China chose me.

The story of Xintiandi actually starts in Miami Beach where

a decade before the Mayor had spearheaded the creation of a public-private partnership to revive one of its most important thoroughfares, the Lincoln Road Pedestrian Mall. The popularity of the Road was down dramatically from its 1960s heyday, half the storefronts were boarded up, the result of a lack of maintenance of public spaces by the city, greedy landlords, and the expansion of land area zoned for commercial use. The new Partnership appointed a committee to select the architect for Lincoln Road's renovations, and my firm was selected at the end of three days of presentations and interviews with twenty different designers. Two elements played a role in my firm's selection: My previous ten years of experience working for the great architect Benjamin Thompson, and a recount of my personal visit with Lincoln Road Mall's original architect, Morris Lapidus. Of the more than one hundred people participating in the selection process, including the mayor and members of the special committee, I was the only one who knew that Morris Lapidus was still alive.

When Ben Thompson was awarded a Gold Medal by American Institute of Architects a couple of years previously, architect Morris Lapidus had sent him a letter of congratulations which Ben had shared with me. The day before the Lincoln Road interview, after checking into my Art Deco hotel on Ocean Avenue, I asked the front desk if they had a local telephone directory. There it was, Morris Lapidus' home address and phone number. He answered my call and invited me to a late lunch with him at his apartment.

In the 1960s, Morris was a famous architect who spent winters in Miami Beach. He gained international fame when he designed the Beach's most famous new hotel, the Fontainebleau. This amazing, wildly eclectic, "boogie woogie" streamlined, modern, playful, over-the-top, architectural, anti-minimalist improvisation, danced onto the cover of Life Magazine. Morris' next major Beach project was Lincoln Road Pedestrian Mall. It was another "boogie woogie," this time dancing down the middle of the Beach's equivalent of main street. A post-war mass exodus to the suburbs had badly impacted the commercial viability of local merchants dependent on all-year, non-seasonal business, and the 1960s pedestrianization of the Road attracted hordes of beachgoers and suburban visitors looking for leisure entertainment-related venues.

At lunch I sat across a swirled color, wave etched, glass table from a mid-modern marvel of creativity in a wheelchair, then aged ninety-seven. Listening to Morris' Lincoln Road story made me think of the ten years I had spent with my mentor, Benjamin Thompson. I worked with Ben creating over a hundred successful food and entertainment destinations beginning with Century City Marketplace in Los Angeles, renovation of the LA Farmer's Market, Westwood Village, the Union Station renovations in Washington DC, revitalization of Brisbane's Fortitude Valley, London's Spitalfields renovation Master Plan, additions to historic Covent Gardens, Marylebone Street Neighborhood Master Plan, eight High Street Master Plans for a UK-based asset management company, and many other projects in the United States Japan, Australia and Ireland. The beat went on and on.

Morris Lapidus' elegant, refined, charming personality reminded me of Ben Thompson, and I went to the interview the next day knowing what no one else knew, that I already had the job. I had only to tell the selection committee what Morris and Ben had told me (not their exact words): "Imagine the future, I do every day." Working with Ben, finding and talking to Morris, getting the Lincoln Road project, was one more, open-and-shut case of cultivated serendipity for a Southerner for life.

The point of the Lincoln Road project involved was to take existing architecture in a down-at-heel urban district and rekindling the vibe, creating a fresh but grounded environment with al fresco bars and eateries, fountains and walkways, a place that felt like old southern Florida but also modern, open and lively. I needed some help, so I called up the mayor and told him I needed a local architect to work with and he gave a phone number for Carlos Zapata, I called him and I was standing right under his office. "I can see you," he said.

Carlos was born in Ecuador and we worked on Lincoln Road together and then created our own practice, Wood & Zapata. He is an incredibly talented architect, although he had a way of annoying clients by always referring to the building under discussion as "his" rather than "theirs." He basically never had the same client twice. We were doing a project with Robert Redford in cooperation with a New York firm, and somewhere between the New York firm and Carlos, Redford was alienated and we lost him as a client. A little bit too much attention was paid to how famous he was and not enough to what we were actually doing for him.

By the time the renovations of Lincoln Road were complete, Morris Lapidus was unable to propel his own wheelchair, so I sent a limo-van and nurse with an off-road wheelchair to bring him to the Grand Re-opening. My "roadie" friends and I hosted a party in his honor, and guests were invited to attend a "Boogie Woogie, Dance All Night, Bash" for the architect who had written "More is Never Enough."

The Xintiandi project, and actually the whole rest of my life, started with a dinner I didn't attend in 1998 on Lincoln Road, five years later. Vincent Lo, the CEO of Shui On Land, one of Hong Kong's biggest real estate developers, was in Miami for a game of golf and he was invited to dinner at a restaurant on Lincoln Road. He asked his host, a city councilman, who had done this amazing project, and the city councilman said, I'll get the mayor of Miami Beach on the line and find out. The mayor gave Vincent the name Ben Wood, and Vincent told his Director Planning and Development Albert Chan to go find Ben Wood. He contacted my former firm BTA, and they said, "Ben Wood is not here any more and anyway he wasn't the designer, he was basically the business manager."

Albert smelled a rat. He wasn't sure who was telling the truth, so he did some research. A few days later on a late spring morning, I was with my partner Carlos Zapata in our Boston studio working on plans for Chicago's new Soldier Field stadium when I received an overseas phone call from a total stranger, a "man from Mars." Vincent Lo introduced himself as a Hong Kong real estate developer.

"You, Mr Wood, need to come to Hong Kong," he said. "I have a major project in Shanghai that I want to discuss with you in person."

Mr Lo had pre-arranged and pre-paid a round-trip, first-class ticket for me to Hong Kong. The ticket was waiting to be picked up at the downtown Boston office of American Airlines. I requested one night to think over his offer. The airline office was located on the same street as our design studio. Minutes after hanging up, I was holding the ticket in my hand. I did not need a night. I instantly made a decision that would change my life. That night, while packing my roller board, I told my wife, I was going to Hong Kong.

Thirty minutes after the Vincent Lo phone call, our studio received an electronic message from Albert Chan. Included was an outline of a Preliminary Concept for the Shanghai project by architects Skidmore, Owings & Merrill, SOM, one of the largest architectural firms in the world. Albert, Mr Lo's in-house architect and urban planner, instructed me not to clear Immigration on arrival in Hong Kong, I was to go directly to the VVIP lounge nearest my arrival gate and Mr Lo would meet me there and spend a few minutes discussing the Shanghai development before putting me on the next flight to Shanghai. That's what happened. A company executive met me outside the baggage claim area at the airport in Shanghai, and he checked me into a company-owned hotel amd told me the following morning would be spent touring the site. We would then return to Hong Kong in late afternoon and the following day starting at 9 am, we would meet with Mr Lo and his board of directors in a series of interviews. Four other international architect firms had been invited. Each architect would have thirty minutes to pitch their firm's qualifications and present their ideas for the Shanghai project. At 5 pm that day, Vincent would announce his choice of architects. I knew from reading this message that Albert's boss must be what in the US Air Force is referred to as a top gun, one of the best. And Vincent was indeed a top gun. His strategy and tactics for choosing an architect were daring, bold and wholly unconventional.

Before my Shanghai host left me in the hotel, he gave me a map of the city with the location of the site and his project office circled. The project office was only ten blocks away. Instead of being picked up by his driver the next morning, I said I would walk. Up early, I peeked into the hotel's dining area and saw four foreigners having breakfast at separate tables. Two I knew were architects, and one of them was my ex-partner at Ben Thompson's firm. The other was a SOM senior partner. The other two were middle-aged, reasonably handsome men, smartly dressed in all-black. They had to be architects. All of us were in the same hotel, same day, for the same reason.

On the walk over, I passed through a wet market. One vendor was standing over an open cardboard box of live chickens.

Hanging above Mr Chicken was a string of chicken feet. I looked again in the box; all chickens appeared footless. I quickly left the live fish, fowl, snake, and frogs market, walking fast, not wanting to look back. At the project office, in a modern high-rise building owned by Mr Lo, my host introduced a company intern. He was a young, bilingual, Shanghainese guy with a degree in Architecture. He would be my tour guide for the next five-hours.

My guide and I had only walked a half-block when the smell of human waste began to permeate the air. After another one and one-half blocks, we entered the site via a narrow lane. On one side of the lane a long row of identical pairs of wooden, black lacquer doors, were spaced three and one-half meters apart. The doors, framed by three solid granite stones, guarded small courtyards. The only way to enter the long line of two-story brick row houses was through one of these courtyards. On the lane's south side were as many kitchen doors as there were courtyards. Outside every kitchen door was a carved stone or metal wash basin. Judging from the amount and variety of laundry hung out to dry on cantilevered bamboo poles one story above these basins, these row houses must be overcrowded. My guide informed me that since 1949, each six-to-eight room row house had been converted to a tiny apartment building with a different family in each room. Everyone shared a single common kitchen. The sole kitchen was equipped with a butane, two-burner cook top, iron pot, black steel wok, and small upright refrigerator. Missing was any place for a "hole in the floor" toilet, indoor shower, or other sanitary facilities. I watched while a worker in overalls picked up buckets of night soil, left outside the kitchen door. He dumped the human excrement into an open-top hand wagon. When he had a full load, the stink stew was shoveled into a waiting dump truck. Within hours, produce farms outside the city bartered with dump truck drivers for healthy portions of

The north block of Xintiandi as it was ...

...and after reconstruction. I tried to retain buildings, alleyways and spaces as much as possible

Miracle Grow. Bucket-to farm, farm-to-market, market-to-table, belly-to-bucket. Circularity.

I looked on as men and women, still in pajamas, brushed their teeth in the outdoor wash basin outside every kitchen. Each basin's water tap was on a separate meter. None of the tap handles were the same. When the tap was not in use, the handle on a lanyard would go back on a hook inside the kitchen door. My guide chuckled when he told me you could tell where someone lived by the shape and form of the tap handle attached to lanyard.

Living and navigating life in these extremely close quarters had to be hard. Space was at a premium. Every square meter was used, every balcony had been enclosed, enlarged, and made part of the living space. Every roof had been raised to make more room. By Western standards, the place was a slum.

But something about the place struck me as different from America's inner-city, chock-a-block public housing. Everywhere I went, even in alleyways one-meter-wide, there was life and a sense of order. Small children rode trikes and played while old people, on tiny bamboo chairs, sat and watched. The men and women who minutes before had been in pajamas now started to emerge from these humble abodes to go to work. They were clean and well-dressed. How was this possible when they had no indoor, three-fixture bathrooms?

My guide and I walked every lane and alley of the site that morning. Hidden underneath the many ad hoc layers, incremental territorial encroachments, and unintentional obscuration due to age, and filling in the gaps left by lost, missing, or stolen baubles, I discovered beautiful brick details, elegantly thin, hand-struck mortar joints, the remains of intricately carved wooden screens, traces of parquet wood and tile floors, engraved corner stones, and finely corbeled solid granite foundation stones.

The young daughters of the owner of Xintiandi area's House No. 1, an opium dealer, photographed in the 1950s.

Seventy years later, the same daughters sitting on the same steps in the new Xintiandi.

The twin jambs and single lintel three-stone-frame around the courtyard doors were crowned with ornate decorative motifs carved in terra cotta. Laymen had not designed and built these row houses. This was the work of expert artisans following detailed drawings. Every structure older that fifty years was a remarkably inventive, lusciously eclectic, hybrid mix of styles. Originally built by French Concession developers, design styles and details, like gambrel roofs, semi-circular stairs, bubbled and curved balustrades, had been smuggled in from the West. The master builders and architects took cuttings from the elegant townhouse neighborhoods of mid-and-late 18th Century Paris and grafted them to host stems of the social hierarchy manifest in the traditional typology of a Chinese courtyard compound. In China, a private courtyard means the sky is yours. True even in a scaled-down, urban version, with the ceremonial main gate reduced to a three stone doorway.

One resident invited us to enter her home. Inside the tiny courtyard, she let us peek into her ground floor, one-room, apartment. Every possession she and her husband owned was in this room. There was a small, roll-up mattress leaning against a wall. Her son slept on this blanket-thin mattress on the floor under the room's only window. She and her husband slept in a raised bed with woven reed springs hidden behind a couple of wooden wardrobes at the end of the room. The husband and son were not home. One had gone to work at a bicycle repair shop, the other to school. She worked at a part-time night job from 9 p.m. until 2 a.m. unloading vegetable trucks for a market a few blocks away.

The small courtyard we were standing was one of over 8,000 specimens of this unique cross-cultural architectural typology extant in Shanghai on that day. Few architects in the West had ever been inside one of these courtyards. Excited, astonished, and dumbfounded, I was a foreigner in a foreign land momentarily held hostage by my eyes and ears. Veins filled with an intoxicating elixir of curiosity and wonderment. In this single courtyard was enough hubris of life, left behind by five generations of Shanghainese, to gag a maggot. Lichen-like, it clung to every brick, stone, and piece of wood, chipped porcelain pot, and rusty bicycle, and bent umbrella in this vivid and visible small world.

The golden days of a Paris of the East were over. But that day, seeing the people of this neighborhood struggling for dignity and a better life, stirred my soul. This amazing, three-dimensional, spatially complex, built and unbuilt, human-scaled corner of the world deserved a new lease on life. From my mentor Benjamin Thompson I knew that for this neighborhood to escape the wrecking ball would be "big work." What next?

Haul your fat white American ass back to Hong Kong and get

appointed the architect of Xintiandi. Second, assuming the first goes well, secure from Vincent Lo and his company the resources necessary to strip, sift, screed, and ruthlessly lay bare the truth and beauty of a historic Shanghai neighborhood's steaming, pungent, deliciously complex, compost piles of living and dead cultural artifacts. No job too small, no march too long, no sky to dark to derail a Southerner hell-bent on crossing a bridge for a client who searched the world to find him.

Back in Hong Kong, I stayed up until well after midnight writing a long letter to Chairman Lo. Stakes were high. Next morning early to rise, I went to the hotel's business center to print the letter. Shortly before 9 am, I gave the letter to Vincent's executive assistant. He would get "Minor opus, 24 hours in Shanghai," that morning.

I went downstairs and joined the four other architects in a large conference room. We were fetched one-by-one and taken to adjoining smaller interview rooms. Following the afternoon presentations, we waited together in the same large conference room for 5 pm to arrive. We barely spoke. At 5 pm sharp, Vincent's executive assistant walked across the room and quietly asked me to follow her. Vincent was waiting outside his corner office door. He did not return to his desk, inviting me to sit across from him at a small tea table. He had read my letter, spoken with each of his directors, and looking straight into my blues eyes.

"Ben, you only got one vote, mine. I want you to help me be famous for something besides being rich."

Leaning over the tea table he added, "The money for this project is coming out of my pocket. None of my bankers were interested in getting involved."

Bold and brave words.

Most of my hastily written, life-changing letter to Vincent ended up in lost-and-not-found hard-drive heaven, but here is the gist of it:

"One block from Shui On Plaza in Shanghai is a place that could tomorrow begin a remarkable transformation. I cannot say this strongly enough...one needs to see past the obvious: the dirt, the decay, and the crowded unsanitary conditions of your site. On these two city blocks is a treasure trove of cultural artifacts that could, for generations to come, symbolize "East Meeting West" on the vast delta of the Yangtze River. The only other place I have been that holds the same power over visceral reactions are the hill towns of Tuscany. The intrinsic character and beauty inherent in these remarkable, vernacular, non-pedigree built forms is breathtaking. Most virtually abandoned a century ago, all of Tuscany's hill towns have been resuscitated and revived down to the last cobblestone. In most of these Tuscan hill towns, you need an advanced reservation for private parking.

Vincent, you will make money but to compete in the Shanghai marketplace, you will need to avail yourself every competitive advantage. I reviewed the preliminary designs that were sent me, which suffer from a heavy broad brush of Western post-modern pastiche facades. Visiting the actual site was a revelation. No need for fake facades. I urge you to consider a more incremental, and more efficient, responsive approach to the project. What is generally being proposed, saving a few historic structures while clearing the rest of the site for new buildings, is wrong. If someone gave you an Italian hill town, it would be a mistake to tear it down and then rebuild a modern facsimile of the town atop an underground parking garage. Any hope of attracting people would be lost. The space and time of centuries of built form evolution that epitomize all the richly diverse and endearing character intrinsic to human scaled environments, cannot be imitated or reproduced.

The site's existing urban spatial structure, defined by lanes, alleys, and small public squares, is a rich, diverse, panoply of living culture. The preliminary plans misled me to believe that the old buildings on the site were nothing to shout about, nothing but trouble. I disagree and believe I was asked to be here today for a reason. I have a hunch you see something in those old buildings that SOM does not. On a clear day I bet you can see forever. I can bring to the table the skills, knowledge, and experience necessary to help you and your company transform this historic French Concession era neighborhood into the pre-eminent, retail, dining, and entertainment, destination in China.

I have asked myself countless times why Vincent Lo placed his trust in me, an American architect who was not famous, does not speak Oxford English, enjoys a penchant for wide-brim panama hats, holds a grudge against necktie nooses, and prefers American whiskey over fine wine. Perhaps spending three-weeks with his family in the Tuscan countryside a month after our interview in Hong Kong, must have tipped the scales for Vincent. Who would have guessed that during those same three weeks, a few Tuscan kilometers away, my family and I were ensconced in a century-old farmhouse, sharing sunsets? Extraordinary coincidence or cultivated serendipity? I raise my glass to both.

BENJAMIN WOOD

My Dad

5

First We Take Your Land

When I was fifteen, the backyard parties were suddenly put on hold. In 1960, John F Kennedy was elected President and the new Secretary of the Interior asked my father to move to Washington DC The Secretary had been instructed by Kennedy to appoint my father to a high-level position within the Department, presumably because my mother had devoted a great deal of time and energy to the Georgia Democratic Campaign to elect JFK.

JFK's Secretary of the Interior, Stewart Lee Udall, was at the time busy lobbying Congress to protect the Everglades National Park down in Florida. The park had been established in 1947, the same year as my birth, becoming the first area within the US to protect flora and fauna native to a region. But in the early 1960s, encroachment by new residential and commercial developments along with a plan to relocate Miami International Airport, was threatening its very survival.

Kennedy and Udall strongly believed the Everglades' value to the public as a protected park, and my father was instrumental in preserving its complex and magical natural world from encroaching urban sprawl. Preventing the colossal man-made environmental disaster that would have resulted from the death of the great swamp required the acquisition of thousands of acres of private land. My father, who was born on the same date in December as myself, was lured to Washington to use his Southern charm, story-telling skills, powers of persuasion, and passion for the great outdoors, to help get this job done and done right.

The Everglades is America's largest freshwater aquifer. Its nine distinct and interdependent ecosystems constantly shift in size, owing to the amount and mix of water types present. The delicate balance of salt and fresh water supporting rich biodiversity changes season to season, year to year, decade to decade.

In 1850, an Act of Congress took this great swamp from the Seminole and Miccosukee Indians, and gave it to State of Florida. Settlers moved into the Lake Okeechobee area and southwards, and for them there was no room for the Seminoles, known as the "wild ones." Most native Floridians had died of white men diseases long before 1850. Most of those who were left were resettled on a "reservation." First we take your lives, and then we take your land.

By the 1950s, hundreds of thousands of acres of the Everglades had been destroyed and continuing development threatened the survival of the largest subtropical wilderness in North America. But my father's purpose was not to stop development. That is impractical and impossible. The point is to take into account the needs of humanity and the value of nature and strike a balance.

Developers Jim Light and Jim Chaffin were among the early pioneers in environmentally sensitive resort development. They were years ahead of their time. Their mentor was Charles Fraser, who was a good friend of my father. Fraser's family owned tens of thousands of acres of timber land in the Low Country, the long stretch of low-lying land along the coast of South Carolina and Georgia, Charles took this family legacy and turned it into what is now Hilton Head Resort which he started in 1956. My father, representing the US Department of the Interior, worked with Charles to develop a plan for Sea Pines, the first post-war resort/ residential development in the Low Country. My family went there as Mr Fraser's guests for the Thanksgiving Day holiday the year before we moved to Washington. The two Jims worked for Fraser on his sales and marketing team.

While we were there, and thanks to tickets provided by Mr Light, I played, with my father, my first-ever round of golf. My father hit a hole-in-one, an eagle, on a par three. And on our last morning at Sea Pines, I saw an actual non-golf American Bald Eagle. The eagle came running out of the thick underbrush at the edge of a golf cart path to snatch a Thanksgiving meal before taking flight across the marsh. It's not often an eagle walks on terra firma. Mr Light told me the great eagles nested on a remote island nearby. The eagles frequent the resort's preserved natural environs that surround the golf course in search of their next meal of wild turkey. With no hunting permitted, the birds did not feel threatened.

On that trip, I also got to experience first hand what would become the benchmark for contemporary conservation-minded real estate development. Charles fundamentally changed his architect's master plan for Hilton Head's Harbor Town just to save an ancient live oak. Twenty-five years later, I worked with Chaffin and Light to re-design the Snowmass Club and Golf Resort in Snowmass, Colorado, and I was able to get the Town to approve an increase in density for new condominiums in trade for the acquisition and preservation of an important wildlife habitat. Fifty years later, I built a house around a 100-year-old Copper Beech tree on Martha's Vineyard. Today, together with two partners, I own a Low Country limited development wildlife reserve, an island of 550 acres frequented by American Bald Eagles. They don't nest there, but they lunch there. Their nests are eight miles away, on the other side of a tidal river marsh in the ACE Basin, one of the largest undeveloped estuaries on the eastern seaboard of the United States. What's the point? The point is respect for nature and the needs of human development, the need to balance preservation of what is valuable from the past with the demands of the future.

Prior to his political appointment in 1961, my father's G.S. (Government Service) Pay Grade had a maximum cap. Overnight, he was able to better provide for his family and also set aside some money for his own private land purchases.

He found us a home on the Virginia side of Washington DC, in Fairfax County, a few miles south of Alexandria. Our new home was a brand-new, subdivision tract house with four bedrooms and a two-car carport. He bought the house for $20,000. For perspective, a brand new E-Type Jaguar back then cost $1,900. Part faux-colonial, part modern ranch, the main level of the house had a gable roof while the split-level, two-story wing had a hip roof. On a cul-de-sac with four other houses, everyone knew everyone, and almost everything about everyone.

The entrance to our subdivision, Mt. Vernon Forest, was a half-mile from the terminus of Mt. Vernon Parkway. The Parkway ended in a large roundabout, with off-lanes to a visitor parking lot and the main gate for George Washington's Potomac River mansion and plantation. On the riverbank opposite Mt. Vernon stood Fort Washington, from the War of 1812. Commander-in-Chief on one side, President on the other. George designed them both.

One hot summer day, a buddy and I scaled the tall south wall of Mt. Vernon. The finely laid masonry wall formed the northern border of our subdivision. We wore shorts and were barefoot. It took around twenty minutes of walking around before we were spotted by a security guard, who walked up, looked down at our feet, and asked where we'd left our shoes. Before we could say anything, he told us that no one wearing flip-flops or barefooted was allowed to enter Mt. Vernon. "How did you get in, climb the wall?!" We were busted, and he escorted us to the main gate. He called the Parkway Police and reported he had two fifteen-year-old trespassers in custody.

My father drove up to the Main Gate guard house fifteen minutes later. With him was my buddy's father. Our dads spoke with the police, and politely requested they not press charges. My buddy and I gave the police our word that we would not climb the wall again. Happily, my father found this misdemeanor, mis-adventure, rather amusing, and said it took "moxie" to do what we had done. Anyway, in his opinion, charging admission to the home of the father of America was unpatriotic.

I made the best of my life in the suburbs, making extra money selling stacks of firewood cut from oak logs left behind by new home site clearings. The same buddy who hopped the wall with me was my firewood partner. Neither of us wore proper safety equipment when using a chainsaw. In the summer, I even cut wood barefoot. One time, I was using a chain saw on a partially toppled tree when the saw, pinched by a sudden trunk shift, kicked back. I lost my grip on the saw's forward handle and the saw dropped, severing the bone and all the ligaments in my big toe. A bit of skin kept my toe from falling off. I took off my T-shirt, tied it around my foot, and sat down on a big stump. My buddy flagged down one of our neighbors, who was in her car running errands. The nearest hospital was very close, so I still have my toe.

In the early morning hours of a hot and humid day in August 1963, I left our suburban neighborhood, still on crutches with a cast to my knee thanks to my severed toe, and traveled by bus with my firewood partner into the District of Columbia to attend "The March on Washington," the historic gathering of people to call for better treatment socially and economically for Black Americans. When we arrived on the Mall around 8.30 am, it was raining, and we found temporary shelter from a rain shower in "Tent City." Erected by early arrivals, the tent encampment looked like a scene from a Civil War re-enactment. By mid-morning the rain had stopped, the sun was shining, and by noon there were over 200,000 people on the Mall. The event ended just before sunset with Martin Luther King's "I Have a Dream" speech, and history was made.

Just three months later, in late November of 1963, I attended the funeral of President John F Kennedy. Dressed in my Eagle Scout uniform I served as an usher at a Congressional Box on the route of the Funeral Procession. After the Procession passed, I walked together with several Congressman and their guests to Arlington Cemetery to witness the lowering of the Presidential Casket.

One year later, my father and I visited the Capitol building to pay tribute to a Georgia Congressmen who voted for the Civil Rights Act of 1964. My father and mother, although no longer living in Georgia, had campaigned for this US Representative.

Governor Jimmy Carter, who would one day be President, had an Aunt who lived in Roswell, Emily Dolvin. She was the Principal of Roswell Elementary School, my school. It was one of a handful of public elementary schools in the state of Georgia with a full orchestra, string, wind and percussion, and joining the orchestra in the third grade, my first instrument was the viola. The teacher then moved me to the cello, and finally to double bass.

After the family's move to Alexandria, I was invited by three high school friends to join their folk music group as the bass player. Two years later, the summer before our senior year, we went electric—following Bob Dylan, who had made the switch two years earlier. Roll over Kingston Trio, we're moving on up, reeling and rocking.

With our fake ID's my best friend in high school, Jeff Bryson, and I would go weekend double dates, to M Street in Georgetown, Washington DC Our dates were with "girls who did." And I do not mean that they did go to church on Sunday. Our number one favorite destination for a pitcher of beer, chips, homemade guacamole, and great music was the legendary Cellar Door, an intimate venue that was central to the folk music boom of the 1960s and to some extent beyond. Greats like Pete Seeger, James Taylor, Carole King, Jimmy Buffet, and the Eagles, were the level to be expected on any given night. Sunday nights at the Cellar Door were "live mike" hootenannies, and if your folk group passed an audition, you were allowed to perform three songs. While still in high school, I regularly performed with my folk group at the Cellar Door. Our "girls who did" were served free by the management.

That summer we did one last folk music gig at a hugely popular seafood restaurant on Old Town Alexandria's Market Street. After an early complimentary surf and turf dinner, we retired to the bar and lounge to perform. During a break, I met a girl. After our last song, she took my hand and we went together down the street, to a second-floor, communal crash pad. The rock band below us played until 2 am. She was young and wild, a mid-west, teenage runaway, with Luna moth eyes. After Luna, sex was never the same again.

To Luna's Everywhere

We can dance all night
We can get it right
The band is tight
The timings right
In the morning light
We can walk
To a Beachfront King
With sunrise silk sheets
Breakfast in bed
Eggs over easy
Cheese grits, bacon bits
Truffles and caviar
Run a bath hot
Smoke some dope
Dream of Days to come

I want to be your lover
Pretty Baby
Make it shake
Like an earth quake
Right here right now
Bang bang, boom boom

In the fall, our new group, Beethoven's Fifth, won a regional battle of the bands. In the audience was an independent talent scout from New York. A week later he booked us six hours in a DC recording studio. On our own dime, we recorded a 45-RPM, two-sided demo of two songs we had written. The talent scout swore he could find us a record label. He promised to get back to us, and he did.

Post 2000 Times Square and New Age Peep Star Marky Mark

6

Times Square Facades

Times Square in New York City is a place everyone has an image of in their head, in a way that they don't necessarily have of Xintiandi in Shanghai, and I'm responsible for how that huge intersection in the middle of the Big Apple looks today.

First, a bit of history. By 1990, the theater district of New York had died, the victim of urban blight, crime and shifting social patterns. Eight of the most historic Broadway theaters had gone bankrupt, and while there were still a couple left, the old Broadway of dazzling musicals and brilliant plays was basically gone, replaced mostly by pornography. There were triple-X movie houses, squalid sex shops and "model viewing" cublicles with sticky floors. So in 1990, a project was created to claim back Times Square and 42nd Street, and a public-private partnership was created, very similar to what happened with Lincoln Road down in Miami Beach at around the same time. It was a very popular idea at that time, putting the government together with private property owners to try to come up with better ways to revitalize urban neighbourhoods. The one in New York was called the 42nd Street Redevelopment Project and it brought together two of the biggest property owners in New York, Prudential Life Insurance and a guy named George Klein, who was probably the most successful real estate developer in the city, far more successful than Donald Trump's father.

George and Prudential didn't own the historic theaters but between them they owned almost all the property around them, and they owned most of 42nd Street, and both sides of Times Square including the building from which the ball drops on New Year's Eve. At that point, most of the upper floors of the buildings were empty as the office tenants had fled the blighted area, and all that was left were the ground floor and second floor tenants, mostly sleaze-oriented. Which is not good if you want to attract people of all ages and families wanting to go see a Broadway musical next door.

So the mayor of the time got elected on the platform of cleaning up Times Square. and everyone knew the year 2000 was coming in just a few years and that was going to be a major celebration, with of course Times Square the global focus. This was around 1992, and the private part of the partnership hired BTA, the Boston firm I worked with, and the public part of arrangement hired Robert Stern, who was at that point the dean of the School of Architecture at Yale, a very famous post-modernist. In other words, he believed in retro architecture. They were going to select a master planner for the makeover of Times Square, and it was going to be one of the two, BTA with Ben Wood leading the charge, or Bob Stern.

There was an all-day presentation, and Bob Stern was first and I sat through his presentation, and he based his proposal on old historic pictures. He basically wanted to take Times Square back to the way it had looked in the 1920s and 1930s, including a re-creation of the flashing neon billboard style of that bygone era. He thought that going the history renaissance route would make Times Square into a major tourist attraction. Of course, I thought just the opposite. I saw his idea of retro billboards as being antithetical to the real purpose of Times Square, which is to integrate into its culture the latest advertising media featuring current fashion and current trends, and not Camel cigarettes.

"You've got to take New York into the next century," I urged them. "And the way you're going to do that is to take every available square foot of facade on every building you own, Prudential and Mr Klein, and you're going to sell it as a billboard."

At first, they looked at me like I was crazy. Who is going to buy massive billboards in Times Square, was their message, because this was the early 1990s and Times Square was a disaster area. My answer was: everybody, because we are going to clean this place up and bring people back to Times Square. We've already been told by the city to get rid of all the porn shops, so there's no choice anyway, and we're going to renovate the ground floor premises and bring in restaurants and hot dog joints and then we're going to attract the fashion business and music stores. Then I did the presentation which clinched the deal. But before I explain that, let me back up a second and explain some of the technology I used.

When I was flying my jet fighter spy plane, we didn't have GPS, but we had what was called an internal navigation system, based on gyroscopes that could sense your location in three dimensions. It broke down all the time, but Hollywood took that same gyroscopic technology and applied it to cameras. Then in 1978, the Defense Department awarded a contract to a precursor of MIT's Media Lab, a group called the Architecture Machine, to build a full 3D model of the city of Aspen in Colorado, so that tank commanders could train in a totally simulated environment created with photos taken in all directions at each location from a truck equipped with four cameras. It's quite standard now in terms of Google Earth and similar apps, but back then it was groundbreaking, and it worked so well, they did simulations of

Peepshows and sticky floors – the old Times Square.

all the cities behind the Iron Curtain, including Warsaw and East Berlin so they could train tank drivers who had never been to these cities to know exactly where they were.

The Architecture Machine, headed by Nick Negroponte who eventually became a superstar as head of the Media Lab, was in the next room to my design studio in Boston when I was doing graduate studies, and I used to wander in and watch Negroponte develop the precursors of the Media Lab, so I had an idea of what was happening. Then there was a movie called Blade Runner directed by Ridley Scott who hired some Architecture Machine graduates who were on top of the new digital technologies, and also special effects master Doug Trumbull. They built a huge warehouse near Stockbridge, Massachusetts in which they built the set for Blade Runner, a huge scale model of a city and they would run cameras through it. They used a gantry crane on which they mounted a 16mm camera which could move in any direction through the model. Trumbull pioneered the whole idea of special effects using scale models, and his assistant was a young man named John Borden who I had met when he worked with Negroponte.

When I was asked to work on the Times Square project, I said, what would be magic would be to film Times Square like they did Aspen, Colorado. So I hired John Borden, the chief designer and engineer for the motion control systems developed by the Archiecture Machine, and he installed cameras on a pickup truck with gyroscope mounts designed by him and drove it through the streets in and around Times Square. We had to do it at the crack of dawn on Sunday mornings before everyone got up ands it took several weeks to get all we needed. We compiled a gigantic database of images covering Times Square from every conceivable angle, and took the huge numbers of images we had collected and put them on a laser disk with software that could provide a 360-degree panorama from any location. Today it seems very simple, but back then it was revolutionary. Then I went through lots of fashion magazines and grabbed images of all the best ads including one of Marky Mark, the singer who was also a model for a famous underwear brand back then. I scanned them all in and then placed them on the facades of all the Times Square buildings on the laser disk.

So on the day, Robert Stern mostly just stood in front of the audience talking with a few renderings and historic photographs to illustrate his ideas. Then I came on with a projector, Surround Sound and three screens, and I led them through a 3D vision of an entirely new Times Square, freeze framing as I went, stopping on the Marky Mark billboard… and then they got it.

"Wow," they said. "That's what we're going to do." They knew they could lease the ground floor places to restaurants, but they didn't know what to do with the upper floors, and I said, "You don't have to do anything with them! Leave them empty!

The wall is worth more than the inside!"

At the time, I had an office in Japan, and I also showed them a lot of pictures of intersections in Tokyo. "We are entering the age of the giant billboard," I declared. And we were.

Those billboards today are so valuable. But even then, you could do the math and realize that you're going to make a lot more from the billboards than you ever could collecting rent from a shop or a hotel. It was a cross-cultural transplant of an idea. The key was that my proposal wasn't nostalgic, it wasn't about old Times Square, it was about 21st Century Times Square. And that was during a period when the fashion amongst architects was post-modernist retro. They couldn't see the future. It was slightly contrarian in retrospect because my name in China now at least is linked to the idea of preservation of a sense of the past, and of integrating existing old structures into new designs. But in Times Square, I was working in the opposite direction. My goal is always to come up with the best solution for the problem that needs to be solved, and it just so happened that in that case, it was to put as many billboards as you can on every square foot available.

So, we drew up the master plan, and on January 1, 1999, the morning after the New Year's party, they closed down everything because they wanted a clean break with the past rather than having the peep show joints and porn shops close one by one over time.

That day, we went though all of the shops and porn places because I wanted to see what the insides of the buildings looked like. When they were porn parlors they were dark, but that day, we turned on all the lights, and we found the booths the girls used to sit in, with the customers watching the private perfomance through a window into the wall. You couldn't touch them, and they couldn't touch you, but the floors were sticky. I went into the manager's offices in each joint and the filing cabinets were filled with pictures of women with a number you could call.

Over the next year, we tore out all the interiors of all the ground floor premises in all buildings and re-leased the places to proper tenants. By the time the ball dropped on the following New Year's Eve, the whole area had changed and was full of cafes and restaurants, the kinds of places you would expect in a theater district. And all the billboards were up there, too. It had become the Times Square we know today.

There was a little dress shop on Lincoln Road in Miami Beach called Imperfect Utopia, and I thought about the name a lot. If something is perfect, my definition, you can't change it or improve it. So the only utopias that are going to survive are those that you can change, which is an imperfect utopia. I am an optimist but I seriously believe that the human race will exterminate itself during the next hundred years, the race will vanish from the planet Earth. But there is still hope because it will only take a hundred years for the planet to recover, to mend itself, so if we can somehow colonize Mars, they can come back and start all over, but with all the advantages of advanced technology. Just like the movie Wall-E. Why not?

Old Yellow

7

Old Yellow

I graduated from high school in May of 1965, and was accepted into the School of Civil Engineering at North Carolina State University. But I was not due in Raleigh until the second week of September so the summer was free. Our rock band's talent agent had not called back. Dreams of becoming a rock star were on hold. How should a seventeen year old prepare for four years of math, physics, advanced differential equations, and civil engineering classes at a predominately male institution?

Jeff, my best friend and the band's lead singer, suggested we make a road trip to Colorado where his father, "Rock," a career Marine Corps Officer, had retired after thirty years of service and bought a cherry orchard and farm house in small town, Paonia, Colorado. A summer under a clear blue, Rocky Mountain high sky, it would fly. There were bound to be one or two farmer's daughters around, fair game for a couple of traveling troubadours. Southern jokes and petticoats—different strokes—one colored by culture, the other by design.

If we were going to go and visit his parents, we needed money and a vehicle. My own parents were still living in Virginia. Our rural farm house outside Roswell, Georgia was empty and being looked after by a caretaker. The wooden windows and clapboard exterior needed a coat of white oil enamel. My father offered us grocery money and $300 a week for three weeks to scrape, prime, and paint the house. We worked like dogs and managed to finish on time. We then paid $275 for a 1947 International Harvester Metro with 40,000 miles on the clock—a step-up and step-out, milk truck. If I leaned my head to one side, I could stand up in the rear cargo cabin. The driver's seat was a lean-to stool on a spring-loaded post. Mounted on a metal divider, a jump seat folded down for a front passenger. The engine was accessed from inside the front cab via a large metal cover which stretched from the driver's dashboard to the passenger side door. The top of the engine compartment was a perfect table top. Before heading north to head west, the seventeen-year-old milk truck got a fresh coat of caution sign yellow paint.

Young, wild, long-haired and bearded, and with house painter's tans, we had the world by the balls. Time to call our Fort Hunt High girlfriends. They would soon be juniors, two years behind us, but both had turned sweet sixteen. Somehow Heather and Wendy persuaded their parents to let them go to Colorado with us. In Heather's case the line was "let me go or I will run away."

With two gorgeous women aboard, we resumed our journey. Jeff and I took turns driving. The synchronizers on the truck's manual transmission were worn out. Changing gears required manually synchronizing the transmission's input engine RPM and output speed (driveshaft speed). In the middle of a double clutch, two separate shifts of the gear lever, a punch on the accelerator pedal, and a good guess of the RPM based on engine noise did the trick. If you got it wrong, the sound was like dropping metal scraps into an electric meat grinder. Jeff and I bet daily on bad shifts—the daily loser was the one with the most fuck-ups per turn at the wheel. Losing meant picking up the tab for everything except gas and oil at the next Pitstop-Plus.

Minimum pitstop requirements: public flush toilet, bagged ice bin, and self-service pumps. A Pitstop-Plus: a variety of unhealthy snacks, sandwich meat and processed cheese, bread, four ice-cream sandwiches—and six-packs of "open with a church key" canned beer—Miller High Life. We did not risk carrying any righteous weed. But Jeff and I rolled our own "cigs" with Sir Walter Raleigh tobacco and Zig-Zag papers. The girls were filter-tipped Marlboro Men. We slept in tees and underwear in light sleeping bags on thick foam mattresses in the back of Old Yellow. Top speed for our poor man's RV was a mean fifty miles per hour. And that was downhill. Average flat-land cruising speed was 42-miles-an-hour. Anything more than a 3-to-5% grade required at least one downshift, and gas-pedal-to-the-metal.

We picked up an Interstate Highway in eastern Pennsylvania. Not long after crossing into Ohio, we were pulled over by a State Police cruiser. A policeman in a Smokey the Bear hat told us were going too slow for safety. Smokey wrote us a "Warning" and escorted us to the nearest exit. First stop, a pit stop. While the girls used a pay phone to place collect calls home, Jeff and I studied our $8-dollar Rand McNally Road Atlas. We penciled in two-lane highways all to way to Paonia.

The closer we got to Colorado, the higher the altitude. Keeping Old Yellow from overheating on hot afternoons was nigh impossible. We learned the hard way to carry several gallons of water. And when and how to safely remove the radiator cap. Driving all night to beat the heat, our timetable West got a whopping kick-in-the-butt. Crossing the Colorado State line, we switched to Coors, the first beverage I ever drank from a ring pull, all-aluminum can.

We arrived at Jeff's parents farm shortly after sunrise on the 3rd of July. The day was still young when we emptied the milk truck, moved our stuff into the barn hay barn loft, and jumped in the back of Rock's pick-up truck. We were off for a tour of the town. Main Street was busy with volunteers stretching banners across the street, getting ready the 4th and the annual Cherry Days Parade. The whole town and every rancher and family for fifty miles would line the sidewalks at high noon on Independence Day.

We found a fabulously authentic, ready-to-wear, cowboy/cowgirl store. An hour and one-half later we walked out wearing richly carved, real leather, stirrup heeled, toe metaled, thigh high, "shit kickers." Add to the menagerie, strap-on spurs, leather braided bolos, and calico bandanas and the sum was two, first-rodeo,"dudes," looking for love. When Rock saw the pair-of-sweet-sixteens don button down-the-front, tight-fitting, white, pink-piped, fancy flap front pocket, western shirts—tucked into light blue denim short shorts, he had an epiphany. His wife Naomi had insisted he keep a couple of donkeys on the farm for grand children visits. Why not invite the girls to ride the donkeys in the big parade? Riding bare back, save for an Indian made saddle blanket, the girls in short shorts would be a hit. Jeff and I could walk in front, tethered to the jackasses by halter and rope.

That night, Naomi cut Jeff's and my hair. We shaved clean. We got up the next morning, at the crack of dawn. The girls braided the donkey's manes with Christmas gift ribbons and fresh wildflowers. The gorgeous babes did the same to their own long tresses. Naomi, half-Italian and half-Maui, made Jeff and I multiple Hawaiian style leis. For raw materials, she cut long strands of an invasive flowering legume vine. The vine got its ticket punched by the County Water Rights Association. Meant to control erosion on the banks of the principal irrigation ditch, the vines defied authority.

Directed by the head Marshall to "bring up the rear," our four person, two animal, foot and hoof marching sextette, entertained bystanders. The girls sat straight-up on the donkeys. With backs arched, they strutted their stuff and returned every tip of a hat. When we saw we were a couple of blocks from the end of the parade, the girls turned sideways and dismounted by high-kicking a leg over the jack's back. Back on asphalt, they got out front to dance fandango down the street. For music, Jeff had Rock's ukulele on a neck stop. I had a key of G harmonica.

Our gorgeous babes were "rubber-necked" by young and old pokes alike. Seeing two young men wearing flowers around their necks and cowboy hat bands did not set off any alarms. They did not know what they did not know. Easy Rider and Woodstock were still four years off. Four Dead in Ohio was five. Our idols, the Beatles, went on the Ed Sullivan show in suits and ties.

The Cherry Days parade ended at the Town Park. Filled with food stands, bake sales, and ready to roll cottonwood stumps, every local grinder and grifter with an angle or an angel was present and accounted for. A US Army Recruiter passed out mini-stars and-strips flags next to a "lost kid" corral. We were waiting in line for ice cream and cherry cobbler when a local newspaper reporter asked for an interview. The interviewer, a college journalism major, was incredulous, astounded to learn we were interlopers, Paonia, Pitkin County summer stock.

What fascinated her most was Heather and Wendy's dance step. Got a name for it? I took the question.

"Not really," I said, "but take a juke joint jitterbug, a rocky mountain shuffle, a Chuck duck walk, a shiffle and a shout, shake it up, work it out, that's what is it's all about."

The aspiring journalist, bemused, amused, went with the flow. Next day the paper published her article in a special Cherry Days edition. Lead line: "Back East Suburban Slickers Charade the Parade and Steal the Show."

Twenty-four of the thirty-eight acres of Rock's farm were

devoted to hundreds of prime-of-life cherry trees. We spent mornings in the orchard picking cherries alongside a half-dozen migrant workers. Picking started a 6.30 am and with a half-hour lunch break, was over at 3 pm. Paid by the pound, we earned beer money and change. We earned extra money helping Rock maintain the farm's gravity fueled irrigation system, as well as mucking out the stalls of Naomi's horse and the two donkeys.

On picking days, after a brief siesta, we pumped up our truck tire inter-tubes, and went skinny-dip tubing in the icy, snow melt water of the Water Association's main canal. We kept a couple of six-packs cold, tied in a potato sack, trailing the biggest inner tube. On weekends, we ventured into the vast environs of central southwest Colorado's arid, semi-desert, plateaus, green river valleys, and Rocky Mountain alpine lakes, forests, and streams.

She Had Earth All Over Her

In a corner of Oklahoma, a woman
is plucking at the earth. She
is naked, and gardening. She
has land all over her, for she
has also been making pots, and
her long Bohemian hair is
blondly gummy with clay. She
kneels down and messes with a
place in the earth.

—James Dickey

One very hot August day we drove Old Yellow south for three hours, until we were in the vicinity of the Gunnison River Canyon. We didn't have a map, and were unable to find any signs for roads leading to the Canyon. We stopped for directions at a roadside gas station. Up the road a mile, we turned down a local farm access road. At the first hard bend in the road, a fence line led us a mile due south, to the Canyon. We walked the fence line to the brink of the Canyon. Sitting on a large boulder, looking down at the river 800 feet below, we ate our packed lunch and consumed what was left of a six-pack. We decided to descend the steep canyon walls for an afternoon swim in the river, picking a steep gully as our route down. We descended into the abyss, sliding, tumbling, and stumbling. In less than an hour, Jeff and I managed to get the girls and ourselves to the bottom. After a glorious swim and sex on separate sandbars, we decided to start back up the gully. About halfway up, the girls decided they had to rest. By now, both girls were badly sunburned and showing signs of dehydration. Jeff and I gave the girls all the water left in our canteens. I began to get worried. I feared if we rested any longer, we might be facing the prospect of being stuck in the gully after dark—making it impossible to proceed safely. Spending a night out under the deep sky would sap any energy we had left. We had to somehow get the girls to the top as soon as possible. Adrenaline kicked in, and Jeff and I managed get all four of us to the top just before sunset. I could see a farmhouse in the distance. I knew Big Yellow was only a mile away, but figured we should go the farmhouse to get water. I took off running, and, as I approached, I found myself staring, across twenty yards of sagebrush and tumble weed, at a naked woman. She had earth all over her, standing next to a potter's wheel. Wet clay covered her hair, face, arms, breasts, and thighs.

She hadn't seen me approach. After an awkward moment, I decided to take a couple of steps backward, and waved at her. She saw me, reached for a blue denim shirt she had put on a nearby chair, covered her upper torso, and in a voice loud enough for me to hear, said hello. I explained my situation. She disappeared into a nearby tool shed and came out, with her face and hair wet, wearing jeans. I walked with her to her kitchen. She filled my two canteens. She handed me a blue bandana tied and filled with fresh-baked oatmeal cookies. I went to get my friends, and my new friend drove us all, in her pickup truck, to get our milk truck.

Watching a naked woman, a stranger, covered in earth, standing in wet mud, took me to the other side of seeing: *two people meeting were simply two people meeting*. Just as Gertrude Stein and Alice B. Toklas changed the history of literature by writing the lexicon for understanding the meaning inherent in coincidental phenomena, whenever asked what I draw on for design inspiration, this stranger's humane compassion comes to my mind. Humane architecture belongs more to a world of concurrent experiences with others than a body of academic, architectural ideas. For my Master's thesis, I ended with a poem called Now, which included a line inspired by Gertrude, referring to unshod moments of densified "now." In a way, that's how I think about the experience of being in a well-designed environment. After you've studied the past and looked into the future, your first responsibility is to make Now as meaningful as possible. Because it is never not Now, and my goal is to make the experience of a place mean more than architecture, or style, can ever do on its own.

8

Islands and Planes

In 2008, I found an island in South Carolina that had once been part of a plantation and later used as a hunting club for shooting dick and deer. I bought the lion's share of it, as I mentioned, with a couple partners. It's called Little Edisto, next to Edisto Island, a part of the tidal flats in South Carolina, just south of Charleston. The property is called Brittan Point and covers 550 acres. The only way to get to Edisto is over a bridge over the inner coastal waterways. It's a very high bridge to allow sailboats to go by underneath. I was visiting a cousin who lived in Edisto for a while, and from the top of the bridge, I looked out and saw this huge undeveloped piece of land, and I went down and found the driveway, and there was no sign of life, but there was a small sign that said For sale," half-buried in the bushes. I noted down the phone number and called the guy, he was a broker who said, yeah the whole island is for sale. It's owned by three brothers from out of state, who had bought it to go hunting, and they built a small runway so they could land a private plane. It was a fascinating property because it had a deed that went all the way back to the King of England. If you owned a deed to property on an island that predated the revolutionary war, you own all the way to the middle of the river. Today, it is only to the mean tide mark. they originally put it up for sale as three separate pieces

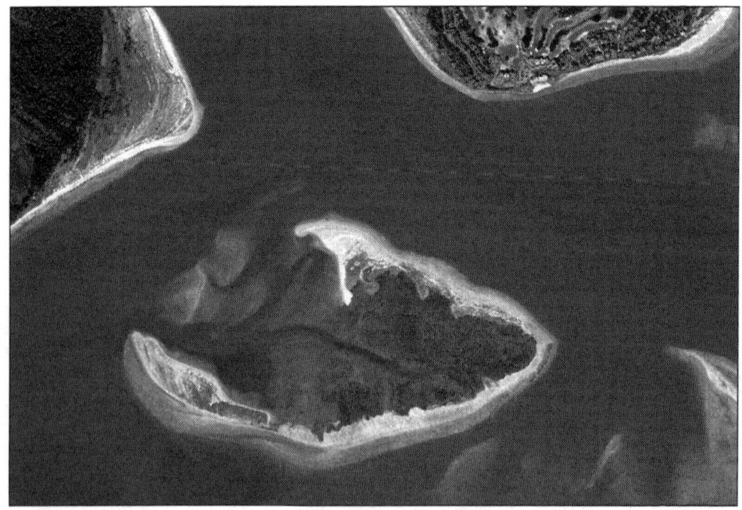

Edisto Island's Dragons Mouth Deveau Bank and Ground Looper Dooper

but land has a greater value altogether than split up. I offered half of what they were asking and they sold it to me. One night, I looked around the bar in Shanghai, and two friends were in there, and I said, I'm going to South Carolina next week to close on an island, and they both said, "Can I buy some of it?" So we went thirds on it.

I walked the whole property in snake boots up the crotch, because there were rattlesnakes everywhere. It was clear someone had owned it at some point. There was no house, but there was some farm machinery lying around. Evidently there had been a plantation house and it had burned down. I studied some old aerial maps and found where the runway used to be. There was no runway when we bought it, the old runway was overrun by several species of fast-growing trees. I rented a gigantic bulldozer which got rid of the trees and I rebuilt the old runway. The conservationists wouldn't have been happy if they'd known, but it had been an airstrip before and I was reviving it. I also built a hangar that can hold at least three small planes and renovated a decrepit old hunting cabin, took it off the grid, installed solar panels and some wind turbines which provide enough power for air conditioning, which is very rare for off-grid houses.

Then I saw in a magazine a new small aircraft that can land or takeoff in less than a hundred yards, made in South Carolina by a man named Troy, and I ordered one, and he offered to fly the plane down for me. It's a tail-dragger, with two wheels at front and one at the back, which is about ten times harder than flying a jet fighter. So in 2016, I started to learn to fly the plane and one day, and I invited Troy and his partner to meet me on Little Edisto. We had lunch there and then Troy said, "Let's go fly to an island somewhere, let's go land on a beach." I should have smelled trouble, but I had an instructor and these are all experienced guys, how bad could it be?

Anyway, the three planes took off and flew to an island about three miles off the coast of South Carolina that is totally deserted, no buildings, nothing, and much of it underwater at high tide. And strictly off-limits to everyone. We must have broken twenty different regulations that day, but people like Troy are fast and loose with the rules.

My instructor was sitting next to me, but it was the first time I had ever landed on a beach. We line up for the landing, the tide was about halfway out, and when I landed, I had one wheel on wet sand and one on dry sand, and the plane immediately did a 360 turnaround and also went up on the tip of one wing, one wing in the sand, the other vertically above it in the air. After a fraction of a second, the aircraft came crashing down, and we got out of the plane, and nothing looked wrong with it, just a small dent on a wing tip. The other two guys landed safely on the wet sand and did a check, and Troy took out a screwdriver and opened an access panel, reached up inside the wing and found a

wing spar had broken.

"Ben, you're not going anywhere," he said. If I'd taken off, the wing would have fallen off.

There was a sign near where we landed saying that the island was a Federal wildlife refuge and no one was allowed to set foot on it. It was about five in the afternoon, so we left the plane where it was, jumped into one of other two planes and fly back to my place. But that time, it was almost dark, but one of the guys took an anchor from my boathouse and flew back to the crippled plane and tied it down, just in case. Then next morning at the crack of dawn, Troy went down to the shrimp dock and talked one of the shrimp fishermen into taking a barge over to the island with eight other men, they hauled the plane onto the barge and brought it back to the dock. The plane barely fit on the barge, but they got it on, and lifted it off onto a sea ramp, and then the engine was started and we drove it into the parking lot and then off down the highway for three miles to a friend's place where we could remove the gasoline from the wings, which we had to do to get the plane onto the trailer to get it back home. Six months later, I had it back fixed. If we had been caught landing on the island or taking the plane down that highway, we would all have lost our licenses. Another roll of the dice pays off. We got a way with it scot-free.

But Little Estido is a wonderful piece of Low Country estuary land. I have a caretaker there who is a veterinarian and the son of one of the three men I bought the property from. He looks after it in return for the right to go over there and shoot deer when he has a mind to do so. Every year he wins the South Carolina award for having shot the biggest deer, because he knows where they are, and he chooses the oldest and biggest and feeds it up specially. He worries that I might sell it, and sent me an email recently in which he talked about his love of the property and about its fragility as urban sprawl looms.

"I have a lot of time to think when I'm at Brittan Point," he wrote. "My friends think I'm crazy for spending so much time working out there for no compensation, but no amount of money could provide the peace that the land gives for free (or sweat equity). I've seen things that no one else will see—a bald eagle attacking a blue heron, whitetail bucks fighting in the marsh, otters chasing fish in a tiny creek, dolphins teaching their young how to hunt mullet, bobcats with kittens, etc, etc. The land is a paradise that I'm afraid will not survive once you are gone. If you protect BP while you can, you can preserve it for whatever time it has left before rising sea levels claim it. Just like your dad saved the Everglades, you can do that for Brittan Point."

But I don't want to sell it. It's one of the Last Great Places, as they call them. In fact, in terms of ski resorts, someone once called me the Last Great Place master planner. I was hired by the city of Aspen, the city of Park City, Utah, at least five major ski resorts to do what is called a Last Great Place plan, to save the last great places from development. And here I am, holding one of those places. It would be incredibly hypocritical for me to subdivide it to make a few dollars, and anyway it's been proven to be true in many places, including Martha's Vineyard, that a big piece of undeveloped property is worth more per acre than a small piece. The bigger the piece of land you own, the more wealth you are perceived to have. There's a certain largesse implied, where largesse means living large, striking a balance between Nature and Humankind. Another way of saying that, and it's something my father said a lot, is "live and let live." Enjoy the land and let nature be your partner.

But the problem with that island is that the water levels have risen every year since I bought it. I've had it eighteen years, and the mean water level is well above where it was. The island is only five feet above sea level, so at the current rate, there won't be anything left of Brittan Point or the Low Country in general by the end of the century. This change in sea levels is going to eliminate the human species. Not because they don't have higher ground to go to, but because it will upset the food chain to the point where there wont be enough food to feed people, and there won't be enough fresh water. You can talk about sustainability, you can say you're carbon-free, which is bullshit, but until they solve the greenhouse gas problem … we're doomed.

The band

9

Metro Golden Machinations

I had one elective per semester at NC State, and for four semesters in a row I elected Creative Writing. Told to write a non-fiction short story, mine was entitled "The Churdie Berdy" about that Paonia Cherry Day parade starring two uninhibited sixteen-year-old hotties who choreographed their own parade popping showstopper.

"Churdie Berdy" was an entry-level crack at literary spoonerism, a play on words related to cherries, Chuck Berry's famous walk, and the word "bird" which at the time, thanks to the Beatles, meant a hot young girl. But it was not my first effort at wordplay, I started slipping and sliding on words in high school in Alexandria. My favorite sophomore class was creative writing. We were required to read and then write an essay on Keats' "Ode on a Grecian Urn," and Ms Teach selected mine as "best in class." I was asked to give a brief oral presentation, and my opening line, "Buth is Truety," got a big laugh—everyone thought it was a faux pas from a hick with a flat top crew cut and a Southern drawl. I almost lost my composure, but then made eye contact with Ms Teach who had both thumbs up, and that saved me.

My A+ premise was that if "Beauty is Truth, and Truth Beauty" then...The phrase really made me famous in my high school, my teacher thought I was brilliant. That's when I discovered the power of words.

I scored a victory that day. "Stupid is as stupid does" were the classmates who laughed. Making fun of a skinny kid from Georgia made them feel good. I did not care about being elected to class office. I had no time for beauty contests, female or male. But I did not want to be crowned a country bumpkin either. I wanted to be a writer, musician, artist, or actor. Would it be out of character to lose my Southern drawl? I decided I had to. I worked hard at shifting my accent into northern American, and that's what I speak today, unlike the other members of my family. Looking back, I should not have given a damn one way or the other.

At the end of the summer in Paonia, the two girls and I bid adios to Jeff, his parents, and Old Yellow. We took a commercial airline back to DC I spent a couple of nights with my parents before boarding a Raleigh-bound Greyhound. My parent's send-off gifts were a portable typewriter and $200 in cash. Engineering students were required to have a mechanical analog computer, the slide rule. The gold standard was a ten-inch K&E Deci-Ion which came standard with a handsome, tan leather case with belt loop. I grabbed one of the last second-hand slip-and-slide K&E's sticks for the bargain price of $38. Throw in some miscellaneous school supplies and there was still enough dinero left to join three of my four-bedroom, two-to-a-room, suites only, flatmates for a Friday night tap-beer slugfest at a nearby, off-campus, watering hole with a three-piece rock-a-billy band. A one-dollar cover charge and two more George Washington's bought the first pitcher of beer. Unescorted coeds got in for free, but in those days women engineering students were as scarce as two dimples on one cheek.

In late October, the talent scout called Jimmy Oseth, our lead guitarist, and three days later he hand delivered a MGM contract for our signatures. One codicil stood out. All band members must be ineligible for military draft for a minimum of two years (they assumed we were all enrolled in college).

Jimmy and Tom had dropped out of college before finishing their first year. Tom had knocked up his girlfriend, eloped, and got a job as a baggage handler for Northwest. Tom moved in with his wife's parents so she could finish high school. Eddie's wealthy father got a doctor to petition the draft board to classify Eddie 4F. Physically unfit for service due to bone spurs to be exact, a bogus, hocus-pocus, Trump-like, sleight-of-foot scam. Blinded by starlight, we conspired to lie to MGM. What were they going to do if the truth got out? Sue us?

Over eighteen, our parents bore no responsibility for our conduct. After the all-day MGM recording sessions in New York City over New Year's Holidays, I imagined dropping out of college to become a rock star. "Come Down," written and performed by Beethoven's Fifth, shipped to over 150-DJ's and over the next couple of months "Come Down" got enough air-time to keep MGM interested in our future. They booked us into two NYC clubs, for one week gigs, starting in June. If the gigs went well, we would then go on the road for the rest of the summer as the opening act for one of MGM's top-forty rock bands.

We were five nights into our first gig at a sold-out popular gay club in the Village, when Jimmy and Tom learned they had been drafted. Within a week, both shipped off to boot camp with orders to deploy to Vietnam. One got a cushy job as a typist. The other donned head-to-toe camos, covered exposed skin in oily mosquito repellent, and smeared cheek bones with black shoe polish. Jimmy in jungle boots armed with hand grenades, a M-16, and a machete, followed a rookie second-lieutenant into jungles and rice paddies bordering the Ho Chi Minh Trail. McNamara's cannon fodder, our lead guitarist was lying face down in a pool of blood and rice water less than a month later. A brave medic dragged him to cover. He was unconscious when a corpsman, dangling from a Huey, lifted him from harm's way.

After MASH emergency treatment, he was put aboard a flying hospital. He and dozens of other gravely injured GI's were bound for a nation divided by "whose side are you on" Kent States of the Union. Ambushed in broad daylight, a machine gun bullet had entered Jimmy's shoulder, traveled down his arm, penetrated his upper thigh, and exited his lower calf. My bandmate underwent three major surgeries in three months, and spent the next six months hopping around on one crutch, burdened with the dead weight of a partially paralyzed arm and leg. After nine months, my friend went home to the warm embrace of a loving mother. She prayed for him, cared for him, and cried every time she changed his bandages. He father, a retired officer, blamed his son—not Congress or the US military and arms manufacturers—for what happened. Had his son stayed in college, joined the ROTC and gotten a degree, he could have served his time, possibly the rest of his career, as a Commissioned Officer in the Army.

Before my friend's last operation, I crossed the Potomac to visit him, the day after spending Thanksgiving at my brother-in-law's house in Alexandria. Jimmy was in an amputee ward at the National VA Hospital. A fully ambulatory patient volunteer led me down long corridors lined with wards of patients hooked-up to two IV's: one for blood plasma, the other for pain killers. In the longest hall was a sea of gurneys restraining invisible men bandaged from head to foot. One soldier, his face missing, had an unlit cigarette sticking out of a hole where his mouth should have been. A volunteer caregiver was standing by, making sure he did not burn his burns.

I spent a couple of hours with Jimmy Oseth. He was still hoping they could repair the damage to his right arm, and wanted to get our band back together again. After the two longest hours of my life, I told Jimmy I would be back again, and would bring his guitar with me. Next to Jimmy there was an infantry soldier with similar ambush injuries. The soldier lay motionless, heavily sedated.

Jimmy did eventually go back to college. When he left hospital, Jimmy enrolled in a trade school and subsequently got a job as a computer systems technician at the National Health Institute in Bethesda. As fate would have it, Jimmy went to work as an IT engineer for the National Institute of Health in Bethesda, Maryland where he kept track of Clinical Research Studies, including investigations into the long-term effects of Agent Orange exposure, a jungle defoliant used in Vietnam. He married, raised a family, and learned how to play guitar with one good hand. Jimmy died just before last new year. I hope he lies buried at the Arlington National Cemetery.

After the MGM starship fiasco, I buried myself in engineering classes. My freshman year roommates were now the only two sophomores in the six-man suite. Students were upperclassman. They ran the gamut of family backgrounds from rural farmers to country club elite. None were poor, Black, or Hispanic. The ink on the Civil rights of 1964 was as fresh as a new stick of spearmint gum.

The all-female staff who cleaned and changed the linens in our suite were 100% minority Americans. I learned from one of the Black women that she and her colleagues worked six five-hour days a week. Considered part-time, they did not qualify for the federally mandated minimum wage of $1.25 an hour. In my junior year I befriended their supervisor when he asked for a volunteer from our suite to be the sole student, non-voting, member of an internal performance review committee.

In my fourth and final year at N.C., the Editor-in-Chief of *The Technician,* the University's student newspaper, Peter Burkheimer, and I organized a "sit-in" of the President's Office. The "sit-in" was staged to call attention to a possible civil rights infringement for all custodial staff, regardless of race. Pete and I were joined by several of the School of Engineering's top academic students. After announcing the reason for our visit, the President's assistant asked us to take a seat in the Visitors Waiting Room. A few minutes later she asked our group to select two spokes-people. It was myself and Peter.

I had never met the President. But he knew Peter. Elected Editor-in-Chief for three years running, Peter introduced me to the President. Two eye-to-eye handshakes. Pete asked the President to officially accept our formal petition, citing unfair wages and lack of advancement opportunities for custodial labor, both full and part time, under contract to the University. After reading the Petition the President got up from his desk to leave his office briefly. I saw him hand his assistant a note. He returned to find Pete, leaning over his desk. Pete's finger was pointing to the "accepted by" line on the Petition's signature page. The President got back in his chair behind his desk, reached into his in-box, and starting reading his mail. Pete retreated to the chair next to mine. But not before telling the President we would only leave after he gave us a signed copy of the Petition. We then got the silent treatment for three hours.

At 4:30 p.m. the assistant came in, walked across the room to raise the venetian blinds on a large window. She nodded to the President and pointed out the window. A large crowd of students had gathered on the lawn of the North Campus Quadrangle. Clearly visible filming the crowd was a camera crew from a national network affiliated local TV station. We left with a signed Petition and a gentleman's agreement not to discuss the exact details of the "sit-in" with media outlets.

In the days following the "sit-in," a group of local attorneys stepped in "pro-bono" and successfully negotiated a more favorable labor contract for over 1,500 workers.

I teamed up again that year with Peter, and also a guy named Darryl, to win first prize at the N.C. State Engineering Fair by generating a computer program which showed without a doubt that a State tax-payer funded plan to extend the main runway at Raleigh Durham Regional Airport was wildly inaccurate in terms of the cost and the millions of cubic feet of trucked-in fill dirt required. Then there was the threat to the environment. A large hollow filled with virgin timber and wildlife habitat, the only virgin forest left in that part of North Carolina, was on the chopping block. Our program consisted of 650 punchcards fed through an IBM 360 computer, which was as big as a living room, a BIG living room and the result of it was that the Bill to fund the extension was defeated in the North Carolina State Legislature. A revised runway scheme was submitted and built by a large Raleigh civil engineering firm which also made job offers to all three of us, but we had all decided to move on to post-graduate studies unrelated to engineering.

Ben SideCar 2006

10

Shots Fired

In 1998 no one in China knew I had accidentally almost killed my sister when I was twelve. It was my secret to keep. I was fifty-one, struggling to pay tuition for a daughter in Wellesley College, and a son in a famous, elite, private high school in Cambridge, Massachusetts. I arrived in Shanghai two weeks after my appointment as Xintiandi's chief architect. My contract stipulated that the design of Xintiandi would be done predominately in Shanghai and drawings and specifications would be annotated both in English and Chinese. My "orders" were to organize a Shanghai-based design team ASAP. I needed architects who were fluent in both Chinese and English. My client and I determined the fastest way to make this happen was to "borrow" a half-dozen architects from the Singapore Office of Nikken Seikkei International. My association with Nikken Seikkei dated back to the early 1990s when I was with Benjamin Thompson's design firm. I, and three other colleagues, spent the better part of four years in Nikken's Tokyo office and then in Singapore. Traveling back and forth to the USA several times a year, I worked on projects all over Southeast Asia, collaborating with Nikken Seikkei's International. In Nikken's Singapore office, I worked with several young, bilingual mainland Chinese architects who had left China to get foreign experience and higher wages.

Everything fell into place. Within a couple of weeks, I was at the helm of a Xintiandi team of twelve people. The Singapore "imports" were back in their native country, eager to work with an American architect. I brought two colleagues from my Boston office. The client found the Singapore and USA "imports" places to live and gave us all an allowance for additional expenses. Our international team included a local Shanghainese architect, a management intern from my client's company, and a representative of the construction company responsible for executing our vision. I named our team the Peace Bridge Studio after the XTD neighborhood's original name, Taipingqiao. Taiping (Peace) was also the name of one of the bloodiest civil wars in history in which at least twenty million Chinese lost their lives in a failed, mid-19th Century attempt to overthrow the Qing Dynasty. The Peace Bridge to living history, spiritual regeneration, and authenticity were the themes we pursued philosophically as a studio.

The offices of Peace Bridge Studio were on the eighth floor of one of Shanghai's first top class commercial office and retail complexes, Shui On Plaza. One of Vincent's first real estate developments in China, our Plaza office windows had an unobstructed view of the Xintiandi site. One of the first things I purchased for the office was a huge set of binoculars developed for use by the Chinese Army during the Korean War. The 14-kilogram binoculars came with a heavy wooden tripod which we placed next to our largest window. We would get up from our drawing tables and CAD computers several times a day to troll the site with the optics provided by this low tech, pre-drone, aerial view platform. Leave it to an ex-USAF spy pilot to improvise, in the heat of battle, a way to gather timely site "intelligence." Typically, in a project involving the evaluation of existing structures, a set of "as-builts" would be produced prior to starting design, but we did not have that luxury. President Jiang Zemin's visit to the First Party Congress site of the Chinese Communist Party would be in late 1999, in commemoration of the fiftieth Anniversary of the Peoples Republic of China.

It was late May of 1998 when our studio began producing drawings. We were on a very tight schedule and needed to complete all demolition needed prior to construction and renovation before the end of the year. Our first presentation to the Luwan District government officials was less than six weeks away. Luwan had convened a panel of "experts" to critique the project design. The experts selected were purported to have the prerequisite knowledge and experience to assess the merits of our vision for Xintiandi. Part of this assessment meant evaluating our proposed "means and methods." They were charged with protecting historical artifacts. Achieving commercial success was our problem, not theirs. The site of the First Congress of the Communist Party was in the middle of the two-city-block area allotted for the proposed Xintiandi project. Intellectually, the experts were most comfortable when focusing on this highly sensitive issue, adamant that all buildings that existed in 1921, the year of the First Congress, had to be returned to their original state. In 1998, no Shanghai historic neighborhood had ever been commercially revitalized. Urban design professionals in China, domestic and foreign, then and now, who enslave developers with the strict tenets of preservation, are mostly the equivalent of cultural morticians. Give me creative conservators or grant me a pardon and let me leave the meeting.

I used to jokingly (with no disrespect) refer to the panel experts as grave digging, shovel over the shoulder, embittered, non-recovering, Cultural Revolution, re-educated refugees. I argued repeatedly that culture is a living art. Historic artifacts of the past are inanimate reminders of the way things were. Successive generations should be encouraged to express themselves in conjunction with these artifacts. Each new generation, through the life choices society affords them, should be given an opportunity to define new culture. Contemporary expressions of art, music, architecture, and literature, with roots deep in the past, should not be muffled by tone deaf nostalgia. Making radical alterations to the spatial framework of a historic neighborhood's existing urban fabric; adopting a "Leave nothing behind" redevelopment strategy; or embalming culture by "Freezing time and space" with strict preservation, result in "dead on arrival" urban regeneration strategies.

Among Shui On's upper echelon, only Vincent Lo fully appreciated the enormity of the challenges facing the company. Xintiandi was a "first time in China" project, and looking back, it was a "first time anywhere" project. Not only was the future of a historic neighborhood in Shanghai at stake. With the world watching, the course of the largest urbanization in the history of civilization would be forever altered, as long as Xintiandi proved to be a commercial and cultural success. We had a few weeks, maybe a few months, to deliver to Vincent a watershed, "first time," game-changing, redevelopment strategy. Try and imagine Vincent "losing face," suffering financial ruin, and coping with runaway ridicule, in the middle of a life lived only once. I cannot. Not born the youngest son of a legendary Hong Kong tycoon, it took me fifty years of modest means to wake up with "a face to lose" in the Dragon's Mouth.

In urban design, the ground, the void, the space between buildings, the unbuilt form, is harder to design than the figure, the solid, the building, the built form. Any musician can read and play the notes. Only the great ones read, imagine, and play for you the three-dimensional spaces written between the notes.

These spaces are inked invisibly, by masters of the universe. Einstein was one of those masters but of a different universe. Einstein believed that the space and time of galactic universes are intertwined in an infinite "fabric." This fabric, deformed by the gravitational pull of massive planetary objects and collapsing stars, causes light to bend.

My first experience of actually understanding this phenomenon was in Japan, when I bought a Sony CD Walkman in a Tokyo electronics store and I took a bullet train to Kyoto, listening to Vivaldi's Four Seasons on the way, the earphones feeding the music straight into my brain. The train followed the coastline, and we were going through tunnels, in and out of darkness and light, and suddenly in my mind, I could hear Vivaldi breathing, and I could hear the space between the notes. In the same way, it is the space between buildings that defines an environment. Very few people in my profession understand that. It's probably the thing that distinguishes me most. When I was a jet fighter pilot, it was the three-dimensional space that defined that experience for me, not the speed, or the proximity to built forms. It was navigating the unbuilt sky. From the day I first looked up through the treetops, the sky has always played a major part in my life. And hence in my architecture.

History, not gravity, bends and shapes the urban fabric, the lightness of living, in our cities. Built forms shelter us. Unbuilt forms are our spatial locomotives: our "move" places. Both are synonymous with the terms used to describe the components of any fabric's structural system: solid and void. I cannot resist making a human, anatomically correct, heterosexual, structural, analogy: intercourse. I know there are others, but I am not going there. But if that thing called Bluetooth asks if you want to "pair with another device," ask Alexa if you need a solid or a void condom.

One Luwan expert surprised me. Tongi University Professor Zheng Shilin was familiar with a more contemporary alternative to strict preservation's cryogenic suspension of time. The professor had recently read a few scholarly papers on a relatively new urban regeneration strategy known as "adaptive reuse." What exactly is "adaptive reuse?" There are other, more academic, definitions. Mine: recycle the existing urban fabric's spatial framework using inventive, carefully crafted, design alterations to accommodate commercial and cultural uses. Liberally apply this entrepreneurial-based design process to the built and the unbuilt. Like a boxer, stay light on your feet. Look for existing fabric voids where you can escape the long reach of winter shadows. Use new or enlarged openings in the solids to bend light around and into the dark corners of the existing lanes and alleyways. Comb ruthlessly through the hubris of the past for evidence of authenticity. Build on this evidence when selecting materials and finishes. If an existing window or a doorway is not large enough to provide sufficient shop-front transparency, make it bigger or add new openings. If a roof over a large open courtyard facing south extends the season for al fresco dining, add a simple glass shed roof around the perimeter. Nothing is sacred except the conservation and adaptive reuse of existing human-scaled space. Recycle found objects rich in intrinsic character. Source locally natural indigenous materials, keeping intact beautifully crafted decorative details. And take seriously anything that might contribute to creating a hopelessly romantic, humane environment.

On my client's side there were several very capable people I could turn to for help. Albert Chan, the young architect who gave Vincent a shortlist of potential Xintiandi design architects, had a Master's Degree from Columbia University. After graduation, Albert worked for the New York City Urban Planning Office, and was well-versed in the means and methods of "adaptive reuse." I suspect it was Albert who first introduced the concept of re-purposing for commercial use of historic residential urban neighborhoods. He was witness to the transformation and gentrification of many of New York's urban areas, many of them in mid and lower Manhattan. We shared a great admiration for Jane Jacobs, author of *The Death and Life of Great American Cities*. Professor Emeritus Luo Xiaowei, from Shanghai's Tongji University, shared with us her forty-five years of research into the historical evolution of architectural and urban fabric typologies of the Foreign Concessions. She wrote the definitive book on the Shanghai Lane House, the Shikumen. A scholar's scholar, Xiaowei, was universally admired and respected by all around her. She was an indispensable asset from start to finish.

In January of 1999, Vincent Lo was poised to go where no developer in Shanghai had ever gone before. To facilitate the permission process necessary for the start of demolition and the start of construction, he added to the team a native of Shanghai, Mr Zhou. Zhou was skilled in the art of communication and had years of experience working with real estate developers. Zhou's mission was to find effective ways to help bridge the gap between the often onerous demands of the government and the practical and aspirational needs of the developer. We counted on Mr Zhou "to get the sign-offs chopped and the building inspector's red pens tucked away in their vest pocket protectors." Mr Zhou, like Professor Luo Xiaowei, proved to be invaluable. With his silver tongue, and his Shanghainese dialect, Zhou could have chosen to "go under the table" to do his business. He could have limited his communication skills to lavish praise for a Hong Kong prodigal son. Instead, he chose the high road, taking on with impeccable integrity the complexities of obtaining literally "ground-breaking" permissions needed to allow us to get underway. Mr Zhou did not help navigate the public-private bridge; he was the bridge.

On the other side of the table, Dr Sun Jiwei, a young architect and urban planner, quickly emerged as our guardian angel. At every formal presentation to the Luwan District Architecture and Planning Review Board, and there were many, more than one a month, Dr Sun would voluntarily "translate" our team's ideas. Dr Sun would, with impressive dexterity, interject his own explanations to further our cause. It was apparent from his comments that he had traveled extensively abroad. Over an informal lunch with his daughter and a couple of my colleagues he said: "I stepped up to the plate because they do not know what they do not know." That comment stuck with me. Even today, it has validity depending on how "far" one is from having a passport. Or if they have one, how many blank pages remain. I have dealt with countless "experts" in the course of getting over 200 projects built in China. The bigger obstacle, other than what they do not know, is getting them to admit it. Not a single expert has ever uttered the words: "I don't have a good answer to your question, Mr Wood. You are asking about something I know nothing about."

Work to partially demolish or remove some existing buildings began in January of 1999. This work attracted a great deal of attention, both good and bad. The entire development team including construction managers, contractors, engineers, and architects, gathered on the site to burn incense, eat roast pig, and pray together for good fortune. Morale was high despite heavy flak from some of the experts who continued to claim that the Xintiandi project was tantamount to cultural genocide. The removal of buildings not suitable for adaptive re-use or the modification of them amounted to killing the neighborhood's inherent mockingbird of "innocence." The most outspoken expert told the Luwan District that no one would ever visit Xintiandi unless it was properly preserved as a museum of architecture. The non-executive directors of Shu On Land's board who had not voted in favor of my selection feared that no one except poor people would show up on opening day. Who would want to drink and dine al fresco in the historic alleyways and lanes of a neighborhood that only recently had been an overcrowded slum with no indoor sanitary facilities? As far as Vincent's "suits" were concerned, no amount of money could transform a pigsty into a commercially successful entertainment destination.

I was not only in the fight ring with detractors from Shanghai and Hong Kong. Commercial space planning gurus, marketing, and leasing Pirates from the First World were feverishly looking for a Chinese door to knock on when I gave my mother a hard hat tour of Xintiandi. I had given the same tour to my partner Carlos two months before my mother. Born in a "third world" country in South America, he grew up in NYC and come to Shanghai intending to stay ten days. He stayed less than three.

"It took me my entire life to get out of a third world country and you've brought me back to one," he told me. "You've got to be kidding." Like many Americans in the late 1990s, he could not imagine China ever being anything else but "third world." He didn't say it, but I am certain he was thinking: Why is Ben wasting his time and valuable partnership resources on this selfish adventure?

Many of Xintiandi's naysayers relented after *The New Yorker* magazine published a favorable review in 2003, written Paul Goldberger, a world acclaimed architectural critic. It would take longer for the more cynical to relent. Some never have, convinced that Xintiandi's success has regrettably led to the over-gentrification and an ever-increasing high cost of living in Shanghai. My answer to them: if you choose to live in a first-world city expect to pay first-world prices.

Xintiandi won Vincent's company, Shui On Land, its first Urban Land Institute's Award of Excellence. It has since received four additional Awards of Excellence. My studio, BenWoodStudioShanghai, BWSS, was the principal design architect for all but one of these award winning mixed-use projects.

At a company seminar on urbanization soon after being given one of these coveted awards, Vincent Lo led a discussion of the merits of fair business practice, effective communication, responsible risk management, and the importance of good design. During the Q&A session, one of his executives raised his hand.

"Xintiandi could be far more profitable if we covered the entire two-blocks with a glass roof," the executive said. "Our profits plummet on a rainy day."

Chairman Lo came from behind the lectern and walked down the aisle toward the executive, stopping one row away. "Are you really that dumb?" he said quietly. "A glass roof would kill Xintiandi."

The executive, a senior project manager, was relieved of his responsibilities within the year. This is what happens to people who Vincent no longer believes in. The fired executive went to work for a mega-mall developer, taking a couple of junior staff sycophants with him.

The Shanghai 2010 Expo imagined a "Better City, Better Life" future where ordinary people are given the opportunity to realize their full potential while enjoying ordinary lives. The 2008 "One World, One Dream" Beijing Olympic vision promoted the idea that bigger is better when competing for dominance on the world's socio-economic stage. Shanghai, on the other hand, is not a "One World" city. It means many things to many people, and Xintiandi gave the people of the City of Shanghai a place in which to express this individual diversity. On a good day, over 80,000 people come to Xintiandi to parade on, not compete for, this multi-world stage.

The pomp and circumstance associated with crude oil fueled opulence and hedonistic pampering palaces of OPEC royalty, the much-hyped trips into space by high-net-worth 21st Century tech rocketeers, and the "one-percenters" who attend Margo-a-Lago black-tie fund raisers, have never a better city, or a better life, made.

Wannabes have hired unscrupulous design and marketing firms to purloin the Xintiandi name. And if not the whole name, then the brand suffix, "Tiandi," which means heaven and earth. Despite the many impersonations, Xintiandi still reigns as China's premier paradigm for historic neighborhood re-development. No number of faked pastiches, 3-D printed copies, or bogus petri-dish cultures, cultivated in DNA modified, artificially intelligent virtual worlds, are going to change this fact. Nor will facades adorned with faux artifacts carved on CNC routers, underpinned by pickle jars of strict preservation-branded embalming fluid.

The socio-economic value XTD's unique interpretation of adaptive re-use continues to be self-evident. The tangible, fungible, nature of an older, pre-automobile urban fabric allowed an early, brilliant, and intrepid Great Urbanization pioneer to reach his full potential. Vincent Lo knew he was in a class of one. Vincent's guiding principle was: "He who flies highest, sees the farthest." Xintiandi was his Everest to climb. Thank you, Vincent, for letting me come along for the ride of my lifetime.

Dead Drunk Moon shiners

11

Dead Drunk

The last President my father served under was Jimmy Carter. My mother was a member of the Peanut Brigade and traveled all over the America campaigning for a peanut farmer from Plains, Georgia. Jimmy grew up around folks far less fortunate than himself, but he was accused of being a Southern liberal snob. The absurdity of this accusation is easy to prove—just ask anyone who has ever lived in Plains, Georgia. Jimmy Carter is a Southern liberal who has never hated or looked down on anyone: not even his bigoted, redneck neighbors. Jimmy preached picking peanuts, not fights.

Serving as a high-ranking civil servant in a Democratic administration, my father lost his Washington job after Kennedy's successor, Lyndon Johnson, decided not to run for a second term and a tricky Republican took over the White House. My mother and father moved back to the Woodstock Road farm for a few years.

My father's best friend Charlie was happy to have them back, knowing it meant the famous backyard BBQ would be back in business. Charlie, who had pinned an Eagle Scout medal on my khaki Boy Scout uniform, was no longer the troop leader. His own sons, both Scouts, had grown up.

Eight years after making Eagle, I was living near Phoenix,

Arizona, learning to fly for the USAF. I went home to visit my parents and siblings over the Christmas and New Year holidays. Sometime after midnight on New Year's Eve, Charlie woke up everyone in our house, banging on the front door. Out of breath and smelling of whiskey, he told us he had just run over two men a couple of miles away, and had left his convertible top-down in the middle of the road. My father and I agreed it was a matter of great urgency to visit the site of the accident and see if anyone was still alive. We told Charlie to sit on our front steps and wait for us to come back.

A few minutes later my father had his headlights shining on the front of Charlie's car. We could see no damage except for a few small dents on the front hood above two broken headlights. We could see shiny glass shards left in the headlight frames were covered in what appeared be blood. We pulled our car over, got out and walked down the middle of the road. After following the narrow two-lane road's white line for sixty yards, we found two motionless men lying face up. It was very dark, but I had a flashlight. Bending over the men, lifting their eyelids and checking for signs of life, I saw tire marks across both faces. Their feet were bare except for socks. After concluding they were stone-cold dead, we walked another fifty yards to find an overturned sedan in the roadside ditch. Both doors were wide open. On the ground were several glass mason jars of corn liquor. Some were unopened, a few were broken, and two were open with a little whiskey left in them. In the middle of the road, opposite the ditched car, were two empty pairs of shoes.

I surmised that Charlie's car had struck these men with enough force to lift them out of their cheap loafers. The impact of Charlie's speeding car had pinned one man against the front bumper and left headlight, the other man against the opposite bumper and headlight. Before Charlie managed to come to a stop, both had been dragged under the front wheels of his convertible. The men had either been thrown, or had crawled, from their car after a high-speed rollover. Dead drunk and staggering home, they were killed when another drunk behind the wheel, Charlie, came racing around the bend. It was game over for these bootleggers.

We picked up Charlie and took him to his house, telling him to call the police after he sobered up. Then we went back to bed. Shortly after sunrise on New Year's Day, I heard sirens. But I stayed in bed, not wanting to rat out one of my childhood heroes. The local newspaper reported the accident. Charlie was charged with leaving the scene, but his case was never brought to court. The local police found several cases of moonshine in the trunk of the dead men's car. For the police, the accidental death of two moonshiners was justice served in a rural farming community.

The year after Charlie's manslaughters, I was to be married in Alexandria, Virginia, and I sent Charlie a wedding invitation. Charlie, whose wife had left him behind to drink himself to the grave, took a cab from National Airport. He got as far as the Alexandria Presbyterian Church parking lot. He never made it inside. He passed out, leaning against a tombstone in the church cemetery just a short distance from the church steps. Charlie, like my father, died too young. But I didn't attend his funeral. Nor did I attend the funeral of his eldest son, a friend of mine, who died a drunk, too young. Charlie and his son both left this world as lonely men. Seeing the tire tracks on the faces of two dead men robbed me of my youth. And today, the BBQ pit, the track and field pitch, and the century-old oaks are long gone. In the move to Virginia, the treasured Civil War cannonball was lost. After the death of my father in 1986, the Woodstock Road farm was sold to a strip mall developer. Today, the butcher counter of a famous grocer occupies the ground under the bedroom I shared with my

Uncle Ben Waltzing his sister Matillda

brother. Any evidence of our beloved homestead has completely disappeared.

My mother, Matilda King Wood, moved into a new house that I designed. My brother built the House of Wood with lumber he cut and milled on-site, with a vertical band-saw mill. The principal living areas were designed around a stone chimney with three fireplaces. All the stones came from abandoned, plantation era chimneys. The largest fireplace anchors a two-and-one-half story high, wood paneled, cathedral ceiling dining room that can sit twenty-eight people at one long oak table. We put a sign over the main entry doors to the dining room: "Welcome to Tillie's Ballroom." We thought about calling the room "Waltzing Matilda's" Ballroom, but no one had ever called my mother Matilda except her brother Ben—who had "Matilda" painted on the noses of every USAF fighter plane he flew in World War II.

That backyard, and Tillie's ballroom, live on in my work as an architect. In those rooms, one outdoor and one indoor, the art of entertaining, storytelling, and live performance was always in plain view. I took from these spaces everything important that I ever needed. So did my sister and my brother. My brother got elected Mayor of Roswell after his annual all-night-all-next-day pig roast made him famous. My sister entertains family and friends in an open air, timber framed pavilion that overlooks horse country in the rolling foothills and blue ridges of north Georgia's Appalachian Mountains.

In the Ozian woods next to the Pavilion, there are dozens of gremlins, goblins, hobbit houses, fairy castles, and fantasy figures handmade from clay and colored with love by my sister. MaMa Mary Jo is every child's Good Witch Lollipop.

If your mother Matilda is waiting by the side of the road for you to return from school in a yellow bus, take her by the hand. When the yellow school bus brought me home from school, my mother would be waiting me at the foot of our driveway. She would take my hand, pausing for a minute or two to smell the heady perfume wafting from the stamen of a blooming beauty, the Japanese honeysuckle. This tuber thrived in the semi-damp soil at the bottom of a drainage ditch at the foot of our driveway. Suckles, like tall buildings, need a lot of air and they need full sunlight. Our suckle got both by hitchhiking a ride on a nearby neighbor, and Oriental kin, the Rosa rugosa. Using spiraled, suture-like threads, suckles rope-up, cling, climb, and tie-off at the top of the rugosa's deadheaded stems. A brawny, hardy thorn bush, with tiny white, non-aromatic rose blooms, Rosa rugosa is the ugly beast of botany. The rugosa's concertina of barbs helped keep our livestock in the pasture and us children in the yard. A ruby-throated hummingbird watched as my mother, Matilda, waltzed my tongue across a Japanese pollen-dusted edible pink kimono as sweet as clover honey. Wild songbirds, picking the rugosa's itty-bitty red berries, danced and fluttered their wings, some swooping our way as if to ask: call out my name. Baltimore Oriole, American Cardinal, Bluebird, Yellow Tanager, Warbler, Goldfinch, Chickadee, and Carolina Wren, names my parents taught their children, are my first memories of living color. Mother made bird suet, from scratch, to fill wire mesh feeders she hung from tree branches outside our kitchen windows. She serenaded anyone watching with "You'll come a-waltzing, Matilda, with me."

The beauty and the beast, the suckle and rugosa, were planted by my father. My mother had a master's degree in botanical science, and she wrote a thesis on the morphology of several species of mushrooms unique to North America. But she was too pregnant with me to blow the whistle when an agent from the State Agricultural Service met with my father and recommended suckle and rugosa as less expensive alternatives to barbed wire fence and metal erosion control weirs. These two plants were new-to-Georgia interlopers. No one was aware that both were emperors without clothes, wreaking havoc and choking everything in their path. Years later, they were officially recognized as extremely invasive bad actors. Shawshank-ed by a State Agency, my father spent thousands of hours on a Ford Tractor pulling a Bush Hog trying to halt the merciless advance of the beauty and the beast. Whenever he could not get the tractor down a trench clogged with mud, leaves, covered over by thick suckle vines, he called in the cavalry, and into the killing fields of a rural Georgia farm rode the Emperor of Death, Generalissimo Monsanto, leading a band of herbicidal warriors with links to non-Hodgkin's lymphoma.

Summer Of Love

12

Summer of Love

My graduation from N.C. State University in May of 1969 ended my undergraduate draft deferment. I was in the University of Colorado Law School library studying my final exams when a blue plastic ball with my month and day of birth, was put in a basket with 365 others. Held on the evening of December 1, 1969, the first military lottery of the Vietnam War had started without me. When I finally returned home to watch TV, the Lottery was on number 160. Five balls later, there it was, December 4th OMG, F—k me!!

I immediately moved out of my expensive Boulder apartment and went to live in the basement apartment of a large, two-story Victorian, in north Denver. A classmate named Bill who had decided to drop out before taking his first semester finals, lived upstairs with his wife and fourteen-year-old stepsister. Finishing my first semester exams was a real chore. I had a daily, one-hour commute to-and-from Boulder.

The move to Denver almost ended my life. Bill and his wife were both needle freaks, addicted to crystal meth. Bill's step-sister was becoming a woman. Already in a free fall from innocence, she spent her after-school hours flying high and low, from light into darkness. One day her angelic, gossamer wings of youth held her aloft, the next she struggled, motherless and alone. Bill's dual universe became hers. And, for a time, mine too. On one end of a warm gun loaded with crystal meth was life, and on the other, death.

Three days before Christmas, I left Denver and drove for twenty-nine hours straight. Alone in my two-seat Karman Ghia with a radio that did not work, I stayed awake singing, strung out on the residual traces of crystal meth in my bloodstream. When I got home to my parents, I slept for two days. My father woke me on Christmas morning. Amazed to be among the living, I never again stuck a needle in my arm. Four nights later, Charlie knocked on our door, dead drunk.

Certain to be inducted into the US Army half-way into my second year of law school, I applied for, and was granted, an indefinite leave of absence from Law School. Officially, I was still enrolled in law school even though I had not attended a single first year, second semester class. The war in Vietnam was raging, body bags were coming home in droves to funeral homes across America, only a few months stood between my life as a civilian and a minimum two-year tour of duty in Vietnam.

I returned to Denver and my basement apartment, but I stayed off hard drugs and found a full-time job at a Civil Engineering firm, Sellars and Grigg. I worked as part of a team working on a new state highway and local interchange design. I went back to my basement every day, did a lot of reading, and played vinyls for Bill's step-sister. Twice Bill overdosed and his wife and I had to take him to the emergency room.

When he could not pop up an arm vein to shoot on his arm, he started on the top of his hands. When he went to the bank to withdraw cash from his divorced mother's trust fund, he wore gloves so the bank officers and tellers could not see the tracks.

I asked my boss Dave Sellars for enough time off to make a late spring trip to see my best friend, Jeff. Jeff was the high school buddy who had co-driven Old Yellow on our summer of '65 trip west to Paonia. Jeff and Heather were attending college in Durango, Colorado. On my second night in town, Jeff and I played joined a pickup band to play for an unsanctioned, off campus, Ft. Lewis College, coed dance. The cheap wine and keg party was held in a large Victorian mansion locally known as the Gable House. Abandoned for over ten years, the house was in rough condition. The current owner, Durango's postmaster, illegally rented out the house for parties. After the party in question, with the band equipment locked safely in the back of a rental van, I unpacked my sleeping bag and crashed on the floor of the big, ground-floor living room.

The next morning, a Sunday, Jeff, Jeff's brother Robert, Jeff's girlfriend Heather, and I, explored the mansion's three floors and basement. We found posted on the front door a 120-day Condemnation Notice. July 1st was the deadline. I told my three companions we should see if there was any chance of buying the house. It was going to be torn down soon, so the owner would probably sell the house for a song. I suggested Jeff and I visit the city's Building Department, when it opened in the morning. I wasn't a home repair expert, but a degree in civil engineering would be of help when deciding if any conditions for getting the house "un-condemned" were impossibly onerous. If they weren't, the next stop would be a visit to the post office to speak with the owner. By the end of Tuesday, after enlisting the aid of a local attorney, we signed a contract with Mr Postman. He agreed to sell the house for $15,000. We had five days to come up with a $2,500 downpayment, with the balance due on the July 15.

The Gable House was a Victorian Queen Anne with seventeen rooms and seven gables. Built in 1892 from plans adapted from a popular Victorian pattern book, a wealthy family lived in it home in the beginning. A decade later, the house was sold to a private tuberculosis clinic owner, Doctor Ochsner, from New Orleans. The good doctor converted the Gable House into Ochsner Hospital, with an X-ray room, operating room, and pharmacy. Three decades after that, Durango's largest Queen Anne was purchased by the county. Renamed Community Hospital, for almost three decades all of Durango's newborns were delivered in the Victorian lady. Community Hospital moved into a new facility in 1960.

We scrambled to scrape the money together. We pawned two spare Fender guitars, one Epiphone bass, and an extra amplifier and microphone. We borrowed money from friends. We took what we could from our personal bank accounts. And before the downpayment had been delivered, we had already begun removing rusted pipes, cracked radiators, broken furniture, and piles of fallen ceiling plaster. I went to a hardware store, bought plumbing tools and the hardware needed to repair leaks in the coal-fired steam boiler. A retired plumber who worked part time at the hardware store helped me choose the right stuff. Underneath layers of paint, wallpaper, and linoleum, were beautiful oak floors, rich heart-pine wainscot, and solid hardwood raised-panel doors with brass hinges and hardware. These discoveries helped kick our asses into gear. We were determined to derail the demolition of our new home. The biggest obstacle was a new roof. Replacing broken windows and getting the coal-fired furnace working again seemed like a walk in the park compared to putting all-new shingles on a steep roof with an upside-down, ice cream cone, corner tower. We were in desperate need of help. I called my brother in Georgia and invited him to come to Durango. And asked him if he could please, please, bring along a friend who knew something about carpentry.

We pinned notices on bulletin boards and telephone posts, offering Gable House beds to young people who had come to

Durango in hopes of landing tourist season jobs. Our notice stated we would accept part-time house repair labor in lieu of rent. All chose the work-in-lieu-of-rent option. With this labor windfall, we had at least an outside chance of crossing the condemnation notice finish line on time.

The Summer Dinner Theatre, in the ballroom of historic Durango's Grand Dame, the Strater Hotel, had hired a group of actors and actresses from Yale University's School of Drama. The Theatre offered them bunk beds in male and female dormitories in the hotel's dank, dark, windowless, basement. With pocket money to spare, the Yalies opted to join the Gable House Gang. Wearing safety harnesses and moving scaffolding around, our house mates used ropes and pullies to hoist bundles of roofing shingles up to the roofing crew: my brother Jeff and me. Drawing on mountaineering and rock-climbing techniques, I devised a fall-protection rig. We worked like aerial acrobats, rappelling up and down to pound copper roofing tacks into straight lines of thousands of overlapping, random-width, square-ended, factory-split, cedar shingles. Working ten hours a day, seven days a week, the Gable House had a new roof one week before the condemnation deadline.

The other war, the Cold War, was buried deep in the ground near Durango. The sagebrush deserts south of Durango were dotted with top secret, underground, concrete silos with nuclear warhead ICBMs. By mid-July, the United Gable House (UGH) Gang had swelled to twenty-eight people. And we, the people, believed love was free and both wars were for other people to prosecute. Our sovereign charter: be kind to others and enjoy a summer of sex, skinny dipping, and rock-and-roll.

We had few rules, but one was cardinal: no drugs in the house. Others were more benign. If you missed your turn washing dishes or preparing meals, you had to put a dollar in a jar for party beers and tortilla chips. The UGH coed team played in the local summer Parks and Rec softball league. Our opponents were mostly all-male clubs from fire, police, and roads and sewer departments, the chamber of commerce, community hospital staff, and Ford, Chevy, and Dodge pickup truck dealer employees. In the above photo, the dude in the white Nehru jacket was our team catcher, and my Gable House co-owner Jeff Bryson. Shortly after this UGH gang photograph was taken, Jeff had his jaw broken by a bat. He spent the rest of the summer with his jaw wired shut, sucking down shakes and six-packs of Coors with a plastic straw.

I am the one sitting in an antique wicker rocker wearing a brand new, wide lapel, white cotton suit made by a local tailor. I wanted to be Tom Wolfe in the Wild West. My right hand is on the back of the UGH mascot, a black Labrador name Afro, the other on a finely woven straw cowboy hat. Surrounding me are the 1970 "Summer of Love" UGH nation. The lanky kid with the ten-gallon hat wearing painter's overalls is my younger brother, Jere. To my right, on the lawn, are two women. The curly redhead worked as a waitress in one of Durango's many Western movie set seasonal restaurants near the famous Durango-Silverton Narrow Gauge Train Depot. Behind the waitress is a summer-stock actress from the School of Drama at Yale. Her boyfriend, a black-teed, velvet top-hatted, bearded, actor, and Yale classmate, is standing directly behind her. The fellow standing to my immediate right with his hand on the back of the chair is Eddie Williamson. Eddie, like Jeff and Heather, was a high school classmate and an original equity partner in the Gable House. Last I heard, twenty years ago, Eddie was living in Eugene, Oregon. The woman with curly long blond hair kneeling on the grass to my left was my number one girlfriend. Alas, I have forgotten her name, but remember we made love like rabbits. The others in the photograph will have to go unnamed, their names lost, but remaining friends forever. The handsome dude standing with his legs crossed was a serious ladies' man and the best table billiards shooter in the bunch. Took a lot of small money from me. Jeff's girlfriend Heather and my Gable House co-owner, is not in the picture.

We constructed a sweat-naked lodge and sauna yurt outside the rear kitchen door, behind a shrubbery fence. We put hot rocks from a small bonfire in the kitchen driveway inside the yurt, and spread them out on the lid of a metal trash can. When cans of stale beer were poured over the rocks, the aroma of wheat was intoxicating.

A grandmother who lived next door, with her adorable husband, told us great growing-up-in-Durango stories. She showed us how to make a pie filling from the rhubarb that grew along our joint fence line. We converted the old carriage house into a painting and pottery studio.

Gable House magic hours were well after midnight, when a game of musical beds was played up and down the second-floor hallway in two-to-a-room bedrooms reserved for females and the Yale couple only. The two Yale love-birds did not play musical beds. Neither did my two co-owners, Jeff and Heather, who slept in the only ground floor bedroom. But me? I went full monty, filling dance cards 7/7. Not for the faint-hearted or inhibited, we let it all hang out. That summer, things got more than raunchy and ripe as the innocence of youth oozed from every orifice and pore of our bodies.

After the building inspector took down the notice the morning of July 1st, news traveled fast. Within a week everyone in the town isolated in the only four-state corner of the American Southwest with a lone Dairy Queen knew we had managed to meet the condemnation deadline. The postmaster's wife went ballistic. She had set her heart on one day moving into her grand dame, having convinced herself that her loving husband would find a way around the condemnation issue. She threatened Mr Postman with divorce if he didn't hire a good lawyer, one who could dig deep for a legal excuse to sue us. Mrs Postman wanted our signed purchase and sales agreement annulled. Poor Mr Postman had bet on us falling flat, smack down on our long-haired, hippie faces. Confident that we would walk away from the deal, forfeiting our down payment, he bet on his own high horse and lost.

Left with only one card to play, Mr Postman knocked on our door: "Where's my $12,500?"

We told him the money was in an escrow account at the Bank of Durango. We had sent love letters and pictures of the Gable House to our parents. Our letters included a detailed description of the work we had done. We begged for money. Even before any of our parents could respond we got a call from the President of the Bank of Durango, who was a good friend of the lawyer who helped us with deal with Mr Postman. Mr Bank President knew we had achieved the impossible, and congratulated us. The next day, in his office, we signed a $14,000, fifteen-year mortgage. The bank threw in an extra $1,500 to pay off our outstanding charge account balance owed to one of their best customers, the Durango Building and Lumber Supply Company. Mr Postman's wife left him.

The UGH Gang's first public act of civil unrest was the Free Dean Movement. Dean was the son of the head of the Drama Department at Durango's Fort Lewis College, Southwest Colorado's sole institution of higher learning. In early June, Professor Drama had received a letter from his ex-wife informing him that their son was going to Durango to live with him. Drama had a live-in girlfriend. He asked if his son, Dean, could room and board at the Gable House.

When the group photograph was taken, Dean was in the county jail. He'd been charged with trespassing on Federally owned property with intent to vandalize. Dean had been given a summer job as a day laborer by an earth-moving company under contract to the US Forest Service. On his first day at work, Dean was instructed to clear broken-off tree limbs as the trees were dozed by a big Caterpillar. But Dean, a kindhearted soul, chased down the dozer, deciding to lay down on the ground in front of the machine to try and stop the carnage. A Forest Service ranger was called in by the contractor. The ranger took Dean to meet a Durango police car waiting nearby.

Father Drama had not told us his son Dean suffered from a severe mental disability. Dean was tall and handsome, but his mind was moving through space on the way to the other side of sanity. But we knew Dean was not a malicious person, and didn't want to see this harmless man go to prison. The second day after his arrest, our gang made a big "Free Dean" banner. A dozen of us walked together, line abreast, holding the banner out front, several blocks to the city jail. Standing outside his narrow cell window we chanted "free Dean, free Dean" in between choruses of "We Shall Overcome" and "Kumbayah." It took a few minutes for the police to arrive. We were on public property and peacefully protesting, so initially no words were exchanged. After thirty minutes, the police suggested we move on. We did, but came back three more times. At Dean's pre-trial hearing, a Federal judge dispatched from Grand Junction released Dean into the custody of his father. Professor Drama gave his pledge that he would take Dean for regular visits at a private psychiatric clinic.

Our second "public" act only took a few hours and was

executed under the cover of darkness. Fort Lewis College was on top of a mesa one-half mile from town. On the slope of the mesa facing town, written with white paint on large, hand-placed, flat rocks, were three, fifty-foot-long, letters, "F," over "L," over "C." No freshman class football player escaped the pre-season "re-paint the letter rocks" ritual and keg party.

No fake white stone were left unturned the night seven men and one woman turned off the headlights of their trusty yellow milk truck and drove to the end of a steep, gully side, dirt road. We were on a mission: to decimate beyond recognition an un-artful, undignified, immature, super-sized piece of graffiti. We pushed and we shoved until every white stain was slid out of line. Pummeled by low-punching, hunched over, role-reversed, raiders, the daubed alphabetic defacement of a hillside by leather-sleeved, letter-jacketed jack-asses, was transformed into a random giant bird poop facsimile. We made it back to the Gable House before sunrise claiming victory for our side, the Other Side. The only female on our team, who had a degree in philosophy, joked we had successfully put to bed a Sisyphean, rookie freshman Raider ritual.

This second public act was never make public. No FLC Raider archival reference commemorates this victory by a motley crew from the UGH nation. I look back on this act as one of my finest hours. Leading a light, horseless brigade, I unmercifully emasculated an entire football team. Magnificent performance in perfect harmony with the Ute, Hopi, Navaho, and Apache spirits that haunt the white man's killing fields in the Animas valley to this day.

In retrospect, the Summer of Love was a fascinating lesson in sociology. Twenty-eight people, from all parts of America, all within a couple of years of age, lived, played, and worked together under the same roof. We lived on a staple of oatmeal and scrambled cheese eggs, fresh vegetable soup, peanut butter and jelly sandwiches, homemade bread, and chili with rice. On Friday nights we played eight-ball, drank Coors on tap from chilled mugs, and munched on pickled eggs dipped in rock salt at a main street pool hall. But by far the most memorable events of the Summer of Love were the daily evening meals. Dining together at a big, long table, made from sawhorses and plywood, was our life raft. We were a mutual support group unafraid to share our joys and our sadnesses. All in the same boat, close encounters, unabashed emotional outbursts, and impromptu confessions kept peace among us.

The slightest criticism of anti-war activist tactics by a gang member could ignite a heated debate that would last for hours. The only member of the UGH facing the darkness I knew was coming, I listened quietly, and prayed silently that the Shadow, the evil that lurks in the hearts of powerful men, would pass. I hoped against hope that the War would end before my number came up. I counted on the Yalies, masters of improvisation, to interject levity and hilarity when things started to get ugly. Some good comedy, or a fine-tuned impersonation, made bearable the angst of my secret debate: file as a conscientious objector, escape to Canada, or serve the country I loved? How do you go on loving a country when "first they take your freedom, then they take your life"?

The Summer of Love went by quickly. Each time we said our goodbyes to a "family" member we cried. Everyone went their own way in the end, proud of their part in staging a comeback for a Durango landmark. All except one, who never had to say goodbye. Heather Bryson, Jeff's ex-wife, an alumnus of the Summer of Love, is today the house's sole owner. Royally ensconced in a glorious mansion, Heather meticulously maintains this stunning artifact of a bygone era. More than 130 years of history live on at Heather's Gable House bed and breakfast. Her guests return year after year to enjoy her hospitality and listen to her amazing stories, including of the infamous 1970 Summer of Love. Long live the Gable House, and hats off to you, Heather!

Wind up Tin Toy Carpetbagger from Little Shop of Curios

13

Damn Yankees

China's Great Urbanization attracted architects and urban planners from all over the world. Executives and equity partners from international design firms came and went, never staying long enough to get tired of their hotel room. Many came on tourist visas. Getting a work visa meant having to file a Chinese tax return. Staffing their Chinese offices with less expensive locals, the "carpetbaggers" insisted that their Chinese clients pay them offshore in US dollars. When given design responsibility for one or more city blocks, they chose the most expedient and profitable solution: repetitive variations of a single theme. Tall, fat, or skinny, the skin is a curtain of glass, framed by extruded lattice in one of fifty shades of grey. One aesthetic, one world, one dream. Three- and four-letter by name, foreign firms presented their designs like a box of chocolates or a Reagan jar of jelly bellies: pick your favorite. All the ones you leave behind will eventually find a home.

Coming from the South of the United States, this unscrupulous approach was not foreign to me. The Northern carpetbaggers who rushed south to feast on the funds being poured into Reconstruction following the Civil War didn't care and didn't stay. Nor did these allegedly world-class architects, renowned for their stellar design of high-rise buildings and mega-malls.

Adopting the podium-tower as the prime building typology for block-by-block commercial redevelopment was a colossal blunder. It is a building type which compares to one of the most toxic pesticides ever invented, a "miracle" drug which was taken off the market after class-action lawsuits brought the chemical companies to their knees. To this day, no one knows how many people died from its use. The company made a conscious decision to keep the toxic killer on the shelves, buying time as they frantically developed an alternative, non-toxic formula.

Any architect who tells you they can design an environmentally sustainable "green" city block podium with or without towers, is full of shit. One day, I hope humanity files a class action lawsuit against the owners and operators of these indoor, life support, terrariums for captive homo sapiens. This lawsuit will not bankrupt anyone. Like all invasive species, they are too prolific, too systemic, to go quietly.

Residents of existing urban neighborhoods, living with the unhinged visual pollution of windowless, big box, opaque podium walls plastered with outdoor advertising, are owed a public apology and some level of financial restitution. China's commercial podium towers are like the Berlin Wall before artistic graffiti replaced coils of barbed wire as the principal decoration. Hostility can imitate art. And art can intimidate hostility. The Wall came down, so can the Chinese cousin. Artful, friendly, fresh-air, street-front alternatives are multiplying exponentially down every shady street in the former French Concession and beyond. Boutique shops and rogue micro-flagship stores, run by colorful, fired-up, wired-in, young entrepreneurs are giving the malls a run for their money. And they are coming in covered in roses. Young eagles and a famous seagull now soar in circles above fields of newly minted Urb-manna. Urb-manna, not from heaven, but from the creative ovens of independent thinkers, is resurrecting an endangered, pre-social media phenomena: people with the ability to make up their own minds.

International "starchitects" were not the only "wow factor" snake oil hawkers to grind the monkey for iconic commissions. A Chinese Master made his bid for "starchitectdom" by painting a stack of gigantic Lincoln Logs Chinese red. He tapered the stack bottom to top and then flipped it upside down. Voila! Instant masterstroke! He then had the Expo Authority insist that magazine and media editors have this red dream photographed only at sunrise, sunset or during night illumination. The rest of the time, all four sides of the inverted traffic cone are bathed in a morbid shadow. Color changes with the absence of direct sunlight. Dip a sun-ripened apple in dried blood. Still want to kiss the bride of the Expo?

A mass exodus to the suburbs plagued many post-World War II American cities. White-male American city mayors made run-down urban neighborhoods sacrificial lambs, subservient to the needs of powerful private interests. City councils all across America robbed the poor to feed the rich. The middle class with two-car garages got fatter and happier.

China and Shanghai are recognizing the lessons to be learned from this American debacle. The human spirit is not invincible. Policies that encourage the destruction of existing urban neighborhoods and rural communities can adversely affect a society's eunoia. What does it mean to be Shanghainese when all around you the city is changing? It is a question that demands an answer.

Few people living in Shanghai have ever ridden a pony bareback, felled a tree with an axe, or lived off the land. But with a colorful and profoundly urbane heritage, the people of Shanghai have always felt "chosen." Chosen, by virtue of birth right, to be forever modern. For Shanghainese, the most valuable commodity their city has to offer is itself. Teeming with mesmerizing man-made attractions, Shanghai ranks with New York, Tokyo, Paris, London for world city status. In Shanghai, where you live, what you do, and who you do it with determines your identity.

Less than a decade after I arrived in China, new construction of single-family suburban houses and golf courses were banned. Developers tried for years to find clever ways around this prohibition. Some are still trying. Beijing has banned gated residential compounds. Gated urban residential compounds in Shanghai can no longer present blank walls to public sidewalks. Only open, vertical iron or stone balustrades are permitted. The new wall requirement is a highly visible, less hostile, welcome gesture of civility. I hope the next thing to be banned are the four strands of electrified fence. I once watched, with horror, a small child climbing a trellis and almost grabbing one of these wires. I screamed from across a narrow side street and the child's mother, who was chatting with a friend, ran and grabbed her child from the trellis.

Sadly, in both Pudong and Pushi, residential compounds and commercial super-block podiums continue to proliferate. Solid black on a Nolli Rome Map, footprints of these "energy guzzlers" figure the ground where small courtyards, kitchen gardens, and potted sunflowers of roof top terraces, once celebrated ordinary life. The leisure wear and fashion palaces, that every day usurp this historical currency, resort to displays of grow-light bean sprouts and fake green stage props to advertise LEED-rated, "healthy," indoor environments.

China's national government has in recent years championed "People Centric, Culturally Focused" urban redevelopment. The mantra is: see clearly the cultural artifacts left behind by past generations. Prevent any further erosion of Chinese cultural identity. Move forward with public sector urban planning initiatives that put people first.

The carpetbaggers moved in like late night prostitutes to seduce Chinese developers. They used every trick in the book. Emphasize form over function, bend, twist, add a second skin but let some slip show. Split the torso and give mister bow legs a pair of giant trousers. If it turns you on, we can lower the neckline. Let the tall tower wow-bow, boom, and zoom. Let it shake-shake, but not in an earthquake. For something more horizontal, find a slinky to snake, curl, coil, bump, grind, and crawl. A famous female architect charged extra for bubble roof prophylactics that leaked. Her lap dance drew attention from all the right places.

The first wave of carpetbaggers set their sights on China's East Coast, first-tier cities, and Beijing and Shanghai were primetime petri dishes for glassy skyline experiments. China's overnight mega-cities and new CBDs got in the queue. The second wave landed on the beachheads south of the Yangtze. Shenzhen became China's "overnight city." The ancient port cities of the Pearl River Delta proved more difficult. Guangzhou, with the third biggest, "go fishing" concession in China, had deeply rooted ancestral enclaves to gerrymander. The carpetbaggers ran the glory gauntlet, from shining East seas to the other side of the Gobi. From Ulan Batar to Xishuangbanna.

In the early 1990s, Shanghai's urban infrastructure engineers and planners collaborated with foreign experts and a Japanese mega-bank to produce a grand vision for the future development of the burgeoning metropolis. Across the Huangpu River from historic Puxi, Pudong would be the new Mouth of the Dragon. Plans were drawn up to open this vast Yangtze Delta outwash to a government-sponsored land rush. Pudong would soon be crisscrossed with six-and-eight lane arteries and veins. Construction of this colossal network of infrastructure would eventually denude the landscape of any traces of Pudong's agrarian, pre-industrial, settlement patterns. Bulldozed and buried, decomposing cultural artifacts provided plenty of false praise and potting soil for successive waves of mutant, colorless, disfigured, shiny shinned, penile, skyline punters.

Symbolically, seeds for these mammoth erections were broadcast from the revolving round observation deck of Shanghai's bubble-on-a-tripod, syringe-on-top, postcard picture Oriental Pearl Television Tower (which I have come to love). Seeds dispersed, time to grow them. Dig a hole, drive sheet piles, and shot-crete a "bathtub." Keep the tub from popping up from the quagmire's ground water with hundreds of friction piles inter-twinned with the microscopic sucking orifices of organic, hypha mucus, mycelium. Smother the tub with a short stack of bookended, mall-rat tracked, atrium pierced, flavor of the day, pancakes. Last to rise was the piece-de-resistance. Knights in shining armor with iconic, hypertrophic, power trip, boners used the podiums as hitching posts.

Branded erections, these ubiquitous, soulless, edifices became symbols of China's exploding global economy. The footprints of Pudong's podiums "figured" the ground where small outdoor courtyards and kitchen gardens of farmhouses had once faced the sun. Fertile ground gave way to indoor atriums lined with grow-light tanning salons and instant noodle vending machines. Nirvanas of commerce, parasitic podiums pogo-sticked willy-nilly down Century Avenue. The son of Third Reich architect, Albert Speer Junior, penned this mesonic, East meets West, seemingly endless axis. The Pudong Development Bank gave the order for everyone to get in line, stay the course, and pay the piper. And they did.

Domestic and foreign currency traders, local and international money lenders, flush with cash, lined-up cheek-to-jowl, opposite the ancestral, neoclassical landmarks of Shanghai's historic Bund. Giant LED flash cards taunted and flaunted wealth for the wealthy. Wannabes seduced with interest-only time deposits. There were stiff penalties for early withdrawals. Banks charged usurious rates not aligned with any cost-of-living index. Eager to squeeze blood from the uninitiated, state-owned banks flogged alternative "paper" investments that promised higher returns but provided no risk protection. Unqualified first time home buyers were sucked in by offers of low-down payments and easy credit. Eager for pre-mature social status, newlyweds gobbled up Pudong apartments. Pudong soon became Shanghai's "build it and they will come" field of dreams. Borrow now. Why wait for tomorrow to live a comfortable, carefree, life? Many buyers faced a lengthy commute to Puxi jobs. Expatriates began to refer to Pudong as Pu-Jersey.

Wealthy Shanghainese, foreigners, returning foreign-born Chinese, and Chinese citizens from other parts of China, seeking the cosmopolitan amenities of big city life, created a market for luxury, mid-and-high-rise apartments in the historic former foreign concessions. Gentrification, an inevitability married to urbanization, was knocking on Puxi's door. Following the success of Xintiandi, other district governments seized the day, and construction of new infrastructure moved to the fast lane. Armed with new guidelines and revenue projections, government empowered prospectors searched the city for dilapidated, blighted, impoverished areas ripe for re-development. Entire neighborhoods of mom-and-pop shops, and vendor-based markets were suddenly looking down the barrel of hovel and hearth wrecker, widow maker edicts.

In the late 1990s an Asia-wide economic recession made it difficult for real estate developers to borrow money. But a few intrepid pioneers knew that all boats float in a rising tide, and temporary mooring during a storm doesn't change that. Vincent Lo was one of a handful of wealthy individuals who elected to risk their personal fortunes. Competition during the Asian financial crisis was limited to long-term investors that wanted to own the rising boats themselves, not leave them to the banks. CapitaLand, Singapore's government-owned REIT, was one of the lead dogs in the hunt, and Vincent's bet was on the development of the Taipingqiao district, a city within a city which became Xintiandi. Vincent could see the forest even as he imagined the individual trees. And CapitaLand was no laggard either. They became great clients, but unlike Vincent, they saw only trees.

At the end of the Asian financial crisis, legions of real estate developers came to Shanghai to collect, not create, value. Building and selling luxury apartments was quick, short-term money. Slowly at first, then faster and faster, old neighborhood lanes and intersecting alleys gave way to economically expedient, pure residential, gated compounds. Perimeter walls, capped with four strands of electric fence, kept out the riff-raff, the barbarians, and the huddled. Lowly, local neighbors strolled the surrounding streets on summer nights in their pajamas. Security guards in drab garb, with time to burn, joined sympathetic compound dwellers to protect feral cats, tossing them scraps of beggar's chicken. Groundskeepers strung monofilament fishing line from tree trunks to prevent wild song birds from alighting on compound garden fountains. Easy prey for the stray cats, but not pretty to watch.

In 2021, Vincent completed Taipingqiao's fifth gated community. All five have walls topped with live, bare, electric wires. In 2005 I moved into the first one, the only one designed by my firm. Nobody's perfect.

An older generation of Shanghainese, living in the historic

East-meets-West former concession areas, had no desire to move to a new apartment in a Chinese version of Houston, Texas. They wanted nothing to do with Pudong's unrefined, cowboy-town manners. Initially the city government argued that updating the existing, functionally obsolete urban infrastructure of Puxi was expensive, and messy. Expats and wealthy Chinese who demanded "modern" became outliers, living in ex-urban gated communities far away from the city center. Nouveaux riche Chinese moved into golf course country club villas. Minhang District southwest of the city, once a sleepy holdover from the Canal and Watertown era, was transformed into a segregated bespoke community tailor-made for expatriates, with international schools and western food emporiums. Kids with foreign passports who did not live in Minhang were "bussed in," swelling the student bodies of expensive, for-profit K-to-12 campuses. My design firm worked with the American School for several years, and they have Carlos and I to thank for their world class Performing Arts Center, a state-of-the art Aquatic Center, new library and blackbox theatre.

I remember my last visit to the Luwan District Flower Market. Visiting this market was one of my favorite weekend destinations. I never went away empty-handed. XTD had been open for less than a year when I went to the market and bought a Bonsai tree and an antique hand-turned, stone grist mill. But this visit was a sad one. At the end of the day, the Market would close forever. Before hosting the Flower Market, the largest building of this French Concession landmark, had been built long ago in the old Shanghai as an indoor greyhound dog-racing track. Dog racing came to an end with the Japanese Army occupation of Shanghai prior to World War II. The Flower Market, with the original dog track oval, under roof and intact, was mobbed every weekend.

With the advent of Xintiandi in central Luwan District, "culture" quickly came into vogue. Flowers, other flora, old-fashioned handicrafts, and antiques were out. The district held an international design competition for a performing arts complex. An American firm from New York City won. Visualize a giant bathroom fixture. Place the fixture's porcelain tiled, bottom half-bowl, endow with a view across a pool of acid rain. Cover the bowl with a concave, white rubber waterproof membrane. Direct the runoff water from this roof down a glass, Venus fly-trap drain. Trim the trap with bright red thread and let it vertically penetrate the center of the main lobby. Burrow under the bowl's skirt, and welcome concert goers through an anal-ring, shape-shifting tunnel. The Shanghainese dubbed the new performance center "the Toilet Bowl." Scrub-a-dub-dub, where have all the flowers gone, Mr Clean?

Gold Mine French Bakery Bar

14

Die, Lie, or Run

As the Summer of Love's boat set sail, it left me facing a harsh reality. I had not notified the Denver draft board of my change of address so technically I was guilty of draft evasion. Why did I commit this crime? Before he became a US Senator, John Kerry, a Vietnam War veteran, anti-war activist, and law student, testified before Congress: "How do you ask a man to be the last man to die in Vietnam? How do ask a man to be the last man to die for a mistake?"

My first high school sweetheart, Sarah, and I got married in Alexandria three days before I was due to report for duty at Zweibrucken Air Force Base, in Germany. Assigned to the 38th Tactical Reconnaissance Squadron, I flew in the front seat of tandem, two-seat, Mach II, RF-4 Phantom jets. Unlike its sibling the F-4, the workhorse of the Air Force's fighting bomber fleet, the RF-4C carried no armaments. It was a "spy plane," designed for high-speed, extremely low-levels missions, and its elongated and fiberglass nose cone was crammed full of sophisticated photographic and electronic surveillance devices. Instead of a co-pilot in the rear seat, I had a Weapons System Operator. But "weapons" was a misnomer. Our mission called for "spy then run," not "search and destroy." WISO, or GIB ("guy in back"), were pilot's nicknames for those who wore navigator's wings.

The limited amount of on-base married officer housing at the AFB was reserved for the top, senior echelon. But we found a house to rent a short distance away, directly off the end of the Base's 6,500-foot runway. We were the first tenants of a newly renovated second-floor apartment in the second-generation house owned by the Stauch family. Our landlord, Albert Stauch Jr., lived downstairs with his wife and daughter. Albert's father had worked all his life making wooden wagon wheels, but by the time Albert was a teenager, demand for his father's wheels had been reduced to providing replacement parts and repairs on horse-drawn farm wagons. At age sixteen, Albert Jr. left home to serve in Hitler's army. When the Second World War ended, Albert found himself in northern Italy. To get back home, he walked over a thousand kilometers, carrying a light canvas rucksack and wearing badly worn, canvas-and-leather army boots. He lived on scraps of food found in bombed-out buildings. He crossed over the Swiss Alps alone and starving. He suffered frostbite, and eventually would lose part of his toes. It was six months before he was reunited with his mother and father. Afterward, Albert Jr. soon married and he and his new wife, Toni, moved in with his parents, sleeping in an attic bedroom. To support Toni, Albert Jr. got a job driving a delivery truck for Parkbrau Brewery, a job he would keep for over forty years.

Whenever possible, I joined Albert in his father's old wood shop, repairing furniture, replacing or re-caning chairs, and restoring antiques. The occasional custom-order for a new wooden wheel made Albert proud. Driving a truck was a job, and crafting a wagon wheel from round, rough timber was an art. At the end of each wood shop session, Albert would lift a basement hatch door in the shop's floor. He would climb down a ladder into the cellar cave and retrieve a couple of half-liter Parkbraus. He spoke no English and I spoke only a little German.

Good German beer, body language, and a few "gute arbiet" toasts were good enough.

Albert and Toni and their daughter, Rosalinde, became great friends with my wife Sarah and me. Sundays were Saumagen day at Toni's kitchen table. Riesling wine from Toni's hometown helped wash down the crispy sow's stomach, spicy cubed pork, and herbed potatoes. Rosalinde was studying English in school. We told stories, and she translated. Albert would pour everyone a glass of schnapps while Toni carved slices of fresh-baked Stollen topped with marzipan icing. A couple of times a month, Sarah and I would treat the Stauch family to a Saturday dinner of pomme frites and wiener schnitzel at a local Gasthaus.

For the four years my wife Sarah and I lived in Germany, we took full advantage of opportunities for travel. I left active duty in 1976 after volunteering for an "early out" program for Air Force pilots following the end of the Vietnam War, but we stayed in Europe for nearly a year. We went beyond the limits of routine sightseeing, became avid ten-speed cross-country cyclists, alpine backpackers, rock climbers, and downhill skiers. We grew expert at navigating language barriers, cultural differences, and political borders. These interests led to community service as leaders of an outdoor recreation program. We published a monthly newsletter, sponsored workshops, and coordinated bicycle and backpacking trips. I volunteered as an instructor for the Air Force's Outdoor Adventure School. Hitler's alpine retreat, the Eagle's Nest, was the headquarters, the old Officers' Club served as mess hall, library, lounge, and office for the school. I taught ski mountaineering and snow, ice, and rock climbing. Four times a year, the school organized week-long trips to the Alps, giving young men and women in uniform serving NATO the opportunity to develop leadership skills while participating in a mountaineering adventure.

On one of our many bicycle camping trips, my wife and I visited Dachau, in Bavaria. After entering the camp under Hitler's wretched "Work Will Set You Free" sign, and finding a memorial stone marking the site of the ash dump near the ovens, Sarah and I fasted for five days. The first Sunday we were back, sitting Toni's kitchen, Rosalinde asked to see photos of our trip. She didn't know we had spent an afternoon visiting Dachau. I looked at Sarah, and there were tears in her eyes. She excused herself, but not before reaching under the table to hold hard my hand.

We said goodbye to our adopted German family in the late spring of 1976. We had our furniture shipped to the Gable House, and spent the next three months traveling the length of Europe via Eurail passes and special train storage for bicycles. We used the rail pass to go to Lapland, hiking a hundred miles under the midnight sun through a vast evergreen forest and grass-covered summer tundra wilderness. We forded five ice-melt rivers, with boots held over our heads, to spend three days above the Arctic Circle. Next stop was the Swiss Alps. We joined the Swiss Alpine Club and went from hut to hut, strapping on crampons for ice crossings at the base of glaciers, donning snowshoes to get past leftover winter snow drifts. We witnessed a great rock and snow avalanche that uprooted trees, wiping out a shepherd's hut before grinding to a halt on a high valley floor. After the Alps, we returned for a bicycle tour of our favorite European environ, the northern Mediterranean seaside. Our last trip before leaving for Colorado was to the Greek Isles. We spent five days and nights naked on an isolated, white sand beach. We shared our sand with a hundred other stark-naked summer nomads. Fresh, sun-ripened tomato on unleavened flatbread sandwiches topped with farm-made feta, a dash of olive oil, sea salt, wild mint leaves, and fresh ground black pepper never tasted so good.

In the intervening years between the Summer of Love and my military service, Jeff had married Heather, his high school girlfriend. They were living on the first floor of the Gable House while the rest of the Grand Lady was rented to college students. My wife and I moved into a two-bedroom apartment over the carriage house. Jeff and Heather had recently purchased a historic commercial building in Silverton, fifty miles north of Durango, with a cast iron shop front. The Victorian Lady, with pressed-tin ceilings, and a central staircase, had stood abandoned for a two decades. During the glory days of gold mining, the building was home for the French Bakery and Grocery Store and the Teller House, a small hotel. Originally a bar, and with rooms to rent on the second floor, Jeff and his brother Robert planned to reopen the bar, beginning a complete renovation and restoration of the building. I volunteered to help with the work. Robert, Jeff, and I worked weekdays, commuting from Durango. Using the skills that Albert had taught me in Germany, I added an additional twenty-eight feet to the existing ten-foot-long bar, duplicating the original design in maple and mahogany.

We converted half the grocery store into a restaurant and delicatessen, and restored the large wood-fired oven to cook pizza and sourdough bread. The other half was converted into an outdoor recreation equipment shop. Out of this shop, I operated a second high-alpine ski-mountaineering school, commuting back and forth to Durango each week. In the summer of 1978, on a trip back east to visit relatives, I visited IM Pei's East Wing of the National Gallery of Art in Washington DC and standing in awe in the main triangular sky-lit atrium space of that extraordinary building, I decided then and there to become an architect.

A much larger building stood vacant on the next block. I invited my Alpine climbing partner, a former airman still living in Germany, to join me in Silverton. We pooled our savings and purchased the Victorian relic, starting work in January 1976. For several days, while rebuilding the coal furnace, we bunked in its small storeroom, huddling at night around a kerosene heater while temperatures dropped below zero. As the highest town in Colorado, at an elevation of 9,300 feet, with an average annual snowfall of 200 inches, Silverton is a very hostile environment in the winter.

The building we purchased was built in the early 1890s, and had a double-wide twin-version of a central stair, and a typical Victorian cast-iron storefront. It housed a hotel upstairs and two hard-drinking bars downstairs. Shortly after the turn of the century, the building was converted into a bakery, a meat market, and a grocery. The hotel became living quarters for the Italian proprietor and his family. In its heyday, several hundred loaves of bread were baked daily in a large wood-fired oven. Twenty to thirty head of cattle were butchered weekly on the premises. Sherry was made by the barrel in the basement, from grapes shipped in by train.

We decided to blend the atmosphere of the old French Bakery and grocery store with the nostalgic ambience of a hardscrabble gold mining town, classic Victorian bar, and cafe. We found the old meat and deli counter in a rear storage shed. We returned the upstairs to its original function as a hotel. The historic names, French Bakery and Teller House, were kept. I constructed two signs using authentic logos gleaned from old newspaper ads.

Early one morning, I crossed the street to get a better look at a boarded-up, abandoned building that was very similar to the one Jeff had purchased. Unable to get a view inside, I climbed through some hoarding at the rear of the building. The ground floor was empty. Nothing was left behind to indicate that it had once been a popular hamburger, hot dog, and beer joint. In the basement, though, I discovered three of the original four sides of a wooden reach-in cooler. Covered in plastic, paint, and the grease of forty years of hamburgers, the icebox was purchased from its absentee Arizona-based owner for next to nothing. Six weeks of work followed. Several rotten stile and rail panels were replaced, and the doors were rebuilt, using rigid foam insulation and redwood for lining. Shelves for wine were constructed from oak, and a stainless-steel bin was made for holding beer kegs. This maple-and-oak, freestanding, eight-foot-high, reach-in cooler became the nucleus for the restaurant design. For a front bar, I dismantled several matching antique dry goods counters. The raised panels and pedestals were joined together to form a continuous facade. A bar top was constructed using red oak and maple that matched the gold hues of the reach-in. A large cabinet with a vertically sliding glass front was found in a barber shop and used to make a back bar. The meat rail that ran from the slaughter shed to the old grocery's meat locker was taken down, inverted, and bolted to the floor—providing a footrest for people choosing to sit at the bar on red oak stools.

The original maple floor was taken up, and several rotten joists replaced. The floor was then repaired, board by board, with damaged pieces replaced by flooring scavenged from back-of-house storage rooms. The stamped-tin ceiling tiles were taken down, stripped of white paint, and given a coat of metallic silver spray paint, then put back up. The old meat locker, with sawdust-filled walls, was converted into restrooms. The old grocery's produce prep area was transformed into a commercial kitchen. The wood-fire oven room was used temporarily as a storeroom, awaiting restoration.

Skilled labor was non-existent in Silverton, a town of less than five hundred adults, so we were forced to learn the basic skills of plumbing and electrical installation. We managed to plumb over thirty fixtures and to replace a pile of molten pennies with a 600-amp, three-phase, commercial service. I gave a licensed electrician, a non-recovering alcoholic, a tab for free drinks at Jeff's bar if he showed up whenever the town electrical inspector was around.

We opened the restaurant in time for the 1976 summer season. I turned over the management of the business to my partner, and commuted from Durango every weekend to continue renovation work on the upstairs, the Teller House. After we had been open several months, a local resident brought me a picture of an early Silverton bar. The wooden reach-in coolers, except at the top, are identical. That was the one part I did not find. The extant hamburger and hot dog joint across the street, in a previous life, must have been the bar in the old photograph.

In the summer of 1977, I accepted a part-time job as the town of Silverton's Building Inspector. Busy with the ongoing restoration of the French Bakery and construction activities in Durango, I was assured that the job required only a few hours each month. Enforcing the Uniform Building Code and the City Zoning Ordinances in a town of less than a thousand residents sounded easy.

Initially, my duties *were* easily discharged. But a thorough review of the Zoning Ordinances changed the situation dramatically. I discovered that the five-year grace period that was part of the city's adoption of the Sign Code was due to expire shortly. And to my dismay, I found over twenty pre-existing non-conforming signs, many of them on the premises of friends' businesses.

Strongly in agreement with the rules and restrictions of the Sign Code, I feared that enforcement might cause voter backlash—resulting in the abolishment of the ordinance. Carefully, and with as much diplomacy as could be mustered, I proceeded to eliminate the offending signs, successful in every case but one. My nemesis was an elderly and strong-willed woman, a life-long resident. I had already rejected her recent building permit application to build a loft apartment in the rear of her souvenir shop. Her plans for the apartment did not include any windows, and had only one way in and out. The steep stairs to the loft were also in the middle of the downstairs shop. But she promptly started construction without a permit. I had the Town Council's support when I issued a stop work order. She complied, but soon enough, she installed a giant billboard on her roof. She made sure it was prominent enough to been seen by the 500 tourists taking the Durango to Silverton Narrow Gauge Train every day.

The Sign Code did not provide any specific remedy for a Code violation, even one as egregious as a giant rooftop billboard. Despite my best efforts, her case ended up in the judicial system. She led a campaign to repeal the Code, which ended with the City Council compromising my position by granting her a variance. Subsequently, I persuaded the Council to repeal her variance. When I left Colorado to go to MIT, the case was still unresolved due to technicalities.

The father of my good friend John Holman, John Holman Sr. owned a lumber company in Moultrie, Georgia, and I met him when my friend Jeff and I were building a house for my sister and her husband, Duke Harris, in the town in the late 1970s. John knew every builder in town and he introduced me to a young Black man name Lonnie Anderson who I employed as a day laborer. Just about every morning for the six months I was there, I drove into town at 7 am and picked Lonnie up from his shotgun house which he shared with a mother and three sisters, all unemployed. This was summertime and the humidity was 90 percent, and we wanted to make an early start while it was still relatively cool. We then went to get take-outs of buttermilk biscuits and gravy and hot coffee on the Square. In those days, at least a decade after the passage of the Civil Rights Act, Blacks were still not allowed even to pick up food.

Lonnie was a great guy, an incredible worker. He mixed concrete by hand because we couldn't get the concrete truck onto the site, and I paid more than anyone else in town would have paid a day laborer. One day, Lonnie said, why don't you come down a juke joint, which was a bar with Black customers and live music and dancing and lots of drinking. That's where Black American music got its start, all those Black singers like Muddy Waters got their start in juke joints. The word juke seems to have come from Gullah, the Creole language spoken by people in Georgia and the Carolinas whose ancestors were brought over from West Africa, and it means something like goofing off or disorderly. I used to think the word came from jukebox, but it turns out it's the other way round, the word jukebox comes from juke joint.

Anyway, on Friday nights we would go with Lonnie to the wrong side of the tracks. We were the only young white guys in the joint, and there'd be forty or fifty young Black men and forty or fifty pretty Black women and we'd dance to live music. We were taking our lives in our hands, and I wouldn't have gone in there alone, but we were safe because we were with Lonnie who was a real bad-ass. He was about six foot six and had scars all over this face because he had beat up so many people. No one screwed with him. We danced with the girls, but I knew better than to go further than that. We didn't want to end up in the reverse of being lynched.

Then on Saturdays me and my friend would drive down to Tallahassee where we could date white college coeds, and Lonnie would go back to the juke joint and he would take his entire pay check and spend it all on vodka. The white police would wait in their squad cars outside the juke joint and when a drunk Black guy walked out they would arrest him for public drunkenness. So every Saturday night around midnight, they'd throw Lonnie in the drunk tank in the local jail along with twenty or thirty other Black boys. They couldn't get out or appear in court until Monday morning, so every Monday first thing, I had to go down to the jail and bail Lonnie out. It was just classic racism, and a way for the police to raise money, but if you didn't have the bail money it meant you could conceivably stay in there forever. The judge was a friend of John Holman Sr., and while he wasn't a liberal by any means, he also wasn't cruel. A couple of years later, Lonnie died of alcoholism, like so many other Black guys have done. The immediate cause of death is the drinking, but it's really the poverty or the sense of hopelessness that kills them. I would have done anything for him, but I couldn't get him to quit drinking. I tried to get him some help but he didn't want any help.

Around that time, I also helped my brother Jere add an addition to his first home. With help from our father and two friends, Jere had dismantled a hand-hewn log cabin my father had bought from a rural Appalachian farmer. The crew reassembled the cabin on a beautiful, wooded hilltop, overlooking a bend in Willeo Creek, only a few miles from our family homestead. With the logs up and a rusty tin roof in place, the crew built large stone chimneys for fireplaces at either end of the cabin. The cabin had a sleeping loft, but lacked kitchen and bath. Jere was planning to get married soon, and no bride would want to move into a house where you needed to use an outhouse.

My brother took four weeks leave from his law practice, and my father took time off from his job with the Department of the

Interior. Together, we built a lean-to addition at the rear of the cabin. We used salvaged timber, rusty tin, wide pine boards from a local sawmill, and recycled fixtures to give it a handcrafted look. We hand-planed boards to make paneling and cabinets, notched and mortised timbers, and fashioned molding with hand drawn knives, turning to many traditional woodworker techniques. We kept fashion and function separate as much as we could.

My work in Silverton was restorative in nature, and helping Jere was regenerative in spirit. Environmental awareness had a different meaning in the past, and staying warm in the winter and cool in the summer was simply a way of life. The vernacular architecture that predated America's Industrial Age was born out of necessity. The log cabin, primitive and sustainable, was architecture by the people, for the people.

After retirement, our father purchased Perry Place, a commercially-zoned property at the north end of what would one day become Roswell's Historic District. The Historic District's history began with the founding of the Roswell Historic Society. The Perry House, at the corner of Woodstock Road and Canton Street, was built by 1877 by the owner of the Roswell Mercantile. When my father took possession of it, there was no one living there and the house needed a new roof and complete interior renovation. Over my first MIT summer, my classmate Steve Lovell and I renovated the main house, and an adjacent one-story farmhouse with original chestnut oak floors was converted to retail shop space. To comply with the Code, we added a fanciful two-story porch and stairs at the rear of the big house. When my father died six years later, he left Perry Place's eclectic collection of built forms to Jere, and today Perry Place is home to my brother's law office.

Soon after Dad was gone, my brother Jere acquired a second abandoned, hand-hewn, dog-trot, log cabin. South Georgia climes are on the verge of subtropical, and "dog trots," relatively cheap to build, were warm in mild winters and cool in hot, humid, summers—in other words, they were ideal primal homes for dirt-farmers struggling to compete with former plantation slave labor. An ingenious design, the dog trot is created by connecting two identical two-story log cabins leaving a large space between them. This gap is bridged over with a second story. When facing the prevailing breezes, the in-between space—the "trot"—provides a naturally ventilated wood-floored vestibule and open-air living room. Entry doors oppose each other on the walls of the "trot" and mongrels eat kitchen scraps and sleep there, too—bow-wow heaven! Trots were built by farmers, red-necked from leaning over a hoe or walking behind a mule and a plow, breaking dirt. Add in a plow mule, a heavy tow rope, a nearby stand of timber, and an American felling axe, and rednecks all over the rural South became part-time home builders.

A Civil War era relic, Jere's South Georgia dog trot was museum quality that had been dressed up some time after World War I. The "true" on the two hewn log sides and the precision fitting of the corner haft-lap dovetail joints were the work of a master log mason. A friend of Jere's was dove hunting with friends when he stumbled across the empty shell. The dress was torn, a couple of clapboards were missing, a secret revealed. Jere paid the absentee owner small money for salvage rights. The find was just in time. Not that long after, the *Atlanta Journal's* Sunday Magazine featured a Ted Turner log cabin restoration and professional "cabin spotters" in heat hit the ground running.

Jere and crew, including me, dismantled the dog-trot and a forty-foot windmill and moved them to Roswell in three-round trips with a gooseneck, forty-foot flatbed trailer, towed by my old Dodge pick-up. My brother and his friends then resurrected the dog-trot and windmill on a vacant portion of the Perry Place compound.

The last buildings to go up at Perry Place included a timber-framed, three-by-five bay, Big Barn Art Gallery with a thirty-five foot vaulted center bay with partial loft. A sand-mold, red brick, full basement was home to Jere's first wife's custom jewelry studio and workshop. A two-story skylighted breezeway connected the Big Barn to a large lean-to, restaurant sized shed. The dog-trot got a large back porch and a rocking chair.

Roy and Tillie's famous backyard parties helped Jere get elected to the City Council, although my father had passed away when Jere was elected Mayor of Roswell. Jere was Roswell's second mayor in fifty years. While Jere was on the Council, he persuaded the City to hire me to help Roswell's City Planning Office draw up a Growth Management Plan. The plan, which was approved, included design guidelines for a Greenway Commercial Corridor expanding the City limits to include our homestead farm on Woodstock Road. Overnight, our farm's value skyrocketed with funds approved for a new regional high school, and several big box retailer centers as our new neighbors.

Ironically, the Jere's predecessor Pug Mabry and his wife, were living in the small house next to the Perry House. Pug sold the Perry House property to my father. Pug is the longest serving mayor in Roswell's history beginning with Thomas King who took office during the Civil War. My father was not a Pug fan, nor he my father's. My father, who proudly wore a Confederate Officer's uniform mounted on a horse in annual Roswell 4th of July parades, did not want the South to Rise Again. Pug did, way down South in Dixieland.

I met Pug during my fourth grade of elementary school. He was "Call me Coach Mabry" Little League Roy's boy. Having the only parents in town who both had advanced college degrees did not make me the most popular kid in Pug's playbook. My parents' liberal politics and my being listed on the roster as a right-handed relief pitcher (with a good fast ball) did not keep me on the bench. I played a mean center field, and after catching a deep fly ball could throw the ball with one bounce all the way to home plate. A left-handed batter, I knew where the ball was headed by reading the catcher's signals out of the corner of my eye and watching carefully the pitcher's wind-up, got a lot of walk-ons to first, and was good at stealing bases.

But before Pug left office, the Council he headed approved my master plan to provide more parking and some additional commercial zoning on backstreets of the Canton Street Historic District. The plan also created a site for a new City Office and Cultural District. Before he left office Pug got his "palace," and the community's performing arts found a home.

In 1980, soon after the birth of our first child, we sold the Silverton property and our one-third share of the Gable House and moved to Cambridge, Massachusetts. For the next three and one-half-years I attended the MIT Graduate School of Architecture. I was selected by the new Dean of Architecture and Planning to design his MIT Rotunda corner office, including the creation of all the furniture, and in 1984, I earned a Master's degree in Architecture and was awarded the AIA Student Gold Medal.

My first and only employer in the field of architecture was Benjamin Thompson. Ben retired in 1994, and I formed a new practice in partnership with his wife Jane. Then in 1998, I left this partnership to form Wood & Zapata which scored two important commissions, the renovation of Soldier Field, home of the Chicago Bears, and the Xintiandi cultural entertainment district project in Shanghai.

DR bar's Girl With No Name

15

The World's Best Bar

I've owned many restaurants and bars in my life. Just about everywhere I have lived, I have owned a bar. The first one was the bar and grill I set up in the bunker in the Air Force base in Germany, then when I got back to the States, I opened a bar and café in Silverton, a historic gold mining town in Colorado. I also owned a share of a bar on the Boston waterfront when we lived there. Of course, my ex-wife never approved of me owning a bar because she figured it was not the healthiest environment for her husband, and she was right. But Ernest Hemingway got all the materials for his books in bars, and I learn from each one, and they get better and better. A good example is my current bar, the DR Bar in Xintiandi. My beloved hole-in-wall was only the third Xintiandi establishment to open back in 2002. It's hidden behind a tall black lacquer door on the long north alley, DR has seen it all.

I have always had bars because they are the best places in the world to meet people. You meet characters in a bar. A lot of architects spend hundreds of thousands of dollars a year either on monographs of their work or on public relations and advertising. I have always relied on a bar to advertise, and also people know they can find me there. If you want your clients to know you have interesting friends, you won't get to introduce them sitting in your office. People don't call ahead, they just know that if you want to meet creative people, the chances are if you go to the DR Bar, you'll meet somebody interesting. Not a lot of bankers drink at my bar.

I'm spent a lot of time making the interior of the DR Bar as good as it can be in terms of its primary purpose, which is encouraging people to talk to each other. You walk into any other bar and the first thing you see is the backs of people lined up in front of a row of liquor bottles. But in my bar, all the liquor is below the bar, and the only thing you see is people's faces.

DR stands for "design resources" and all the materials used in the interior are special in one way or another. The bar top is silver thread, half silver, half copper. The flagstones on the floor are real inkstone, and the ceiling is made of real shoe leather.

From the day I opened that bar, young Chinese people would come and find a romantic corner to sit in. There are three different kinds of seating at DR. You can sit at the bar on a stool, you can sit at the low table where people can see your knees, or you can sit at a regular dining table where people can't see your knees. When people walk through the big black door, I can guess, with almost a 100% accuracy, where they will choose to hang out. A group of friends will choose the low tables. Sitting on low bench seats allows body language to help shape the conversation. Women in short skirts, often leaving their legs uncrossed, relax and enjoy sitting across from men friends. If a young couple come in in a girlfriend-boyfriend mode they'll sit at the high table. They take a table for two, because it is usually the man who is a bit shy. He wants to see his girlfriend's face and chest but does not want to worry about the rest of his body language. People who manage to corral a bar seat are regulars or an out-of-towner who found out about us through an on-or-offline travel guide. We do not offer 2-for-1 happy hours, which attract the wrong kind of customer.

I put a sign on the wall outside the bar when I opened it, and it's still there. It says, "We think a bar should convey honesty, warmth, pleasure, and modesty. Please strip to bare essentials and leave the complexities of life behind. Switch your hand phone to vibrate and engage in the erotic potential of a chance encounter or a romantic rendezvous."

My bartenders have two rules to follow.

Rule One is, free pour every spirits drink, no use of a jigger to measure a shot. Every single is a double, and same for wine. Architects are not often called upon to give financial advice to their clients, especially when many of them are self-made billionaires, but from the time my mother taught me how to make award-winning buttermilk biscuits, I knew you do not make money (or a good biscuit) by saving money. You make money by spending money. You pay peanuts, you get monkeys. Use fresh butter and creamy buttermilk, and you're on your way. Same with drinks in a bar.

And Rule Two is that "What happens in the DR Bar stays in the DR Bar." With no door on the men's room, all contemporaneous "satisfaction" hook-ups take place in the women's room including "ménages a trois."

My own rule is that if a sex worker walks in, the first and only drink is on the house, then after fifteen minutes, it's time to leave. And please do not come back—ever. Many of my competitors try hard to promote a "pick-up" bar reputation. It's the kiss of death. A bar like that opens and closes every day in Shanghai.

We once had a lady boy in drag come in and stand next to a couple of regulars sitting at my end of the bar. He started hitting on two of my best customers, both straight as arrows. They politely asked him to stop. Then came my turn. He put his face in my face.

"Why you not like nice girls?" he asked.

I grabbed the elastic waist band of his girlie dress, reached down, and gave a jerk on his cock.

"That ain't no strap-on buddy." Get lost.

But first, what does the world's best bar have to do with coping with fame and fortune in the Dragon's Mouth? It's all about contact on a daily basis with complete strangers, and fraternizing with people better and worse off than you. The best advice for coping with success comes from modest overachievers. I know the world's always going to live with economic inequality. But there's no reason we can't have social equality. I'll get to why social equality is the corner stone of my design philosophy later. People like Don Gao. The worst of coping with fame comes from obnoxious self-proclaimed masters of the universe. Spanish architect Santiago Calatrava springs to mind.

You can choose to spend time with someone you love, with one or more friends, or maybe a celebrity or a stranger. There are no rules as to how to enjoy these profane or sacred moments. The poetic fodder and romantic hubris of spontaneity and camaraderie, with people different from you, makes you a more interesting individual. To be relevant to your family and friends, in company with others in your society who are, makes life worth living. I think of hell not so much as being alone but as being alone with other people. I want a great many friends in heaven.

The "Drugs" in my repertoire of "Sex, Drugs, and Rock-n-Roll" are now limited to Tennessee Jack Daniels, the occasional DR Bar Hemingway Daiquiri or a rare shaken not stirred Bond man Grey Goose martini. My rock-n-roll is alive, and I still have a copy of the MGM record my band released. Any details regarding my activities covered by the remaining, three-letter word in this famous trio will be left to speculation.

In 2010, I purchased a photograph by artist Yang Fudong to hang in the bar. It's a high-definition black-and-white celluloid image, part of a large installation entitled "International Hotel" featuring the "girl in the swimsuit," shot by the pool of an old Shanghai hotel with a large format camera. For years, my bar customers kept asking me—who is she? Lorenz Helbling, the owner of ShangArt Gallery where the photograph was purchased, had no idea, and he doubted that even Yang Fudong knew her real name. Then one Saturday afternoon in the summer of 2019, I was sitting on a barstool at the end of my bar and watched as two women walked in through a glass side door and went straight to stand in front of the photo, which is visible from outside. One woman turned to the other and, in Chinese, said, "That's me when I was seventeen."

My bartender overheard the woman and exclaimed to me, "That's her! That's 'the girl in the swimsuit'!"

Now, after nine years, I was going to find out her name. It was Javen. She and her girlfriend had come to Xintiandi that Saturday to visit a boutique ice cream café next door to my bar. Serendipity is a beautiful word, one that filled the sky over Shanghai that day. Clouds of serendipity, like the trees that grew the acorn that hit Chicken Little in the head and changed his life and those around him, can be cultivated, both inside and outside our minds. But we need to be wide awake when the door opens, and in walks an opportunity to change the world.

Twenty years in my employ, Sophia manages the DR Bar. Here, unusually, is a DR Bar story that does not feature a beautiful female customer. I was away on business when I got a call from Sophia. She said a customer's rowdy behavior was chasing away our other patrons, many of them regulars. The man was a foreigner, singing very loudly to Doors songs he insisted she play over the DR sound system. She asked me if she could kick him out, and I told her to ask him politely to leave. He left before Sophia could get help from a security guard.

Next evening, a man called the DR and asked to speak to me. "You know who your manager kicked out of your bar last night? Bono."

"Oh," I said. "No one in the bar last night had ever heard of either Bono or U2."

A few months earlier, I had met U2's bass player, Adam Clayton, at the DR. I spent the next three days trying to help him find an apartment in Shanghai. He left empty-handed. Said he would be back. When U2 played to a sell-out crowd at New Soldiers Field in Chicago, Adam called me during the band's break. The Bears Stadium was one of the greatest outdoor rock concert venues U2 had ever experienced, he said. It is too bad U2 will never give a concert in Shanghai. U2's Bono and Adam Clayton only visited Shanghai solo. The obligatory, Dali Lama "neutral" test, was applied to the band, not the man. I'm not in the business of collecting the names of celebrities but I am in the business of providing a place where they can go and feel relatively anonymous.

The bar is relatively quiet these days, but for many years it made a ton of money and was hopping every night. I was able to give $100,000 a year to charity, and underwrote all sorts of musical and artistic events. It was the place to go for many of the Shanghainese and Westerners who wanted to meet each other, and White Fever and Yellow Fever were roads that ran both ways, cross-cultural highways of desire. Lust for lust, lust for money, and money for lust. My father, who art in Heaven, went to a Christian faith church every Sunday. He suspected Jesus could have been a bigot and was certainly not the son of a virgin. He never told me why Jesus might be bigoted, but he did make me aware of anti-homosexual and anti-Semitic discrimination.

His generation was not ready to add one more Adam and Eve, and a vestal goddess of immaculate conception to the Garden of Eden. A 21st Century Old Testament would need an additional two Adams and Eves. A post-2010 woke Bible would need a serious, top-to-bottom re-write. If I was an Gen-Xer, my Pope would have to concede recruits for the world's oldest profession including straight F's and M's plus LGB's & T's.

The most interesting celebrity to ever visit DR was Easy Rider's Dennis Hopper. He sat in the same DR corner ever night for six weeks. He did not smoke or drink. He would arrive before the last show at Raymond Levine's French Cabaret was over, and the Cabaret's star female dancers, one French, one Russian, and one Chinese, were his midnight to 2 am guests. One night, before the women arrived, Dennis and I talked of getting older. We were not of the same generation. Ten years younger, I told him that getting older is a good thing. If you are not getting older, you are dead. That night, Dennis did not know he had prostrate cancer. Although he died too young at 75, Dennis Hopper led a full life. A writer, a director, storyteller, photographer, and artist, he could also act. Hopper married five times. For him it was a pure bite of the apple, no bouts with fever, start to finish. The longest he stayed single was a mid-career thirteen years. Strikingly unorthodox, unusually successful, and avant-garde, Hopper was a gifted renaissance man. Pleased to meet you, Dennis. When I next see you, hope you guess my name.

The Gable House, Durango, Colorado

16

Cultivating Serendipity

James Dickey's poems and writing were introduced to me by my parents. In 1974 their friend Hubert Shuptrine gave them an autographed first edition of *Jericho, the South Behold,* a collection of watercolors by Shuptrine and poems by Dickey, "two Southerners, [who] turn their talents on their land and their people" (from the dust jacket). It was a harbinger for what I had begun to realize was my own human condition: a Southerner is a Southerner for life. For some, like Shuptrine and Dickey, this was a cross to bear that was also a badge of courage, an affirmation of a belief in man's humanity to man. For others, like Alabama Governor George Wallace, it was a cross defining a legacy of hate. Both crosses are alive and well today in an America separated by racial, social, and economic inequality.

Like Dickey and Shuptrine, I was born in the Deep South. James Dickey and I were delivered in the same hospital in Atlanta, he in 1923 and me in 1947. He grew up in Buckhead, a suburb north of Atlanta. He attended public, racially segregated schools in Fulton County. Dickey enlisted in the USAF and served in World Was II as a radar operator with a night fighter squadron. He served a second tour of duty during the Korean War. He then went to work as an advertising copywriter for Coca-Cola and Lays Potato Chips. Four years later, in 1960, at the age of thirty-seven, he returned to poetry and writing.

Life growing up for me was not that different from what it was for James Dickey. Not much had changed for white kids growing up in the Deep South in the twenty-four years that separated our births. My hometown was a few miles north of Buckhead and like him, I attended Fulton County's public, racially segregated schools. I got a college degree in civil engineering and attended law school for one semester, then I served in the USAF, piloting a supersonic Phantom Jet, flying Iron Curtain border night missions. My mission was to gather intelligence on Russian radar installations.

Two years after *Jericho* was published, my military service in the USAF was ending, and my wife and I were planning a move to Durango, Colorado. We wanted children, and Durango, Colorado, home of the Summer of Love, seemed to me like a good place to raise a family. Sarah was not sure, but followed my lead. For months, I'd been in discussions with my Gable House co-owner, Jeff. He was working for a general contractor and making good money. He led a cracker-jack framing team and had quickly learned the tricks of the trade. He was convinced we could set up our own general contracting company. It would be a gross understatement to say that my father-in-law, a retired US Army Officer, was unhappy as out that idea. He considered my leaving a promising career in the Air Force to start a new business from scratch to be an act of selfish lunacy. I told Lt. Colonel Leon K, and my mother-in-law, that there was nothing to worry about. Their daughter and I were young, madly in love, living in the only sovereign nation in the world whose Constitution included the word "happiness."

The next four years were some of the the happiest years of my marriage. Two years after I made her parents unhappy, Sarah and I gave birth to our first child, daughter Amy Elizabeth.

BENJAMIN WOOD

In 1983, at the age of thirty-six, after three years of graduate school in Cambridge, Massachusetts, I began my career as an architect. I went to work for a famous architect, Benjamin Thompson. Ben called me on a Friday morning in June, while I was in my basement study busy writing my master's thesis. He asked if we could meet that same morning to talk about joining his architectural firm. Ben had talked with the MIT Dean of Architecture and Planning the night before on an NYC-to-Boston airline shuttle. I jumped on my ten-speed bike for a quick ride to Ben's office near Harvard Square. After our third before-lunch bloody Mary, he invited me to go to Martha's Vineyard for the weekend. The TIME magazine helicopter, with Editor-in-Chief Henry Grunwald on board, would pick us up at 4 pm I went home, packed a small bag, called my wife at work, and set off on a great adventure: ten years of traversing America and circling the globe. A decade of cultivating serendipity with Ben and Jane Thompson was underway.

In the backseat of a red Jaguar sedan on the way to the helicopter, Ben Thompson offered this advice: "Ben Wood, I learned early in my career that it takes just as many hours, just as many drawings, and just as much energy to do 'small' work as it does to do 'big' work. We will do 'big work' in the future, but first I need your help with the 'small' work."

Since losing their mother recently, Henry's grown children were spending more time with him, and he needed a bigger house. So on my second day as an architect, with a light sea wind blowing in from Martha's Vineyard Sound, I walked a beachfront house site with these two famous men: Henry Grunwald, who helped end the Cold War with his TIME magazine interview of Gorbachev, and Benjamin Thompson, the Cambridge, Massachusetts architect, and founder of America's first lifestyle store, Harvard Square's Design Research. Ben, his wife Jane, and I had stayed the night before at Henry's seaside cottage, five hundred feet from his new house site. Henry's cottage was a modest, one-and-one-half story, three-bedroom, grey shingled cape-cod, with a rocking chair beachfront porch. The house was thirty years old. The beachfront porch, originally several yards from the high tide mark, now set directly over it. Henry feared that a full-moon monster tide, or a New England winter nor'easter, would wash his beloved cottage into the Vineyard Sound. As TIME was the first magazine to publish an in-depth report on climate change, Henry knew what was coming.

After two hours of walking Henry's new six-acre, heavily wooded and secluded site, we headed back to the cottage. We had walked to the site via the beach, but for the walk back we took the upland route, a one-lane, deeply furrowed ancient way, impassible except for four-wheel drive vehicles, and even then depending on the season. For lunch we had deviled eggs, unsalted tortilla chips with fresh avocado dip, baby potato and red onion salad, and smoked bluefish spread on sourdough toast, laced with fresh dill shoots and truffle oil. All bought from a local seafood market. Ben and Henry resumed a discussion from the evening before, while I made notes and sketched.

The house would be all wood, inside and out. Red cedar shingles for walls and roof, swamp cypress wall paneling, four or six raised-panel, southern yellow pine doors, reclaimed heart pine, wide plank floors, aromatic cedar lined, walk-in closets, clear fir kitchen cabinets, maple block and slate counters, and white oak stair treads and risers. A breezeway with a large skylight for drying swimsuits would connect the main house to the three-bedroom guest wing. Each guest room would have room for a writing desk, small sofa, armchair and ottoman; a double steamer-size wicker trunk for spare linens, heated towel bars, individual private outdoor showers, and five-fixture *en suite* bathrooms. An expansive seaside porch, eighty feet in length, would end with a hexagonal pergola with a built-in picnic table. A raised boardwalk would connect the porch to water deep enough for a swimming dock. On the lee-side of the house, on the other side of a large sundeck from the guest wing, four pairs of French doors would open into a gourmet kitchen with walk-in pantry. Locate one half-bath and powder room off the kitchen hallway to the dining room, and another near the back door of a rear kitchen delivery dock for catered food deliveries. Near the one-lane main road, build a simple wood barn for garden tools and a workshop.

The next day, Sunday, over an early morning cup of coffee and English muffins, I showed my sketches to Ben. He put a sheet of tracing paper over the ground floor plan, took out a small box of colored pencils, and sketched his version of the plan. Henry was not an early riser. It was nearly noon when Ben Thompson, sitting at a table in a small sunroom off the cottage kitchen, showed Henry his colored drawing. Henry asked a few questions. "I love it, Ben. When do we start?" This was my second day as an architect. Thank you, N-A-T-U-R-E.

Later that afternoon, the TIME helicopter ferried us across the bay to Ben and Jane's summer estate on Cape Cod. Ben took me on a sunset tour of the grounds. Big barn, little barn, one-room guest cottages, large studio, and main house on a bluff overlooking a wilderness tidal marsh and river mouth. The next morning, I got up very early and after a walk on down to the bottom of the bluff, a fog was lifting over the marsh when I entered the main house kitchen in search of coffee. On the counter next to a primed-to-go coffee maker was a very large pyramid of fruit from the local market and fresh vegetables from the Thompson's garden. On top of this rainbow-colored butcher-block counter-top sculpture was a note attached by two mint flavored toothpicks to a large ripe beefsteak tomato. What a lovely way to leave a note. Ben was a very thoughtful and colorful man.

After three months, I had the plans far enough along to start thinking about who was going to build Henry's new house. I checked with two local lumber yards, and both gave me the same three names. All were experienced, qualified, well-established Vineyard custom home builders. I met and reviewed the plans with each one, and asked them to get me estimates of the construction costs. All three said estimating costs was not common practice on the Vineyard. Custom houses for the rich and famous were strictly "cost-plus" projects, and typically five-to-eight times more expensive per square foot than an average suburban McMansion on the mainland. The Vineyard is an island, Mr Wood. Nothing is cheap on an island.

I decided to go back and talk to the owner of the larger of the two local lumber companies. I asked him which of his home builder customers returned the most lumber. I wanted to know which builder on the island was meticulous when it came to using reasonably plumb and straight framing studs, joists, and rafters. I expected he would give me one of the names of the three I had interviewed, but he stated flatly that "cost-plus" contractors do not return lumber—they mark up all their material costs before billing their clients. Returning lumber would be returning a source of profit. That's when I decided: To hell with them.

I was about to leave when the lumber company owner asked me to wait a minute. There is one young man you should meet, he said. His name is Andrew Flake, and I'll get him on the phone and ask him to come meet you right away. Andrew drove from his home office to meet me in the rear lot of a lumber company with hundreds of clients. He had a load of crooked lumber and a big black Labrador in the back of a twenty-year-old pickup truck. He shook my hand, said he would work hard, do a good job, and charge an honest fee. And today, that young man is a great friend, and the one who built the Grunwald house. Andrew, his wife June, and their three daughters are family to me.

On my mother's side, I am a distant relative of the family that originally owned and operated the Jack Daniels Tennessee Whisky distillery in Lynchburg. Lacking any other source of revenue, the family was forced to sell the distillery during Prohibition. Written on the back label of every bottle of Jack: "Every day we make it, we make it the best we can." Those words describe Andrew Flake's lifelong pursuit of excellence, and mine as well.

Ben Thompson built trophy homes for the rich and famous like Henry. But his true passion was "big" work designing urban downtown "festival marketplaces" that bring joy and an enriched social life for tens of millions of people every year. Ben Thompson was eventually awarded the American Institute of Architects' Gold Medal, the highest honor bestowed in our field.

In his acceptance speech, Ben told the black-tie and evening gown audience: "Over a hundred million people a year visit one of my meccas of urban entertainment. And half of those people are woman. Imagine making love to fifty million women. I do every time I sit down to sketch a new place where people can celebrate life."

Ben had prepared a slide show of his work for this occasion. As he spoke, on a giant screen directly above and behind him, the slide show's grand finale was playing. Ben's slide shows were legendary. This one was no exception. Slides of fireworks exploding over South Street Seaport accompanied by the final refrain from the Star-Spangled Banner were timed perfectly to reach their crescendo as Ben mouthed the words "making love." Ben was a master of his very own, passionately human, and gloriously erotic universe. No great architect, before or after, has managed to cultivate a more serendipitous, orgasmic, seductive, love affair with life.

But "big work" with my mentor would end in tragedy. Nine years after I joined Ben's firm, he suffered his third stroke. He never returned to his design studio. Now permanently blind and unable to walk, he spent the remainder of his life bed-ridden. In the wake of Ben's untimely departure, the firm he founded was taken over by a group of senior partners. I considered staying on, but was not given that opportunity. My partners went to Ben in secret and told him they were going to "fire" me. I was the partner-in-charge of the firm's three largest, most profitable projects. The clients for these projects were powerful private developers. I had built strong personal relationships with all three. With my mentor gone from the scene, the partners feared I would abandon the firm, taking the clients and the projects with me. Ben abhorred confrontation. He conceded, agreeing with my partners that I posed a threat to their survival.

The partners called me the following day before I left the house for work: "You can stay at home, Ben Wood. Come into the studio over the weekend and get your personal belongings."

I immediately got on the phone. By Monday afternoon there was a stack of faxes in each partner's "in-box." The firm's three best client's message: If Ben Wood goes, we go. Next day, Ben Thompson's son, Tony, the firm's attorney, flew from his office in Washington DC to meet with the partners. Before walking out of the meeting, Jane told them it was not too late to try and reverse course. With her husband gone, Ben Wood was the firm's sole "rainmaker." After the meeting adjourned, Tony called to advise me to find a lawyer if I did not already have one. My partners had decided to sue me for "contractual interference."

Negotiations ensued and I did go back to work. Two of the

three clients were among Ben's closest advisors and both were my friends. Paul Del Rossi, CEO of America's largest chain of suburban multi-cinemas, and Chris Shallis, a real estate development consultant for London Edinburgh Trust, a pension fund management firm, quietly went into bat for me. Twelve months later, all three clients terminated their contracts with Ben's old firm. I immediately left the firm with Jane to start a new firm, Thompson and Wood. We signed our first three clients in a matter of hours after legally registering our company.

I have never blamed Ben for what happened that Friday morning. From Ben, I learned a great deal more than architecture. He did not bring a senior partner with us when we joined Henry that first day. When the TIME helicopter lifted off the roof of the North End, Boston Police prison building, gently rolled right, and headed out over the harbor southbound, mentoring a promising young man was his sextant. He had the pilot fly over his Barnstable farm, on the way to the next landfall and a soft landing on the Terminal Moraine of an insular, last Ice Age geologic wonder. The Vineyard was the beginning of Ben's gift to me: the fruit of his unwavering generosity, kindness, and compassion.

If I could give either of my children anything, it would be a full monty bubble bath in a field of strawberries forever bathed in the bright light of serendipity. But they were already given that priceless gift by their mother. Cultivating serendipity got me a bigger boat. It got me out of the Deep South. But it also demanded a price to be paid.

I told one of my former USAF pilot training classmates who was flying for US Airways and still single that I was planning to open an office in Shanghai. He knew my wife Sarah, and, intending no insult, advised me to leave her home on my long trips to China. Taking a white woman to Shanghai would be like taking a ham sandwich to a banquet, he said. Of course, he was joking. Problem is the joke was on me. It was the beginning of the end of my marriage. No amount of cultivated serendipity was going to save me this time.

I cannot sleep now thinking of all the times Sarah tried to reach out to me when our marriage was falling apart and I was not there for her. I did virtually everthing I could to ensure that her efforts to save our marriage failed. Some time during our divorce, which took five years, I watched a movie while on board a flight back to Sarah and America. The movie was entitled "Barney's Version." I had done almost everything that Barney did. I was never accused of murder but I did not have to get married three times to forsake the only person I ever truly loved.

The Family

17

FAMILY

NOT KNOWING how to walk the fine line between a life less short and one cut short can take your life and the lives of others. A twelve-year-old's cocky Shinenola damn near cut short the life of his sister. Using my own money, I ordered a small caliber rifle from a Sears and Roebuck catalog. I stuffed an envelope addressed to Sears with a tear-out catalog stock item number form. Our rural delivery postman was delighted to take my money and issue Sears a money order.

The rifle arrived while my father was on a business trip. My mother saw the package before I did. She handed to me and insisted I remove the brown paper wrapping. Inside was a box with a picture of a rifle on the top. She did not have to say anything. "Wait until your father gets home," was written all over her face. She took the box into the den and came out without it.

Two days before my father was due back and my mother out of the house, I let Shine-nola take over. Knowing my mother was not due home for two hours, it took me less than five minutes to find the box hidden under the sofa. I rode my bike to the nearby corner store and bought a box of rifle bullets. No ID required. I rushed home, took out the rifle, hastily reading the written instructions for loading the bullet magazine. With still some time left, I crossed our hayfield to the gully where we burned our trash. I found some tin cans and shot them full of holes.

I had watched my father clean his guns with a kit he kept in the den's gun cabinet. I decided to do the same before returning my new rifle to the box. I did not check the magazine for any unspent rounds. I was sitting on the edge of the den sofa using my father's gun barrel cleaning rod when my older sister walked into the den and took a seat in a wooden rocking chair. After a few minutes she got up to leave. She had taken one step towards the living room when the rifle went off. The bullet went through one arm of the wooden chair and lodged into the other. If she gotten up a second later she would have taken a bullet in the abdomen. Both my sister and I froze. A few minutes later my mother arrived home to a daughter in shock and a son petrified by fear.

Telling the truth to my father did not set me free. Corporeal punishment was socially acceptable among many families of my father's generation. Bare ass, leaning forward on the wall next to his hall clothes closet, he gave me twenty lashes. His thick black leather belt raised thick welts and drew blood. I assumed I would never see my rifle again. Worse than the belt were the weeks of suspended allowance and extra chores.

I never joined the National Rifle Association. I did not find out until the release of a Michael Moore documentary that chariot warrior Charlton Heston was a weirdo gun freak and had once headed up this organized mob. Screw Congress and the stalking horse they "ride hard and put up wet" every time they reject legislation for more humane gun control laws. The Right to Bear Arms is not liberty for all, but tyranny for everyone. No pursuit of happiness can justify owning a military-grade assault rifle. As one of the parents who lost a relative at Columbine said: "Fuck'em where they spit." Raw, vulgar, and ugly, this profane phrase is what big game trophy hunters call a "money shot." Dead on. Hail a Taxidermist.

My cousin Wren Godfrey Chapman published her memoir in 2021. Her memoir is entitled *Pirate Girl Falls Through Beaver Dam*. Wren's sister is my age, and Wren is my brother's age. Daughters of my father's sister Sue, they were known growing up in Fayetteville, North Carolina as the "Godfrey Girls." Two sisters as different as night and day. From toddler to teenager, Wren would find hell and raise it. Her sister came along only for the ride. Vietnam and the assassinations of JFK and MLK came and went, and the ride was over for both of them. Wren rebelled against the tyranny of war and racism and ran away to sea. After being tied to the crow's nest of a pirate ship running contraband, she ran again. Her sister stayed and sought refuge in the arms of an army infantry officer. One said goodbye and one said hello. Good night and good morning, Vietnam.

Wren and I have been soul mates from the day we first learned how to walk and talk. I am unsure who taught who what. Neither of us was ever just along for the ride. We *were* the ride. Before either of us was legal drinking age, we had raised enough Cain to stop Satan in his tracks. Wren's Earth School (her words) life turn came when her first serious crush broke off their engagement while she was still a teenager. She dropped out of college, drove off in her trusty Volkswagen Beetle, and never looked back.

Slower than Wren and I to throw caution to the wind, my brother Jere's first parental escape came when he took a high school summer job as a tug boat hand pulling barges up and down Chesapeake Bay. His college vacations took him further afar. He joined Wren on the ski slopes of Aspen, Colorado, tended bar for free lift tickets and grub and, come summer, he boon-docked his way across North America. When not working as a lumberjack, he paddled over wilderness three-story-high waterfalls to disappear into dark deep eddy pools. He left behind a gaggle of fiberglass kayaks split in half, wrapped around rocks in Class V rapids. To beat the odds, he switched to a custom-made composite, minimalist kayak. The low-volume kayak can navigate extreme maneuvers, above and below the water. Called a squirt boat by the pros, it provides an ultra-sonic booster seat for one-man Foo-water-fighters.

Jere's lifetime of outdoor adventures has taken him to four continents to conquer world-class, white water, white fang runs, and single track, mountain bike legend trails. His motto is full speed ahead, do not stop to smell the roses. Growing up, I was the skinny kid. I used to introduce him as my fat brother, but I blew past him when I turned fifty and became his fat brother. He nailed top spot on the sibling scoreboard, then he took up kite surfing, and became a human Osprey soaring on the wind. Wading into an early winter Atlantic Ocean rip-tide one time on Edisto Island tide, I threw a rescue rope to my sixty-eight-year-old brother. Banged-up and bleeding, my wet-suited brother waded backwards into the pounding surf to retrieve his surfboard and death-defying flying kite.

I decided he might need to consider a new sport, one that was not so life-threatening, so for his sixty-eighth birthday I gave him a custom-made, light single-engine aircraft. Brother, spread your wings and learn to fly. After logging almost 400 hours in a Cessna 172, Jere was issued a private pilot's license. I had soloed in the same aircraft forty-five years earlier after seven hours of USAF flight training. Considering age makes life more precious. I told Jere what every pilot in the military is told in flight training: "There are old pilots and bold pilots, but no old bold pilots."

Four years after the kite surfing bang up, my dare-devil

brother Jere walked away from a serious single engine airplane crash. Trying to land Blue Bird, one of three custom made bush planes we keep at High Valley Airport, Jere almost became a private aviation, risk of death, actuaries statistic.

The leading cause of fatal accidents in light private aircraft is a pilot showing off for someone on the ground or sitting in the other front seat. Clint was Jere's friend and a pilot. Jere wanted to show Clint a very short landing and bolster his right to brag. When landing on such an air strip, the standard and required practice is to do a pass over the strip to make sure that it is devoid of people and animals. Jere didn't do that, and as he approached for the landing near sunset, he suddenly saw two people walking on the runway right in front of the plane, but with their backs to the plane and with no way of knowing he was coming. He slammed on the brakes and did a hard left turn, and the plane spun around and collapsed on its fuselage. The right wing and right landing strut were a total loss, both ends of the propeller had snapped broken sheared off. Fuselage warped, tubular air-frame pipes above cockpit bent and broken. Tail intact. Left wing intact. Left landing gear strut intact. Engine, avionics, tires, brakes appear to be ok. But basically Blue Bird was FUBAR'd (fucked up beyond all repair). But Jere and his passenger walked away without a scratch.

The next day Jere got back on the horse, rolled one of our spare Bush STOL's onto the grass apron, fired her up, and once again broke the bonds of gravity. Today, if Jere is not sitting behind an antique desk, wearing a bow tie and acting like a former mayor, he is out flying. Low and slow, weather permitting.

Wren, Jere, and my sister Mary Jo and I have survived countless brushes with terminal disaster. Our luck is rarely dumb. In Wren's memoir, I miraculously survive being trampled to death in a wild horse stampede. But it was no miracle. I was raised with horses. Cultivated serendipity and lying flat and motionless on the ground, impersonating FOD, saved my life. If you are a pilot, you know that FOD stands for "foreign object damage" and refers to any foreign object on an airport tarmac that doesn't belong there. Wild horses stampeding down a beaten baked clay path on a narrow canyon floor know they can break a leg if a front hoof slips on FOD. I survived because I "knew shit from Shinenola."

Shit from Shinenola is a fast-fading idiom. Knowing or not knowing shit from Shinenola is the difference between being intelligent or stupid—man, women, horse, or horsefly. And FOD? FOD pierced a Concorde wing tank on take-off causing jet fuel to flow "like shit through a goose" onto red-hot disk brakes. All onboard died.

"Mary, the mother of Jesus, was not a virgin."

My father interrupted a Sunday morning sermon, by our Presbyterian minister to utter these nine blasphemous words. He did so from the choir box wearing a long, red robe and a shiny bald head. When church was over, the entire congregation, as it did every Sunday, gathered outside the Greek antebellum temple of God to socialize and shake hands with the reverend. When it was my father's turn, he said, "Roy Wood, I invite you to give the sermon next Sunday." A week later, from the bully pulpit, my father delivered a fine speech about the joy of living, his love of nature, and the nature of humankind. He praised God and told the congregation not to believe everything in the Bible. He ended by singing "Amazing Grace" a capella.

In a niche off the church's vestibule was a glass cabinet with a few Civil War relics. One was a hand-made checker board whose darker squares were painted in blood. A rusty bayonet, leather bag for black powder, a gold-lettered front covered Bible with blood soaked pages, and some solid lead shot.

The morning of my father's blasphemous revelation, the minister asked my brother and me if we wanted to help him ring the church bell and we leapt at it. The bell tower stairs were built into the back wall of the "slave loft" at the rear of the church and no one ever went up there except for an occasional visit by someone to maintain the bell. We rang it at precisely 10:50 am, giving the adults in bible class or choir practice and the children in Sunday school time to exit the two-story, white-painted brick, white clapboarded, post-antebellum, early 1950's annex. Many of the churches in the town had porches facing south, and after the service, people would stand around in the sunshine and socialize. But the churches with porches on the north side were in shadow, and people tended to go straight home. It was an important lesson I took to heart. A person becomes a good designer by being an observer of people, watching how they use not only the built form, but also the space between.

Whenever my father had extra cash, he bought "raw dirt," or abandoned, homesteads. He was fond of telling his friends that if you buy and never sell, you'll die land rich and cash poor. My father, even though he never sold any land, did not die cash poor. He died too young at sixty-nine, leaving my mother a small fortune. In his forties, following an investment tip from a work-place colleague at the US Department of Interior, he and my grandfather, Pop King, bought shares in the Georgia Power Company. This postwar, privately owned electric utility company was following the lead of the Great Depression-era Tennessee Valley Authority and pouring the money made by selling investment shares into building dams and manmade lakes for hydroelectric power generation. My father worked for the federal agency that approved all impoundments of navigable rivers in

America, and permits to impound were in demand. Relatively cheap, and relatively environmentally friendly, hydroelectric power was quickly gaining traction in a fast-growing, postwar, housing market. Hydroelectric plants substantially reduced dependence by electric utility providers on coal-fired, steam generators. The means and methods of the soft-and-dirty coal strip-mining industry left nothing behind but toxic waste and often spelled ecocide for vast areas of wildlife habitats and bio-diverse natural environments of the coal-rich mining towns of southern Ohio and West Virginia. Buying Georgia Power stock was an investment in a cleaner, air and water, future, for Georgia. And that investment ended up making Pop and my dad more money than a lifetime of paycheck savings.

Working for the Department of Interior, whether in Washington DC, or in Georgia, my father's primary responsibility was the acquisition of private land for public use. My father perfected the art of buying land: keep it simple, make the deal face-to-face. Like a praying mantis carefully sizing-up a larger prey, my father made damn sure there were no predatory lawyers to get in the way when he was negotiating. He would talk turkey with any landowner—good, bad, or ugly, and his best deals were made sitting on the owner's front porch, shooting shit, sipping whiskey or cold iced tea, with a slice of crackling cornbread and homemade jam on the side. He loved sitting under a giant live oak with the owner of a trailer court, motel, or campground. He'd spend hours talking with a "seller" in the shade next to an alligator billabong, with fifty acres of sawgrass hammocks, marri-prairies, and landlocked sandy hummocks deep in the Florida Everglades. He knew which hat to wear for each occasion, too: near Savannah, Georgia, it would of course be a straw Panama for an antebellum verandah negotiation.

The stories he brought home after land buying trips had

enough material for a hit country western song. I went with him on one of these treasure hunts. We drove to eastern Tennessee in our family's '55 Chevy Bel Air. On the way, just south of Chattanooga, we passed by the biggest billboard I'd ever seen: Visit Lookout Mountain. The following afternoon, heading home we saw the billboard's other side: Turn Around, You Just Missed Lookout Mountain. We were going home with a handshake deal for 750 acres. Inside my father's brown leather Gokey briefcase there was a marked-up USGS map. Penciled-in were the boundaries of a pre-Civil War, river-runs-through-it, pioneer homestead. Rich with fertile bottom land, hardwood timber stands, whitetail deer, wild turkeys, and high-water-table limestone-enriched subsoil, this idyllic landscape would soon be bound for better things, to become part of a 55,000-acre Scenic River Conservation Area and Wildlife Refuge, with the farmer and his wife being granted a life-estate by the Feds. They could continue to live, farm, and die in their beloved homestead—knowing they were part of something that no one can put a price on: the intensity and immensity of experiencing mankind's relationship with nature. Natural beauty stretches the imagination, magnifying, and expanding our horizons. And wildlife habitat protection and natural scenic resource conservation deliver us from the sins of wonton environmental destruction. The inverse is a world without us. With the planet's ozone layer depleted, climate change will preclude a re-boot of the evolutionary process of natural selection that created us. We are the only species on earth capable of destroying itself. We are homo sapiens, different from dinosaurs only in DNA. We can become extinct.

For twenty years, Jere served as Mayor of Roswell. Today, if Jere is not sitting behind an antique desk, acting like a former mayor, wearing a bow tie, he is out flying. Low and slow, weather permitting.

Suited Up for Close Encounters.

18

Close Encounters

More military personnel lost their lives in the Cold War than in Afghanistan. Tens of thousands of men and women in uniform were killed in peacetime accidents. I lost four classmates during Air Force flight training. Two more were lost shortly after they got their wings, one flying with the Italian Air Force, the other with Iran's Air Force. Two of my USAF Zweibrucken Air Base mates died in fatal NATO aircraft crashes.

My closest brush with death-by-Phantom came on a cross-country flight to Bodo Norway. I stopped for fuel in Stavanger, where an inexperienced Norwegian Air Force crew chief repacked and installed my aircraft's drag chute. My Bodo Norway Airfield landing was on a short runway in between two fjords. I made a textbook short field approach touching down less than 300 feet from the white strips, holding the stick back and keeping the nose wheel in the air as long as possible. With airspeed rapidly dropping, I pulled the drag chute handle. I glanced at my rearview mirror, horrified to see the chute's cocoon lying still on the runway. Running out of runway fast, and well above recommended hydraulic braking speed, my GIB (guy in the back) made his first intercom call, suggesting we eject. Instead, I stood on the main brakes. In the rearview mirror, we both could see black smoke, an almost certain indication our tires had been

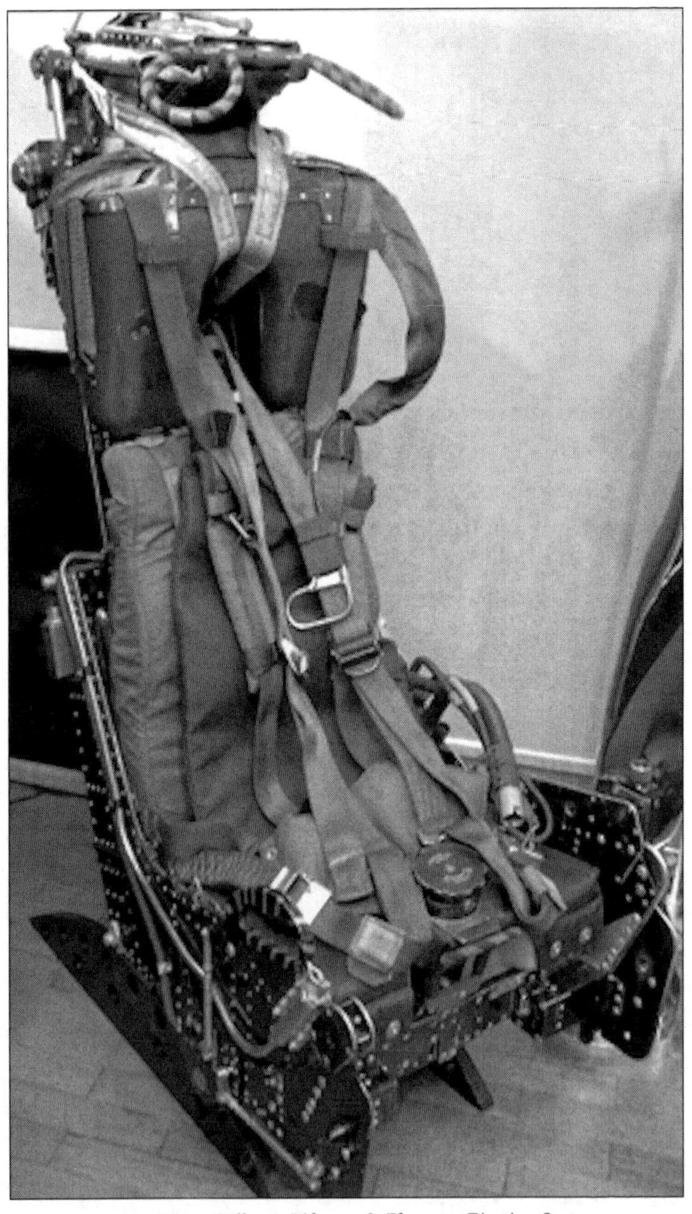

Yes Mercy Killer or Lifesavor? Phantom Ejection Seat

set on fire by red-hot brake drums. Removing the safety, I pulled the emergency brake handle. Next came the trail of sparks and large chunks of rubber as we began to skid down the runway on metal wheel rims—I no longer had control of the aircraft. After completing two 360-degree ground spins, we ran into the grass off the end of the runway. Our Phantom came to a complete stop fifty yards short of a certain-death dive into a shallow boulder-strewn fjord. This harrowing experience lasted less than thirty seconds. For every one of those seconds my GIB was screaming "Eject, eject!" He had his own ejection handle but in the Phantom it can only be activated by the pilot, me.

The decision to eject or remain with the plane depends on the exact situation, and no situation is exactly the same. In a Phantom, ejection is the sole decision of the front-seat aircraft commander. The maritime equivalent of ejection is a captain's "abandon ship" order. The failure of my drag chute set into motion a chain of lightning-fast mental responses and physical reflexes. A landing roll-out (or take-off run) ejection is termed "zero-altitude." In any Phantom ejection, the pilot in command lowers a safety guard, jerks up on a handle partially buried in the seat between his legs. Pulling this handle triggers explosive bolts that jettison the tandem-seat cockpit's thick, heavy, Plexiglas canopy. Next, a 60-millimeter canon shell explodes under the pilot's butt, subjecting the body to 10Gs of force. Strapped in, pilot and seat rocket up a telescoping guide rail anchored to the cockpit floor. At the end of the rail, another perfectly timed blast launches a small pilot chute skyward, ripping a larger chute from the seat-back. The seat and safety harness are released by a tripwire triggered by the force of air filling the deployed main chute. After that, the pilot floats safely to the ground. In zero-altitude ejections this float distance can be as little as six feet. The efficacy rate of a zero-altitude emergency escape is less than that of a third-rate Covid vacinnation jab. Anywhere along the line, even the slightest delay in sequencing, or a mechanical component defect, can cause premature, fatal bodily impact with the ground.

The decision I made that day in Bodo almost killed two people, one of them being me. I bet our lives that it was safer to ride it out on the ground than have a cannon blast us out of a metal bird cage at zippo altitude.

When I opened the canopy, fire trucks and an ambulance were speeding down the runway towards us. Normally, to exit a Phantom, you use a ladder. Not this time. The rubber tires were gone. The main landing gear struts were badly bent and damaged beyond repair. With one leg over the side of the cockpit I realized I was three or four feet closer to the ground than normal. I jumped down, then helped out my GIB. We walked to the end of the runway following alongside deep gashes made in the grass and dirt by our wounded bird. I noticed that my GIB was walking a little bow-legged. He was the first to turn the medics away. Uninjured, we jumped in the back of a pickup truck with a big "follow me" sign. The driver of the truck had seen the entire accident unfold, while he was waiting mid-runway to lead us to our aircraft tie-down and parking spot. We filed an accident report, sent it to Zweibrucken, checked into the BOQ, or Bachelor Office Quarters, changed clothes, and went to the Officers Club bar. After a couple of scotches-on-the-rocks for me, beers for him, my GIB told me he shit his pants when he thought we were going over the edge. When I refused to eject, he was sure we were doomed. He stopped short of threatening to never fly with me again.

The next day we got orders to stay with the aircraft until repairs on our landing gear could be done by qualified technicians. Parts would arrive in a couple of days. Three weeks later, with new landing gear, we got permission to fly the plane back to Zweibrucken.

A subsequent accident investigation board blamed NATO Command for not providing adequate training for Stavanger Air Base ground crew. My GIB and I received Letters of Commendation from the Commander of USAF NATO. We were cited for our bravery, airmanship, and exemplary military conduct in the line of duty. Truth is, we saved the USAF two experienced aviators and a piece of hardware worth 60 million bucks.

After this incident, USAF Phantoms were never again given clearance to fly to the only NATO air base north of the Arctic Circle. But our brush with fate was not what put Bodo into the annals of Cold War history. Few historians, military or civilian, had even heard of Bodo until Gary Power's U2 spy plane was shot down over Russia. Bodo was a rest-and-refuel stop for super-secret CIA U2 overflights. Flying at an altitude of 70,000 feet, Powers was shot down by a powerful new SAM, or Surface-to-Air Missile. His plane broke up, but Powers managed to survive and free-fall to a low enough altitude to deploy his parachute. He had signed up with the CIA to commit suicide, if necessary, to avoid enemy capture. He did what any intelligent mercenary would do: he chose life over death. Gary Power's internationally televised trial and confession "shocked and awed" the free world.

The Gary Powers incident made the Cold War colder. I came close to making it hotter. Every night an RF-4 Phantom from our squadron was assigned to NATO-USSR border patrol, enemy radar detection duty. The mission: fly a parallel course, staying on the NATO side of the Iron Curtain. You approached the border flying very low, below radar detection level. Then, within a mile of the border buffer zone, you popped up into radar detection altitude and waited until the electronic screens in the GIB's cockpit lit up like fireworks. The more fireworks, the more enemy radars had locked on your position. The GIB made a record of the radar frequencies. Some nights, the mission was extended by two hours via air-to-air refueling, which, at night, requires nerves of steel. These missions ended with a return to home base for a 6 am encrypted enemy radar frequency report sent to NATO Command.

Pinpointing your exact position on one of these border runs was not always easy. An onboard INS, or Internal Navigation System, used gyroscopic stabilizers to detect motion. INS predated satellite-based GPS, providing the pilot with x-and-y coordinates. The gyros were mechanical, and not always reliable. The best analogy is our own inner ear, which can be tricked into giving bad information when our body's platform is made unstable by unusual conditions.

One night when flying one of these top-secret missions, my aircraft's gyros were not behaving and we strayed off course. After being locked on by enemy radar, I decided to get the hell out of Dodge and climbed to a comfortable cruising altitude. As I leveled off, I looked to my right and twenty feet off my wingtip was a MIG-21, armed with air-to-air missiles. The Soviet pilot had a flashlight shining on his face. He waved, then peeled away, disappearing into darkness. The MIG could have blown us out of the sky, but our lives were saved by a brave enemy fighter pilot forced into a conflict situation he did not want. An adversary's valor, compassion, and grace had touched the faces of two American aviators. I did not report this incident.

When you fly your last flight before becoming a civilian, you are not informed of this fact beforehand, as Command is afraid you might show off and do something stupid. My squadron leader broke this rule in my case, and even told my wife to meet me when I taxied in and parked my plane after my last landing.

She was there, with champagne and camera. What no one knew is that I had flown below radar, penetrated deep into Switzerland, flew to the face of the Eiger, lit my afterburners, rolled the plane over, and climbed straight up this famous rock face. I admit it, it was a violation of a nation's sovereignty and by rights they could have shot me down. Hours later, NATO Command sent a "request for aircraft identification" emergency bulletin to every air base in Europe. I told no one, and neither did my GIB. The next day, the base commander showed me a copy of a photo of an RF-4C aircraft with the same tail number as my aircraft, taken from an Army helicopter flying in German airspace near the Swiss border. The RF-4C was reported flying just above the tree-line heading north at high speed. I wondered what my commander would do—I had three days of active duty left to serve. My GIB that day was Captain R D "Radar" Copps. If backed into a corner, I'd swear I'd defied Radar's vehement objections to my intentional violation of neutral Western Europe airspace. In actual fact, Radar was flying the plane when we crossed back into Germany. All Phantoms, fighter and reconnaissance versions, come equipped with identical flight controls in both the front and the rear seats. There was no other front-seater in my squadron that allowed his GIB to pilot the aircraft. Radar and I became a team of sorts and were always the first crew chosen to participate in NATO war games, usually bringing in the trophy for the top reconnaissance mission. With my departure, Radar's piloting opportunities would be on hold. Before hanging up my olive drab flight suit forever, I officially recommended Radar for a special USAF program allowing a navigator to retrain as a pilot. A year after I left active duty, Radar graduated at the top of his pilot training class. He remained on active duty serving as the Chief Test Pilot for the Phantom until his retirement. Like my Uncle Ben, R D Copps was a pilot's pilot.

Pop King at Kings Camp

19

Pop King

My siblings and I are post-Second World War babies. War babies owe their existence to the brave men and women who served in-and-out of uniform to defeat our nation's enemies. An underground bunker suicide and a unconditional surrender signaled final victory for the land of the free. Soldiers retuned home, women got pregnant.

My brother and I shared a bedroom growing up. At bedtime, my mother would come to kiss her two boys goodnight. When she turned off the lights, I would hide under the covers with a flashlight, mesmerized by Jack London and Mark Twain stories. I read as much as I could and discovered early that life could, and should, be a great adventure.

My father, Roy, kept a scrap book on all three of his war babies. Mine, entitled "Ben Wood + Happenings" was passed to my mother after Roy's death. My father and I were born on the same day in December, thirty years apart. I was named after my mother's brother, Benjamin. In the "+ Happenings" scrapbook there is a copy of a letter, from my grandfather Pop King, to my namesake uncle Ben. In the letter, Pop informs Ben that he is preparing a Will and not to expect any inheritance money. "But Ben, do not worry, I am giving you the entire United States of America to make a living in."

Pop King spent his last twenty-five years building and operating a fishing camp and marina. King's Camp was a thirty-minute car trip from our house. The Camp never made any real money for Pop King. Everyone who keep a boat tied to a dock or buoy, bought bait, had a boat repaired at the marina, or went to the Camp Snack Bar to eat a cheeseburger, slaw dog, grilled cheese, French fry, or enjoy a bowl of Pop's chili, loved Pop King and his wife Mary. When old enough to follow orders, my younger-by-one-year brother and I worked summers at the Camp. We stayed busy cleaning fish for successful anglers, washing out and collecting trash from returned rental fishing boats. We keep the coin-operated drink machine full of Coke, Orange Soda, and Dr. Pepper. We helped owners tie-up their boats or pick them up from their buoys. Occasionally left behind in a boat were unopened cans of beer. We either sold the beer to fisherman or ferreted some cans away for safe-keeping. When no one was looking, we would sneak off to the woods to wash down, with a swig of beer, a Peanut Butter Cup or a package of cheese crackers. We were naughty, clever, suntanned, swim-like-a-fish, Tom Sawyers. We wore cut-off jeans and white T-shirts. We were barefooted or put on worn-out, sun-bleached, tennis shoes. My mother cut our hair: A flat-top bob for the blond hair, baby blue eyed me, and a straight, buzz-cut, do for my brown, over brown, brother.

When not at the Camp we joined the rest of the family on camping and canoe trips in State parks and National forests. On long vacations we camped with my cousins' family, the Godfreys, from North Carolina. On shorter weekend trips, we camped with my parent's best friends: my Boy Scout Leader, Charlie Nellans, his wife Norma, and their five kids, Nick, Gwen, Michael, Bob, and Vincent. The Nellans, Godfrey, and Wood gang, nine in all, were as close as brothers and sisters. Cooking over an open campfire with this gang began by sharing a pocketknife to cut a straight, small diameter, green wood tree branch or remove the trunk of a hardwood sapling. We put a sharp end on the end of our sticks. These were our skewers for roasting pigs-in-blankets (pork hot dogs wrapped in canned biscuit dough). Dessert was roasted marshmallows, squished between graham crackers, called s'mores. We cooled off on hot afternoons swimming upstream in white water, jumping off rock ledges into deep pools of cold spring water, and once played for an entire day in a neck-deep pond of thick, dark grey, mud.

In the fall, we went on Saturday morning mourning dove shoots. With other young boys and fathers, we formed a long line, each person spaced ten feet apart in fields of brown stalks with dried corn still on the cob. We stood motionless, awaiting the arrival of a flight of doves. When they were in range the shooting started. Spooked doves scattered in all directions as the air filled with the smell of gunpowder. After the shoot, the boys would collect empty shotgun shells. Re-loaded at home, the shells got return tickets to spray lead poisoned pellets into the ground beneath the killing fields. Bunny rabbits, ground squirrels, and chipmunks beware.

On spring weekends, we worked in the family vegetable garden, planting, weeding, and cultivating. We hand-picked the season's first strawberries from patches surrounded by thickets thick with ticks. We gave hand signals to my father, helping him back up to hitch tractor implements. In the fall we put up hay, filling the barn loft with winter food for the horses. When winter arrived, we went Christmas shopping. We never bought a Christmas tree, there were too many free ones among the fallen pine cones that covered the ground under sun holes in the canopy of the thick pine forest near our house. We did not really need a Christmas tree. Our Christmas and New Year

Holidays were spent at Kings Camp. Uncle Ben King would be there with his family, Aunt Tinky with hers, Uncle Godfrey, Aunt Sue, and theirs. On Christmas Day, we woke with our cousins at the crack of dawn. With one parent present, we were allowed to open our stockings and one present. The rest would have to wait under the Tree until all of the adults had gotten out of bed, put on robes, and joined us. With everybody gathered around the big rock fireplace, Santa Claus, in full regalia, would pass out chocolate bars and handfuls of Hershey Kisses to every kid. My father always played Santa Claus. The red velvet suit, hat, and stringed bag was made by our mother. He had to buy the wide belt at a costume store.

For the big Christmas dinner, all the leaf expansions of the big table were employed. Out came the big candelabras and extra long red candles. A twenty-five-pound turkey, basted and roasted golden, resting in a bed of carrots and potatoes, was laid to rest on a homemade cutting board of heart pine. The bird then went under the knife, divided into dark and white meat. The giblets and stuffing were scooped into a large silver bowl, the big drumsticks placed, for show, on a raised hot pot stand in the middle of the big table. After dozens of please pass this, pass that, always to your right, almost every red, green, yellow, or brown, dish was empty. After whipped cream topped pecan pie, fried hot apple pies, cherry cobbler, and brownies, story telling that started at the table retired to sofas and chairs. At 5 pm, two bowls of egg-nog, spiked and un-spiked, were put on a side table next to the fireplace. When the egg-nog was gone, whiskey and rum moved in. The tales got taller and the memory logs burned brighter. It's hard to say who "won" these contests, Pop, Uncle Ben, or my father.

Christmas night the bird dogs were brought in from the late December cold to sleep on the warm stone hearth as the embers slowly died. Allowed inside for one evening, the next morning they would be back outside earning their keep. The day after Christmas was the "Big Hunt." With the sun barely above treetops, my brother and I would jump in a Willys jeep, tail gate down, loaded with cages of pen-raised, ring-neck pheasants. With our father at the wheel, we stood on the rear wheel wells, holding on to the cage tie down straps. Our job was to set the birds in the bush. Beginning mid-morning, many of them would be dropping from the winter sky. Before "planting" the ring-necks in twos and threes, among the low brambles of old cottons fields, the hapless birds needed to be hypnotized. A hand rub job, on the bird's curled neck, with head tucked under a wing, worked the magic. Finished with the pheasant "plant" we went back to the house for a breakfast of salt-cured, country ham, gristmill corn grits, buttermilk biscuits, and red-eye gravy. From mid-morning to early afternoon, Pop King, Uncle Ben, my father, boy cousins and brothers, would walk behind bird dogs. Three English Pointers and one Springer Spaniel, went on "point" when they sensed where pheasants were hiding. When on "point" the dogs did not move again until their hunters walked forward, flushing the pheasants, launching skyward a bouquet of flying colors. Gunfire from pump action, double barrel, and semi-automatic shotguns broke and folded wings. The smell of saltpeter filled the air. Birds fell forward yards from where they were hit with lead shot. Sometimes Jere and I had to bushwhack our way deep into thorny thickets to find a downed bird. If found alive, a quick wring of the ring-neck's neck took care of matters. A few birds got lucky, escaping death by birdshot. But reprieve was short. Foxes waited in the woods for night to fall to ambush the pen-raised, open-space rookies. In moonlight, the iridescent, emerald green, ruby red, agave blue, hood of a ring-neck, glows like a cat's eye marble.

During the ring-neck hunt, womenfolk talked about their husbands and kids until it was time to prepare a hearty meal for the returning hunters. Served buffet style, the hunters lined up for turkey drumstick and vegetable soup, oven-heated, store-bought Hormel ham steaks, Heinz yellow mustard, bread and butter pickles, and another round of quad-colored side dishes. Dessert was day-old butter-milk biscuits, homemade strawberry and blackberry jelly, and left-over Christmas pie.

On cold, windy, raining days, women played Bridge or Canasta, taking breaks to help older kids with cardtable-size jigsaw puzzles. You could find at least four more on the Monopoly rug. The tots were confined to a big play pen loaded with toys and stuffed animals. As I got older, chess and Scrabble became my indoor day favorites. Brother Jere was my nemesis in the former, my mother, or her sister Aunt Tinky, for the latter.

On sunny days, Jere and I and Uncle Ben's two sons, Budger and Nubin, went quail hunting with the rest of the menfolk. We were not old enough to carry real guns, but all had BB rifles. No pen-raised "ring-neck plants" this time. Smaller targets, faster flyers, native bob-whites make the playing field more level. Most bob-whites, like native trout, get away to live another day. If we bagged more than five or six quail, it was a rare day. Over the course of three or four miles of bush whacking, both hunters and dogs picked up a small army of ticks. On the dogs these blood suckers were joined by cockleburs. A lit match head got the ticks to back off but filled the air with the smell of singed dog hair. A sharp pair of scissors cut loose the cockles.

Pop King's wife Mary, "Me-Mo" to her grandkids, kept a closet full of collapsed cardboard moving boxes. Resurrected, they made great Alamos or OK Corrals. We wore chaps, cowboy and cowgirl clothes, and double holster, six-shooter, cap guns. We flipped a coin to see who got to be Davy Crockett and wear

Pop's real coonskin hat.

Near the end of our eight months of reliving our childhoods, Jere, Mary Jo, Claudia and I decided that the Kennedy Resort's main mission was to forever promote outdoor recreation and conservation of the natural environment. Our mother and father dedicated much of their lives to promoting these two campaigns. Unlike our parents, our Uncle Ben was neither a preacher, teacher, or mentor. He was our idol, our American Hero. A fighter jet pilot and veteran of seven different theaters of war beginning with World War II and ending with the Vietnam War, he was a soldier's soldier, a pilot's pilot. Brigadier Benjamin H King retired from the US Air Force the same year I entered the USAF. He continued to fly airplanes until one year before he died. He landed his Mooney "gear-up" at a local airport, walking distance from his home in Florence, Oregon. He got a friend with a truck mounted winch to drag his plane into the grass apron. Time to hang it up. During the winters uncle Ben operated a small marina and fish camp in the mountains of northern Mexico. Large-mouth bass fisherman from all over America, many of them professional athletes and coaches, would come in camper trucks and RVs to his Mexican Kings Camp. The days ended sitting around an open fire pit, drinking whiskey, listening to my uncle's tales of high adventure, victory and defeat, and survival. Beating the formidable odds that every combat aviator faces was material enough for hundreds of spell-binding, hard to believe, stories. A guest could come for three weeks and never hear the same story twice. Pop King had taught his son well.

American hero USAF Lt. Ben King

20

Mono Island

One day in October 2016, I met my brother and sister at the international airport in Brisbane, Australia. With me was a colleague from my Shanghai design studio, whose job was to document the trip—I didn't want taking pictures to be a distraction from what might be the greatest adventure of my life. The four of us transited to a flight to Honiara, the capital of the Solomon Islands, and after a couple of days rest at Honiara's top beachfront resort, we began the last leg of our trip, final destination: Mono Island, the largest inhabited island in the Treasury Islands.

Very, very few people who are not born there ever go there, but in 2016 the three children of Roy and Tillie Wood decided to take a leap together and go to an island described in stories byUncle Ben, our mother's brother, who served in World War II's Pacific Theater. Both my sister and I worked different angles to try to secure passage to Mono. I called or emailed every private ocean watercraft and sea plane charter service in the South Pacific, and all gave the same reply: getting to Mono was too risky. Large expanses of open ocean outside normal shipping lanes would have to be crossed. The amount of money I was prepared to pay didn't change anything.

My sister fared better. After two years of negotiations, dozens of emails, and a great deal of help from a Mono Island-born woman living in Honiara, my sister found a way to get there. The Monoian, Patricia, worked at the US Consular Office, and had seen an email my sister sent to the Consular Head. Patricia persuaded her boss, a career civil servant from Kansas, to contact the CEO of Solomon Airlines and ask them to extend a regularly scheduled flight to Gizo to Stirling Island. During World War II, Japanese troops occupied Mono Island. Near the end of the War, when US Navy and Marine Corps forces liberated the island, the Navy Seabees built an airstrip on Mono's nearest neighbor, Stirling Island.

We left Honiara at seven in the morning, arriving in Gizo on time. The regular passengers disembarked. We waited in a one-room airport lounge for two hours while our pilot had the plane refueled. Just before noon, we re-boarded the Swiss-made Pilatus Turboprop, and thirty-five minutes after taking off from Gizo, we had the broken-up blacktop of the long-abandoned Stirling Island airstrip in sight. At final approach, we could see a large group of natives waiting near the end of the runway. My sister and Patricia had saved the day. Patricia had arranged $2,000 for Mono Islanders to clear the abandoned runway of hundreds of small trees prior to our arrival. Solomon Airlines had done a fly-by a few days earlier to visually inspect the runway. Our pilot, the same one who did the fly-by, told us to brace for a rough landing but assured us everything would be okay. Almost four decades had passed since the last aircraft left Stirling Island. Large cracks in the bitumen-bonded, crushed and compacted, seashell tarmac had filled with thick grass and weeds. The same locals who had cleared the runway had filled several large potholes with small rock and shell fragments. The Pilatus bush plane's aerodynamics, huge flaps, tundra tires, reversible props, and heavy disk brakes did the rest.

Our plane was met by thirty people from Mono's largest community, the village of Falamai. Falamai, Mono's only deep-water pier, was on the other side of a narrow channel from the Stirling Island airstrip. The natives loaded us and our bags into dugout canoes for the short paddle to our host village. Hundreds of natives turned out to greet us as we disembarked from the dugouts. A long line of men, woman and children holding hands guided us up a gently sloping expanse of well-groomed grass to Falamai's community center.

Many locals in the line had made fragrant wildflower string necklaces for us. Festooned with colorful and edible jewels, we gathered with tribal leaders and local dignitaries under a thatch-roofed, open air, communal pavilion. We received an official welcome from the Falamai tribal council. The Wood children, all of us past the age of sixty-five, made short speeches, recalling our uncle's love for the Island and its people. There wasn't room for everyone under the big roof, and dozens of villagers surrounded the pavilion to get a view of the first Americans to visit Mono in seventy-three years. We were served a meal of fresh vegetables, filets from the daily fish catch, boiled crustaceans and sea snails, and bread made from tropical tubers. Eight natives of Mono, women in their nineties, recounted for us their vivid and deeply emotional childhood memories of our uncle.

We spent the next three days feasting, dancing, singing, swimming, jungle exploring, laughing, crying, and praying with a thousand natives. We slept in a native house with no electricity. In the mornings, the women of the village would take turns bringing us potluck-style breakfast and lunch dishes, fresh fruit, fried eggs, homemade jam, and baked bread. In the evening, before the evening's festivities began, we enjoyed happy hour on our porch. I treated everyone (including at least two or three village guests) to fresh squeezed fruit drinks spiked with imported Vodka, served in hollowed-out coconuts.

The island's only source of electricity is a small gas generator kept in a padlocked storeroom adjacent the community center. The generator was run weekly for twenty or thirty minutes to power the island's sole radio communications. A government-funded outreach center, based in Honiara, was updated each week on the island's health and welfare. The only mechanized vehicles on the island were mini two-wheel cultivators that ran on gas, which was in precious supply. The rusting hulk of a Seabee bulldozer served as a roost for local free-range chickens. Pre-World War II Christian missionaries from New Zealand had helped the natives build a beautiful one-room church. The missionaries were also the first schoolteachers on the island, teaching the natives English. A two-room, government-funded school at the time provided children with a sixth-grade education, with classes in English. The church services now encompass all denominations. Everyone we met on Mono had English names, and for males, Ben was the most popular.

In World War II, our Uncle Ben's fighter plane, a Lockheed P-38 Lightning, was shot down during a dogfight with a large formation of Zeros over the Pacific Ocean, just five miles offshore of Shortland Island. He managed to shoot down three Zeros before his both engines were shot up by enemy machine gun fire, managing to ditch the P-38 and before leaving his bullet-riddled cockpit and throwing his parachute pack overboard. The chute deployed and floated gently onto the surface of the water. Two of the Zeros chasing him down spotted his parachute in the water. When they began the first of three strafing runs, Ben dived under the wing the of still-floating P-38. While holding his breath he jettisoned his boots, which were dragging him down. He could see bullets as they penetrated deep below the water's surface. He made two more dives, until he could see the Zeros returning to their main formation.

Ben could see Shortland Island but knew from intelligence reports that it was home to a Japanese seaplane base heavily guarded by enemy soldiers. Thirty miles in the distance, he could see the Treasury Islands. Thirty miles would probably buy him a better chance of avoiding capture.

Paddling mostly at night to avoid exposing his bare hands, feet, and face to the intense sun, the going was slow, the winds and currents were not in his favor. But Uncle Ben survived the next six days in his tiny one-man rubber liferaft bobbing up and down in the shark-infested, open ocean. He had no water and, for the first two days, no food. His emergency rations had soaked up so much salt water he couldn't keep them down. He did have a service revolver and hunting knife, and on the third day he killed an albatross. He washed down the raw bird flesh with minuscule amounts of rainwater he had collected earlier that day. He saved some precious scraps to bait the hook and line in his flight suit pocket survival kit, but the fishing line had dry-rotted, and his attempts to salvage enough to sink a baited hook failed.

On the fifth day, a tropical thunderstorm came up and, just before sunset, the wind changed direction, became very strong, and his raft was carried by large waves towards land. Darkness came, the storm subsided, and his raft stopped moving. He thought he was hallucinating when, in the light of the moon, he saw land on either side of him. He was in the middle of a narrow channel between two islands. But time was running out. The salt left behind by the waves that had carried him into the channel were causing almost unbearable pain to his badly sunburned lips and eyelids. Half-blind, and unable to speak, he lay down in the bottom of the raft to await daylight before attempting go ashore. In a state of semi-consciousness, the first morning rays of the sun woke him. He could see that the islands on either side of the channel had very different shores: the thick jungle and mangroves of Stirling Island on one, the palm trees and sand beaches of Mono Island on the other.

In what must have seemed like an eternity, Ben climbed out of his raft and swim towards the sand beach, raft in tow. Reaching the shore, he dragged his raft to dry sand, stumbled and fell on his face. As he tried to get back on his feet, he saw sunlight reflecting off the surface rivulets of a shallow stream that spread like roots over the beach sand. Too weak to walk, Ben used his elbows to drag himself to drink. Cool spring water soothed his lips and eyelids, soaked his hair, and wet his brow—and quenched his thirst. Soon, he was able to walk again. He saw a trail next to the stream with fresh human footprints. Ben was a couple hundred yards down the trail when he saw a large native man emerging from the brush, only ten yards in front of him. The man had a machete hanging from his waist. Ben raised his right hand to signal peace while he cocked the service revolver in his left hand behind his back. The native, in English, said, "Quick, follow me—there are Japanese soldiers coming down the trail."

He led Ben through a thick tropical hardwood understory to a trailhead concealed behind a fallen tree covered in vines. Ben and the man walked in silence for two miles, up a heavily forested, volcanic rock hillside to a small clearing next to a stream. At the edge of the clearing, sitting outside a thatch hut, were three other downed Allied airmen. The airmen had food and first aid kits, they tended to Ben's wounds and fed him while the large native man looked on. The man left, telling Ben that he would return with more food the next day. That night, and every night for four months, Ben slept on a woven bamboo mat in this safe haven hideaway. Ben's godsend returned the next day with a large basket of food and three more downed airmen. Now there were seven.

My sister, brother, and I arrived in Falamai seventy-three years after Uncle Ben's rescue, and seven decades after Uncle Ben first told his stories of the seven survivors to his sister's three children. We had come to Mono Island, to the Village of Falamai, bearing gifts and tidings of goodwill. We had come to thank the wonderfully kind and compassionate human beings who hae risked their own lives to save our beloved American hero.

Four joyful, glorious, amazing days ended with tears and promises to return. On our last Mono morning, as we walked down to the beach to load into canoes bound for Stirling Island, I looked back to see a large crowd of Mono Island children following us. They started running, passing us on the way to get a place on the World War II-era concrete pier. From the pier they could watch us load into the dugouts and paddle across the channel. Their goodbye waves and cheers will remain in all our memories. Most of them will never leave the island, ride in an automobile, eat ice cream, wage war, or be asked by a beggar for money. They are the flowers; we are the weeds.

As we crossed the channel to rendezvous with the Pilatus, I checked again that my notebook was in my shoulder pack. In my notebook, written for the ages, were the words to a song sung to us by the Falamai Christ Church Choir. Penned by a member of the choir, we saw these words written on a blackboard hanging on the wall next to our front pew seats when we arrived for our visit's special Sunday morning service.

The Flowers of Falamai

Great heroes and fearless Americans
You recaptured our beloved Falamai
The roses of Mono gladly welcome you
You are our saviors

When we suffered from hunger and terrible fear
To our shores you came
Bringing hope
Giving us courage

When sweetly smelling flowers
Shoot out from the forests of Falamai
And dawn breaks over Toloki Point
We remember Ben King and the others

When you go home
Take this song of consolation with you
On our tiny island you won a war
And our love forever

A song celebrating Mono Island's liberation from Japanese occupation by American and Allied Forces during World War II

Written and performed by the Mono Island Church Choir October 2016

Jeffrey Katzenberg making friends in Yunnan.

21

Beautiful Houses

Architecture is one of the few professions that you can get better at until the day you die. Frank Lloyd Wright visited the Guggenheim a few months before construction was completed, but died before his greatest work was finished.

Wright's mid-career masterpiece was the Usonian-inspired Falling Water, which for many architects of my generation was considered the most beautiful house in America. I visited Falling Water while still in graduate school. In 2011, I was invited by Jeffrey Katzenberg to take a redeye flight from Shanghai to Los Angeles and join him for brunch in *his* Usonian Beverly Hills home. He told me that *he* lived in America's most beautiful house.

I met Jeffrey's driver at the airport, and on the way to Beverly Hills we passed by Century City. The open-air Market Place I designed for The Mall at Century City in 1984 was gone, swallowed whole by a big box full of luxury brands. We drove down several streets in Beverly Hills before ending up on a single-lane road, heading up into the hills toward the Hollywood sign. With the sign in view, we turned into Jeffrey's driveway. The driver stopped the car in a turnout around fifty yards from a single-story wood-and-stone house. Beautiful in design, the house and the natural surroundings were as one. Wright's aesthetic was politely present in sweeping horizontal roof and eave lines. This aesthetic, combined with the informality of a northern California wine country estate, gave the house a soft, gentle, even modest feel. Before going inside, I knew there would be no grand staircase, no marble floors, no Oriental carpets, no crystal chandeliers, no great room with two-story high ceilings, and no fluted white columns holding up glossy white mantlepieces covered in candelabras. A narcissist's propped-up, heavy-mascara Beverly Hills mansion, or a tricked-out Mediterranean red-tile roof stucco castle, it was not.

When I got out of his car, Jeffrey was standing at his front door wearing navy blue shorts, a DreamWorks alligator shirt, and Birkenstocks. He had an easygoing and welcoming smile. Hidden away on several wooded acres, the house was every bit as extraordinary as Jeffrey had told me. Every room, except for his home theater and wine cellar, had walls of glass. At the touch of a remote, these walls disappeared into the woodwork. The expansive outdoor views, unfettered by transparent and reflecting panes, exploded. Configured in a large "U" shape never more than one room deep, natural light and fresh, naturally ventilated air flooded every inch of every room.

Jeffrey's chef served us brunch on an expansive deck-and-patio that ran the length of the longest side of his house. We enjoyed a wonderful mixed green salad and homemade sandwich of tuna on freshly baked multigrain bread. The chef brought Jeffrey a tall glass of iced Diet Coke and me a freshly brewed unsweetened iced tea. Jeffrey, on a three-week trip we took together through China, drank five or six cases of the low calorie, highly caffeinated beverage. A dozen or more Diet Cokes a day, along with Jeffrey's 4 am one-hour workout, made it nearly impossible to keep up with him.

Jeffrey's architect was Howard Bracken. I imagine Bracken was a happy man when Jeffrey told him he wanted a house designed for a kingmaker, not a king. Bracken blended Jeffrey's house seamlessly into the Hollywood Hills' aesthetically fragile landscape.

I heard that Bracken credits his longevity to a daily rise-and-shine outdoor cold shower out back of his northern California home. Frank Lloyd Wright, when asked by Mike Wallace in his famous interview if he was religious, answered: I spell God N-A-T-U-R-E. I expect Bracken's answer to the same question would mirror Wright's. The process of "building softly on the land" begins with both client and architect walking the site together through all four seasons. Disciplined observation and dialogue are the hallmarks of an intellectually rewarding client-and-architect collaboration.

The only architect I knew growing up was a member our church, Jim Barker. He was a Presbyterian and he and his wife were my parents' close friends. Barker raised his family in a house made of salvaged, drab green Quonset huts. You entered the Barker home's long gravel drive from one of the town's only paved highways, via a front gate typical of local horse farms. An ingenious contraption, the gate opens when a driver rolls up, and pulls down on a rope. A rider on horseback would do the same, opening the gate without dismounting. Deep in a step-sided-shallow hollow filled with virgin hardwoods, and spared from plantation axes, the Barker hut flotilla was roped together by glass-roofed gardens lush with forest ferns, toadstools, and river rock. A glass-bottom bridge protruded from corrugated arches of the master hut. Half suspension, half cantilever, the bridge hovered two stories over rotten chestnut log moss and a wildflower garden. The bridge ended abruptly, blocked by towering columns of 150-year-old tulip poplars and a red pebble outdoor shower. Barker's cylindrical vaulted maze was punctuated by "Sputnik" windows made famous by the space race. It was the most beautiful house in my hometown. Barker sold this masterwork after suburban bedroom communities of McMansions began encroaching on Hut Hollow's privacy. He sold to a shopping mall developer, and Hut Hollow was backfilled to build a mammoth parking lot.

I do not know when Jim Barker was born. I do remember that he and my father were close in age. That would mean that Jim was around thirty when I was born, in 1947. In 1947, the first credible sighting of a UFO coincided with a proposal to develop earth satellites. Russia had been experimenting with nuclear technology for four years. The Cold War was in its pre-infantile stage, not yet out of the womb. Chuck Yeager became the first man in the history of aviation to break the sound barrier at sea level. Prior to Chuck, the superheroes were Buck Rogers and Flash Gordon, and science fiction cartoonists, writers, and film-makers presented clear Armageddon scenarios. The times were changing fast, not just for technocrats, plutocrats, and democrats—but for free thinkers like Jim Barker, too. The money-grubbing suburban sprawl buyout resulted in Jim Barker and his family moving to his own "flying saucer" atop a cave dwelling carved out of a granite monolith just fifteen miles north of Hut Hollow. Jim Barker became my Flash Gordon.Today, that house is gone, too. On November 8th, 2017, the headliner for a WSB-TV Channel 2, Atlanta, evening news hour feature read: "Flying Saucer House Crashes Down to Earth in Demolition."

If I had not found a bigger boat, I would today be busy designing suburban trophy homes, boutique art galleries, and vacation retreats with barns and boat houses full of expensive toys for the rich. Architecture mimics bad art when used to create homes with three, four, or more times as many rooms as the number of people who live there. Jim Barker never found a

Animas River Valley near Durango Colorado

bigger boat, and didn't need to. Over the course of his career, he designed over a hundred places of worship in towns and cities across the South. He lived in two worlds. In one he believed, in the other he imagined.

The first house I ever designed from the ground up was a built-on-spec venture. I borrowed $50,000 from my father to finance the construction of a home for what had become, with the arrival of our daughter, a Durango, Colorado Wood family of three.

Half-buried in the crest of the glacial terminal moraine, the house looked out over one of the great river valleys of the North American Rocky Mountains, the north Animas. Except for a 220-foot long window facing southwards to the sun, all main rooms faced north with sliding glass doors opening onto valley view decks. A custom printed circuit board controlled a system of operable insulation sandwich panels mounted under the glass ribbon. Like a reverse eyelid, they opened and closed on demand. the sun shone on a giant black painted radiator made from suspended oil well pipes, and the "radiator" gravity fed heated water to a large cedar hot tub that also served as the thermal storage for a radiant, under-floor heating system.

Terminal moraines are rare and precious and very rarely is approval given for a house to be built on one. I have done it twice, once in Colorado and once on Martha's Vineyard far the east. End moraines mark the final point of a glacier's advance, the place to which the ice flow pushed its captive debris and then gave up, retreating back into the mountains. They dominate the valleys they occupy, standing there, proof of nature's power.

I sold the house to a commercial real estate broker and made a profit of $30K after repaying my father. My buyer held the house for a couple of years before selling to a local architect. The first owner ended up in a federal penitentiary, sentenced to thirty years for smuggling marijuana. The second owner published the house under his own name, claiming credit for sustainable energy innovations he had not authored. The latter transgression I consider to be indefensible. I had fun designing and building the house, I made some money of it, and ended up hooked on architecture.

Andrew Flake, me and Mike McCaskey in the Vineyard.

22

More is Never Enough

I met Mike McCaskey while playing in a doubles tennis tournament at the West Chop Club on Martha's Vineyard. My partner was Andrew Flake, founder and president of the tennis club. After the match, Mike invited me and Andrew and our wives to dinner. When it came time to pay, Mike produced a credit card carrying the logo of the NFL's Chicago Bears football team. I asked, "Are you a big Bears fan?" He smiled and said yes. Next day, he came to Andrew's house for a poolside afternoon. My wife and I were staying in the Flakes' second floor garage guest suite and joined the party. Over Happy Hour cocktails I showed everyone a short video I had hand edited that morning. I spliced footage of my god-daughter Alley, Andrew and June's newest daughter, playing on the lawn with moving images of a beautiful summer sun setting over Vineyard Haven Harbor.

A few months later, I found out that Mike was more than a big fan of the Bears, he was Chairman of the Chicago Bears. Mike called me in our Boston studio and requested help in selecting an architect for a new Bears football stadium. He knew that Carlos and I were not sports architects. But from our conversion poolside at Andrew's, his instincts told him that I could help him cut through the hype, marketing flak and promotional smoke screens set up by big name "sports architects" to lure in NFL owners. The commission as Design Architect for this 2-billion-dollar Chicago Bears and City of Chicago, Parks and Recreation project should have, by all rights, gone to an experienced stadium architect. But it did not. Mike, in a fairy tale of a story, chose Carlos and I to design his new stadium. I chalk up my success in this mission impossible to a life of cultivating serendipity. And to teaming up with a brilliant designer and form-giver, Carlos Zapata.

Thomas Jefferson, when asked why it took him only one day to write the Bill of Rights, replied: "I practiced for forty years." Vincent Lo and Mike McCaskey, like all true visionaries, advance their goals by taking carefully calculated risks on people who believe they can change the world.

In December of 1999, Mike and I went to Italy for three weeks. I drove, he sang, from one famous football stadium or Catholic cathedral to the next. We flew into Milan, rented a compact car, and traveled as far south and east as Bari on the Adriatic. Then we headed west to the Amalfi Coast on the Tyrrhenian Sea. Mike the singer was damned good. He had learned to sing from his dad, Ed. Mike's mother Virginia, daughter of NFL founder George Halas, met Ed when he was singing baritone with a semi-professional barbershop quartet. All four men were devout Catholics and toured northern Illinois on weekends performing at Church socials. Mike was also a distinguished alumni of the Yale Glee Club and the Catholic Men's Choir. When not singing a capella, Mike dug into a fanny pack stuffed with custom arranged background music cassette tapes.

The best football and World Cup venue we saw was Bari Stadium, an extraordinary study in the athletic abilities of modern pre-cast concrete by Italian architect Renzo Piano. Winner of the best cathedral stadium double play was Florence. The Florence track and field stadium is a masterwork of symphonic, sculptured, cantilevered concrete, by Italian architect and engineer Luigi Nervi. Every architect in the world who appreciates the magnitude of the Nervi's artistic, engineering, and technical talent, has visited this extraordinary stadium. Piano's Bari inspiration came directly from Nervi's pioneering work with cast-in-place, reinforced concrete. Best overnight stay was the Christmas Nativity Scene and Catholic Mass in Sorento.

Whenever Carlos and I presented him with plans for New Soldier Field, Mike knew the direct origins of many of the design concepts. Had we not made that Italy trip together, the stadium design would have have turned out differently. Mike was always searching for inventive and imaginative ways to intellectually engage the people around him. He spent countless hours with my partner Carlos Zapata and me. He did not want a single cheap "bad" seat in the new bowl of New Soldier Field. Mike's aspirational goal produced the NFL's first modern asymmetric stadium design. There were fifty-yard line seats, with great sight lines, in both the Club and General Admission sections of the stadium. Clubs and Club Lounge on one side, GA's on the other. The Bears' Club seat farthest from the sideline, was closer to the field with better sight lines than the closest Club seat in any other NFL stadium. When New Soldier Field opened, Blair Kamin, the *Chicago Tribune's* architectural critic, dubbed it the "mistake on the lake." But criticism by Kamin came into serious question when the *New York Times* named "New Soldier Field" as one of America's "Ten Best Buildings" of 2003.

Mike and I, and our families, had vacation homes on Martha's Vineyard. Sitting with Mike on his West Tisbury deck or on my hilltop safari camp porch off Lambert's Cove Road, we would talk about our children, our spouses, and our love of life. Andrew, the person who introduced us after the West Chop Club tennis match, often joined these fresh-air and sea-view chats.

Vincent Lo in Chicago

Mike's July stay on the Vineyard was his annual pilgrimage to recharge the soul, reboot the mind, and touch the hearts of an Island community of family and friends.

Mike's stewardship of the Bears came under heavy fire several times over his long span of tenure as Chairman. But Mike had the courage to stand up, defend his decisions, and defend and protect the family legacy of George Halas and daughter, Virginia Halas McCaskey. On countless occasions he came close to being crucified by Bear fans, convinced he was an Ivy League snob. Before he was made Chairman of the Bears Football Club by his mother, Mike was a tenured professor at the Harvard School of Business. I will never forget a family meeting at Virginia's house. The meeting was held in the cramped living room of the subdivision single story, tract house where Mike and his seven siblings were raised. After a lunch of take-out pizza (one of her son's had to drive and get the "not free delivery" kind), Virginia asked me to go down to the basement with her. She reached into a freezer locker and brought out a clear plastic wrapped, solid chocolate, life-sized, football, a gift from the NFL. I carried the heavy hard-frozen, faux pigskin, gridiron bomb up the back stairs to the kitchen counter. Virginia came up behind me carrying an an unopened gift box. Inside was an electric knife with serrated blade. I butchered the chocolate beast, sawing and whacking off bite-size chunks. Before this "chain saw" massacre, one of her children had suggested we get ice cream delivered. No way, not when Virginia had a giant Hershey bar stashed away. Imagine this level of frugality from a woman worth hundreds of millions of dollars.

The main purpose of the family meeting was to get an update on stadium design and construction progress from Mike. I was there to answer questions and provide a detailed accounting of consultant expenses, including the fees charged by Carlos and me. Mike warned me that the meeting would be difficult. It was. Along with the chocolate bits, there was a great deal of money on the table.

But Mike, despite pressure to the contrary, was determined to keep the Bears in Chicago. And was determined to give every Bear fan the best seats of any stadium in the NFL. He did it without the braggadocio common among the owners of professional sports teams. And just like Vincent Lo, Mike thrived in the face of adversity. Moving an NFL team to a new home in a mostly white wealthy suburb is now, and was then, in the playbook of the owner of every dream team. Today, this NFL stadium's joyride from downtown to the more affluent "burbs" is coming soon. Mike died in 2019, a true gentleman and scholar silenced forever. The coast had been clear for years, and now it was finally time. The Bear's executive team went to the NFL owners with a business proposal: endorse our plan for a new 100,000 seat stadium. All Clubs will benefit equally from a dramatic increase in Bears revenues. Revenue from general admissions seats at all NFL games are distributed equally among team owners. The Bears' owners got their wish. In 2021, the McCaskey family announced that Chicago's NFL team would move as a new stadium was completed. Hey, fans of Da Bears! How does the name Da Arlington Bears sound?

In early 2003, the last phase of XTD, the South Block, opened. The same year, Mayor Daley and Mike cut the ribbon in time for an NFL season opener at New Soldier Field. Vincent Lo flew in from Hong Kong to join me and Mike on the football field at half-time. It was a very good year.

Lockdown in Shanghai – a shot from a drone.

23

COVID Pioneer

I ARRIVED in the USA on Chinese New Years Day, January 29, 2020. On that very day, China announced to the world that an outbreak of a deadly virus, subsequently dubbed Covid-19, was killing people in the city of Wuhan. I was among the first international arrivals to go through US Customs and Immigration on day one of World War Covid. Arriving on a non-stop flight from Shanghai to Atlanta, I was subjected to a temperature check with a hand-held, in-the-ear, probe. I passed the test, exited baggage claim, and met my sister-in-law Claudia curbside. She drove me north to Roswell, my hometown. I was planning to stay two months in the House of Wood with my brother Jere and Claudia.

My first night in the guest room was straight from hell. I woke up at 3 am on the floor next to my bed in a pool of blood, still bleeding from a large gash on my forehead. I remember having a horrible nightmare right out of "The Living Dead." Evidently I had jumped out of bed to out-run the Dead, head-butted a wooden door jamb and then crash-landed backwards next to the bed.

Two months before, in late December, while still in Shanghai, I had noticed in just a span of 48 hours that my sense of smell and taste was not up to par. My favorite bar snack, peanuts, had zero flavor. Something was not working. I wondered why, and a couple of days later I began to grow short of breath during mild physical exertion. Nonplussed, I went on with my daily routine, stopping for a couple of stiff ones at the end of the day. On New Year's Eve, I was working on my second vodka-soda-on-the-rocks in my martini bar when I ended up on the bar's rock-hard stone floor, writhing in pain. I gasped violently for breath and then passed out as I tried to stand up. Out cold for a few seconds, with my breath barely back, I managed, with a little help from my friends, to get on my feet. But the dead fall had driven my shoulder and upper arm deep into the left side of my chest. Out of my mind with pain, barely conscious, I summoned my driver and went home immediately.

If I lay down, I could not breathe. I tried in vain to sleep sitting up. Suspecting I had broken a rib or two and might have internal bleeding, I called my assistant at home right after sunrise and told her to send an ambulance. She rushed to my house, helped get me into a wheelchair, and came with me in the ambulance. In minutes, I was in the emergency room of the oldest and largest public hospital in the heart of the city. I was helped out of the wheelchair and asked to lie down on a gurney. I tried, but screamed bloody murder when I twisted my torso to mount the wheeled cot. I put myself back into the wheelchair and was taken to a private room. It took four people to lift me into a bed. They put me on my back. I tried to roll on my side and almost passed out from the pain. The room was on one of two floors reserved for foreigners, but my feet overhung the foot off the 5-foot, 8-inch bed. The floor was for foreigners, the bed was not.

I have no business complaining. Shame on me. The room, linens, and private bath were immaculately clean. Food was back-of-the-bus, airline quality, served hot, and they had ice for my water glass. Doctors and nurses spoke English, A litany of doctors, including the Head of Infectious Disease, visited me. The diagnosis: viral pneumonia. Via IV, the doctors tried every available antibiotic. Nothing seemed to work. Extensive laboratory work concluded that this was a strain unknown in the virus world. Remember, this was before anyone had ever heard of Covid-19.

Meanwhile I was getting no sleep. Every two hours, day and night, a nurse came to check my vitals. I kept asking for pain killers, sure I had at least one broken rib.

"No go, Mr Wood. Except for a massive bruise on your the left side of your chest cavity there is no evidence of a broken rib. Your problem is viral pneumonia. When your immune system kicks in, you will get over the pneumonia and we will wrap your chest in ACE bandages and you can go home."

After several sleepless nights, I asked a nurse for a chair to sleep in. She brought me an aluminum high-backed desk chair. The hospital did not have any "reclining," TV-watching, easy chairs. My nurse tried to stop me, but I moved to the chair anyway. At least I was not flat on my back, or on my side, with my lungs subjected to pressure from a fluid-filled lung cavity pressed against a mattress.

None of their repertoire of antibiotics worked. They found fluid in my lungs but not enough to be life-threatening. But my left lung cavity was 90% full of blood from internal bleeding caused by the fall. The fluid in the lung cavity, not the lung, was greatly exacerbating Covid-related respiratory issues. The first one caused the second one. I was beating the latter battle and losing the former one.

My private clinic cardiologist came to the hospital on two occasions to consult with my doctors. I pleaded with her to get me discharged from the hospital. Convinced I was going to die, I wanted to die at home. After her second attempt failed, I spent one more night in the hospital. The next morning, I called my driver and told him to be outside the emergency room entrance ASAP and to call me when he got there. I got up, took my sack of clothes and valuables into the bathroom with me. When the call came in, I walked out of my room, got in the elevator, and headed straight for my car. My floor's medical staff had not had time to get any security guards mobilized so I walked past all five of them as I exited the building. I went home, arranged for two private nurses, one day, one night. After five days, I was back at work, cleaning up loose ends in anticipation of my Chinese New Year vacation back in the United States. The only way to cheat death is to keep living. Two extraordinary nurses, sheer willpower, and dollops of vim and vigor kept a seventy-two-year-old architect alive.

On Chinese New Year's Day, just around the time China formally announced the existence of the virus, I flew from Shanghai to Atlanta, moved in with my brother and his wife, and had that bloody encounter with the nightmare, which is now known as being a common symptom of the way Covid attacks the central nervous system. But after that difficult first night, I returned to normal and I started working again from their home.

Two weeks later, I went to Washington DC to see a client, a two-day, one-night business trip. I checked into a hotel the night before the meeting, and woke up in the middle of the night after a devastating nightmare, lying on the floor in a pool of blood. Evidently I had had another seizure and run into the wall. I cleaned myself up and went back to bed. The next morning, I took it real easy. I got a bandage from the front desk, did the meeting sporting the bandage round my head with a big bump and a blood-clotted gash on my forehead. Then I went to the airport and took the last flight from DC to Atlanta.

I was in the window seat, and sitting beside me was a very attractive, well-dressed woman who I could see was a doctor because she was reading a medical journal on her computer. We got into a conversation, and she said, what do you do? I said, I work in China, I'm an architect. She asked me when exactly I had returned to the USA. When we leveled off at altitude, I became very dizzy and was having trouble breathing. Then I got up to go to the bathroom and had to grab the overhead compartment hand grips as I made my way forward. I almost passed out getting up from the toilet. When I got my legs back, I stumbled back to my seat, white as a sheet, and as I stepped across her to get to my window seat, I momentarily blacked out, and fell into my seat.

"Sir, if I know anything about medicine I would say you just had a heart attack, or a bad reaction to Covid," she said. "Please promise me you will go straight to a hospital after we land in Atlanta."

She then went up to the front of the plane, and talked to the crew. When the aircraft pulled to a stop at the arrival gate, the Captain came on the intercom and asked everyone to remain seated until a certain passenger could be escorted by security off the plane. Suddenly it dawned on me: that's me! The kind doctor had decided I had had a heart attack. A Covid carrier was her window seat mate.

Two airport security guards escorted me off the plane and two medical technicians both were wearing masks were waiting for me at a security interrogation room. They checked my passport and verified I had arrived from China on the day news of Covid circled the world. The medical technicians had no way to check me for Covid but wanted to hold me in custody until they could find out if the CDC, headquartered in Atlanta, could direct them to a facility for a Covid test. But I had cleared Immigration and asked on what legal grounds I could be held in custody pending a Covid Test. After a flurry of phone calls, they told me I was free to leave.

Chauffeured by Claudia, my sister-in-law, I returned to my brother's house in Roswell. All through a late night dinner of leftovers, I kept thinking about my seatmate's comments and kicked myself for telling the fine doctor that only two weeks had gone by since my brush with death. But there was no way, I had Covid, I was sure of that. My last trip to Wuhan was in November of 2019, although I did meet several people, including the Director of Wuhan's Office of City Planning, on Christmas Eve. I was wrong. Covid was what I had had, and what the best doctors in Shanghai had been unable to diagnose because it was totally unknown.

At the House of Wood in Roswell that night, fresh from my flight from DC, I was in pain. I knew something was horribly wrong. Claudia begged me to go to a hospital immediately and rather than face another rough night or, worse, a stroke or heart attack, I packed a clean pair of underwear and my phone charger and we were off.

Claudia knows everybody who is anybody in Georgia. She made one phone call and, after a call-back, we were headed for Emory Hospital's main emergency room. We had curb-side service when we arrived. The trip to Emory quickly changed any immediate plans I had for a return to Shanghai. The Center for Disease Control "shelter-in-place" directive was not the direct cause. On the afternoon of my second day at Emory, three pints of bloody fluid were suction pumped from my left lung cavity. Over the next two months, I went back to Emory as an out-patient for three more pumps. The last one extracted two pints of clear liquid. In the interim, my China work visa was suspended indefinitely as part the virus lockdown. My two terrifying, sleep-walking, pools-of-blood trips to hell and back again were eventually attributed to Long Haul Covid 19 brain tremors.

As an adult, I had seen my brother and sister only once or twice a year at Thanksgiving, New Year's, July 4th, or other special family events, but during the Great Pandemic when I decided to "shelter-in-place" at Kennedy Creek, a big retreat in the highest valley in the state of Georgia, including an airstrip, which I bought in 2019 and turned into a hotel. My siblings elected to join me, which brought us together for seven glorious months over the summer of 2020. We shared our life stories. One a veterinarian, one a lawyer, and me, the architect, the only sibling to pursue a career outside of Georgia. We talked about our weddings, divorces, children, failures, successes, heartbreaks and happinesses. We connected as the adults we had become, back to the children we once were. We were reborn.

During those months, global travel had come to a halt and China was firmly closed to the rest of the world. But in October, I received word that I was being considered for a Magnolia Award, an award granted to foreigners by the Shanghai City government in recognition of their contribution to the city. On the basis of that, Vincent's company helped me get an official invitation to return to China, and I booked a Delta/Air France direct flight from Atlanta to Shanghai, with one stop in Paris. After deplaning in Paris from the Delta red-eye, I spent all day in the Air France Business Class Lounge at Orly Airport's International Air Terminal ahead of the Shanghai flight's 9 pm departure. But what I didn't know, and what the Air France staff didn't tell me, was that the rules for re-entering China had changed while I was in transit from Atlanta. Without more paperwork and a QR Code showing I was Covid-negative, I could not get on the flight. I returned to the lounge and asked the Air France staff to book me on the next available flight to Atlanta.

"There is a three-day wait, Mr Wood," I was told. "Also, you will have to leave this Lounge soon, closing time is 11 pm

And all in-airport hotels are closed as of last week. I can arrange transportation to an off-airport hotel, but if you go, you will then have to spend a week in self-quarantine, confined to your room before returning to the airport. You can sleep downstairs in the main concourse and when you return at 8 am, we will upgrade you to the First Class Lounge."

After a sleepless night sitting straight up in a concourse seat, I returned to the Lounge, and I was asked for a credit card to pay $10,000 for the one-way flight back to Atlanta. I blew up and started yelling. I was almost arrested by the Orly Airport Police who were about put me in handcuffs when the Air France Lounge Supervisor rescued me.

But I had no choice. I spent three nights on that Orly concourse, sleeping in either those airport seats which have arms to stop people lying down, or on the floor, with the cleaning staff picking up my legs to clean the floor under me. Air France not only refused to refund the $18,000 ticket to Shanghai, but also charged me $10,000 for the flight back to Atlanta, so those three nights in the Orly waiting area cost me $28,000.

Once back in Atlanta, after Orly, I rebooked with United for a flight to Shanghai, taking off from San Francisco on the next Wednesday, and the airline staff told me I needed to take a Covid test before I could board the plane. My son lives in San Francisco, so on Monday I flew there and then found the only PCR test I could get would require a three-day wait for the results. As it happened, I knew the CEO of Abbott Labratories, Miles White, and I called him in Chicago and spoke to his sectarary who said he was in a board meeting and was not to be disturbed. So I called his son in London and said I really need your father to call someone in San Francisco and get me a PCR test. He did it, and ten minutes later an Abbott truck drove up in front of my son's house. Ten minutes! The guys beckoned me into the van, we did the test and eight minutes later I had the results. Then I had to get it to the Chinese consulate, which turned out to be closed, but they said the test result could be submitted by email, with a reply expected within 72 hours, also way after my flight was to take off. But that night, my phone buzzed and I got an email saying approval had been given for me to board the flight had been granted—they had given me a green code based upon the test result. How come? I don't know. So I went to the airport and got on a flight and flew back to Shanghai, and was allowed to quarantine at home.

When I left quarantine in October 21, 2020, having literally faced down death in the year that had passed, the wonderful people of Shanghai, and clients both public and private, gave me a new lease on life. The borders had closed but my sky had not changed, I still had the entirety of China in which to make a living. Spirits lifted, and feeling easy like Sunday morning, I walked through an open door back into the dragon's mouth. A flaneur on the loose, a rebel with a cause, a Southerner for life, I resumed work, stirring my soul with an architecture of humanity.

It was a time to re-assess and re-consider, and this is what I wrote: Use the goodwill and determination of the world's most populous country to make this planet better than you found it. Use your intellect and curiosity to weave a thick carpet of cultivated serendipity, ride this magic sleigh for all its worth. The best way to fight for life, is to cheat death. "Carpe diem." Seize the day.

Quarantined

Behind a Shanghai door
I walk a line
Doing my time
So that I can soon breathe free
In a country not mine
No one here grew up
Riding Shetland ponies bareback
To skinny dip in Spring-fed ponds
Crossing spill-ways and dams
Climbing Red Clay banks
Discovering abandoned shacks
Under old oak trees
On the edge of old cotton fields
Built on the backs
Of blacks and white trash
Today affluent suburbs
a capital city's bedrooms
cover these Red Clay memories
Of my Deep South boyhood
Mine are buried
under golf courses
single family houses
and fast food drive-ins
But now is no time for tears
It is time to make amends
To dedicate our lives
To making the world
A Better Place
For all of Humanity

Authored by an aging American architect
Who In less than 24 hours
Will walk out his door
Into the streets and high rises
of the world's largest city
And get back to work

Morraine's tail quenched by cold salt waters of Vineyard Sound.

24

LAND HO!

THE TRUE measure of wealth is not how much money you have, but how much land you own. And the problem with China is you can't own land. So no one in China is wealthy. You may be rich, but you're not wealthy.

But you can own land in the United States of America, and like my father before me, I have worked to acquire land all my life. He was a civil servant and bought land for the government, I have bought for myself, for my family, and as I re-arrange my holdings, for posterity. I own 777 acres in western Virginia in the Appalachian Mountains and a slice of Martha's Vineyard, and co-own 500 acres of an island in South Caolina and the 40-acre Kennedy Creek resort in air strip in the mountains of Georgia. That is the most scenically magnificent of all of them. All four of these pieces of land are amongst the Last Great Places, gorgeous slices of the planet that I hope to lock into conservation. In architecture, I am all about merging the past with the future, but what the Low Country of South Carolina, the hill country of Georgia and the island shelter of Martha's Vineyard do not need is more human development. To the extent that I can preserve some parts of these serene landscapes, I will do do it, as my small contribution to humankind's murky future.

Martha's Vineyard is the remains of a terminal moraine, the

end of a glacier, the detritus left after the retreat of an ice age. And the first house I ever designed in Durango, Colorado, as I mentioned elsewhere, was also on the crest of one of these unruly geological dumping grounds. On my first trip to Martha's Vineyard in 1984, I helped my mentor Ben Thompson lay out the footprint for a client's oceanfront home. We only stayed two days, but it was long enough for me to fall in love with the place. Only Nature's Eunoia can create a New England Island experience so precious with promises of happiness.

We have a grey-shingled two-story cottage on our 57-acre Vineyard property, Blackwater Cove. But until the ground starts to freeze, I prefer to stay in a large canvas tent on one of seven of the farm's hilltops. The tent is a genuine African luxury safari model sitting atop a raised wooden platform overlooking the ocean. It has indoor plumbing and electricity, and next to the tent is a kitchen with a roof but no walls. All the equipment in the kitchen is stainless steel and was bought used from a large restaurant supply company. We made an outdoor dining table out of a recycled twenty-foot section of a laminated solid maple bowling lane. The table can seat twenty-four people. A large sunset deck, facing west, is cantilevered off the hill, supported by white oak log timbers salvaged from an Edgartown Harbor pier. In the summer, there is no place I would rather be than on this deck at sunset with a glass of whiskey in my hand and a companion by my side with whom I have some common ground.

The farm's next house was designed and built with the help of my son Travis. We call it the "Space Shot" because for a small building there is a lot of "space." A hybrid open-web steel truss and conventional wood frame affords a column free interior, space, 28-feet by 42-feet with ceiling heights up to 21 feet. A semi-transparent aircraft hanger door 26 feet long and 14 feet high with operable awning windows, top hinges, and side mounted hydraulic pistons, opens like the hatch door on the back of a SUV at the push of a button. Another push of a button and a hydraulic scissor lift takes you from the ground floor kitchen up to a roof top green house and deck. If you are in the kitchen and need fresh herbs, go in style to the roof, enclosed in a transparent multi-wall polycarbonate cab. Part of the north wall is "inflatable" and can be opened and closed with a small centrifugal fan. There are three wind turbines on the roof along with photovoltaic panels. All the lighting is low voltage LED that changes to a red color when the flames of the fire in the indoor stone pit begin to flicker. The back-up source for solar electrical power is the batteries in the scissors lift. A second back-up are the batteries of a golf cart used for the transport of supplies from the farm's main car bar. A 60-foot long bridge connects the second floor of the Space Shot to the tent and outdoor kitchen. In good weather, the hanger door opens and Space Shot fills with fresh air and Vineyard space. At sunset, a western sky fills the view west to Lambert's Cove Beach, Paul's Point and beyond. On a clear day you can see the Texas Tower at the mouth of the Intra Coastal Waterway forty miles away.

The farm's last house was built around a hundred-year-old Copper Beech tree. Everyone calls it the Tree House. A perfect specimen of the Vineyard's largest grows up through an opening in the roof of a small, moss-covered garden in the middle of the house. The house feels like two houses: one on the ground and one nesting in the branches. The house is cooled in the summertime by the tons of natural air conditioning created by the tree's own transpiration. It's a carbon negative evaporative cooling system.

Long live terminal moraines wherever you are.

INTO THE DRAGON'S MOUTH

Off the southern coast of Cape Cod
Lies one of North America's
Last terminal moraines
Breaching the waters
Between Vineyard Sound
And Atlantic shelves
Hardwood forests and rolling fields
Adorn Polar Ice Age earth movers
erratic boulder rollers
refugees and wildlife refuges
Night Herons and Piping Plovers
Osprey, Oyster and Fly Catchers
protected from mainland marauders
by open water and hammerhead sharks

Oaks struggle with white pines for primacy
Pockets of Sassafras
with shallow root beer roots
And the whale ship Sailor's savior
The Beetlebungs
Tangle and twist in sporadic patches
Dotting a quilted landscape
Stitched together by ancient stone walls
Sculpted granite boundaries
Some tightly packed
white man's work
Others "laced" with holes
Wampanoag Indian shortcuts
Tracing time back

Buy a trail guide
Select an ancient way
and as the leaves turn
pick a late October day
to weave between gated estates
In silence except for the wind
Walk under the spreading branches
Of hundred-year-old
Copper Beech Climax forests
Bathe in the light from leaves of gold
Dry your hands on silver bark
Let time stand still

In late 2019, I acquired the forty-acre mountain resort in north Georgia, ninety minutes drive from Atlanta which is now called Kennedy Creek. The High Valley Airpark and Resort is in Suches, a tiny off-the-beaten track unincorporated town. Suches is not on the way to anywhere. Home to a proud community of multi-generational, God-fearing, independent-minded, "mountain people," Suches has more churches per capita than any town in the State. There are around one thousand residents, one gas station, and about a hundred churches in or near the town. The nearest hospital, big box retailer or fast-food outlet, is thirty-two miles east, or nineteen miles south. Either way, narrow, winding, switchbacking, two-lane roads snake their way through steep, mountainous terrain. The route east is part of a two-hour loop known to America's Harley Hog aficionados as the Dragon's Tail. Suches children attend Woody Gap School, the most expensive public school in the State of Georgia. Woody Gap has an enrollment of approximately one hundred students a year. An average of eight young men and woman graduate from Woody Gap each year. Woody's main classroom building is almost one hundred years old. Built of local quarry stone delivered to the site by horse and wagon, Woody Gap School is the pride of the town.

Coopers Creek is one valley over from Suches and High Valley Airport. As a teenager, the first day I used a fly rod to fish for trout, I was wading in the waters of Coopers Creek. My father watched as a trout thrashed the water and struck a floating, artificial fly. I snapped my rod high and hand-over-hand, pulled the line in. I was careful to not let any slack gather. Trout can shake loose a hook when they clear the water in an aerial ballet.

My father, ever the wildlife conservationist, believed in "catch and release" for all native trout. Landing a hatchery-raised trout you can take home is rudimentary compared to a "catch and release" operation. You must hold a live, slippery-as-slime trout firmly in one hand, while removing the hook with the other. If you fail to keep the trout in check, retrieving a deep-throat hook can cause severe injury to the gills which can be fatal to the fish. On the flipside, every avid trout fisherman has ended up with a barbed hook buried in his flesh. My first trout with a fly rod was a western rainbow, not native to the Eastern United States. The rainbow had been raised in a Forest Service fish hatchery, and Dad and I took my rainbow and five others home that day.

High Valley Airport is the highest runway in Georgia. The single runway is a 2,000-foot-long grass strip. High Valley Airport, like thousands of other private and public airstrips in the USA, has no control tower. Use of the runway is limited to aircraft capable of short field take-offs and landings. High Valley's grass strip is identified on FAA air navigation charts as GA87.

Kennedy Creek runs through the resort on its way to Woody Lake. The Creek is home to native brown trout. I renamed High Valley Airpark as Kennedy Creek Resort. The new name is a

Rainbow over Kennedy Creek Resort, July 2022

tribute to the art of catch-and-release fly fishing. High Valley Airport remained the name of the grass airstrip.

After two years of the pandemic, Kennedy Creek retired triumphant from the brink. Four new hangers and a Tabernacle have been built, General King Tavern is open, and my sister-in-law Claudia's wedding and special event business is in full operation. Black Ops, a US Army Special Forces team, have started taking over the entire resort on a regular basis, twice a year, conducting spring and fall training camps. Army helicopter troop carriers, operating from the grass strip without runway or on-board lights, fly several sorties a night. And Brother Jere and his taildragger friends have also hosted two invitational fly-ins.

A message to any pilots planning to join a fly-in at Kennedy Creek: keep political sermons of any stripe to yourself, and any guns at all—handguns, rifles, assault rifles, and other assorted assault weapons you might fancy—had better never see the light or night of a Creek day. Your plane is subject to visual inspection by one of the volunteer marshals on arrival. Owning lethal weapons designed to kill people is your Second Amendment right. It is also as un-American as McCarthy's heinous, vulgar, storm-troopered witch-hunt which followed the Second Great War. Also leave any toys resembling guns at home. The only exception: the Resort has a trap range so light-gauge shotguns are welcome. Please bring only shells with #7-steel, clay target loads, and biodegradable casings and wads.

Retired USAF Lt. Colonel Christine Mau was the first woman to fly a F-35 Fighter Jet. She was also the first Air Force woman pilot to fly in combat. Today, Chris is a Lockheed Martin F-35 simulator instructor. During my north Georgia mountains shelter-in-place summer, the communal areas of Kennedy Creek Resort were closed but we did keep the guest cabins open. Chris had driven with her fifteen-year-old daughter to the resort from the Florida Panhandle for a four-day stay. I was living in the cabin next door to Chris', and on the evening of her first day she was sitting on her front porch. I walked over and introduced myself. We started talking about the resort's 2,000-foot-high valley grass strip. She had a small private plane and said she was considering flying it up from Pensacola later in the summer for an airshow the resort was hosting. I told Chris about a few of my Phantom adventures, and she began to tell me her fascinating history.

Chris grew up in southern California, her family home off the end of a runway at a Marine Corps Air Station. F-4 jets, with afterburner flames scorching the air, flew over her house every day. Imagine, as she put it, a young girl looking up at those "roaring loud, big, bad ass F-4s thinking one day I'll fly one." She was eleven when the movie Top Gun was released, and that was all it took—she was determined to be a "Maverick" one day. After attending the Air Force Academy, Chris went to flight training, graduating top of her class. When you graduate from pilot training, a list of aircraft available for advanced training is posted. If you graduate number one, you're the first to choose. Chris selected the F-15 Strike Eagle. In 2011, she made military aviation history, leading the first-ever all-female F-15E combat mission.

For the next two evenings, I returned to Chris' porch. She wanted to know more about China, and why I was still living there. I wanted to know why she retired early from the USAF. Our answers were not that different. I stay in China to stack the chips, to keep in the "better life" design game, doing my best to make sure no one is left behind. Chris retired early to devote more time to her children. She had broken through the glass ceiling of gender-biased, non-combatant restrictions. If humanity is to survive, the work of mavericks, renegades, game-changers and ceiling-breakers is essential. Long live one bad-ass top gun woman: Christine Mau.

I own a small resort in Shangri-La in southwest China. Natives of so-called Semi-Autonomous Regions in China have some level of land ownership rights. Much of northern Yunnan is occupied by these special regions, and in 2008 together with a Chinese partner, Lin Hong, I bought 200 mu of land, about thirty-two acres, from the native Tibetans living in their ancestral homes in a small village near the northeast end of the single three-kilometer long runway at the Shangri-La/Deqing Airport. Negotiating with the Land Bureau, we purchased fifty-year Land Use Rights to thirty of the 200 mu. The remaining 170 mu remain classified for agricultural use, not subject to development pending future purchase of usage rights. Overnight accommodation at Dimu Resort is provided in five large, reconstructed Tibetan farmhouses. We have a local operator who keeps our twenty private rooms fully occupied in the tourist season. The rooms are in re-constructed, traditional Tibetan farmhouses. No new wood was used in the construction of the farmhouses. Log columns, framing timbers, wood for floors, and split, red pine roof shakes were salvaged from old, abandoned houses. Even the furniture is made from recycled wood crafted by the same carpenters that built the window frames. No nails were used. All joinery is mortise and tenon. Dirt for the rammed earth walls was dug on-site. The only things in the house that are not recycled are the electrical and plumbing systems and fixtures. A central canteen provides communal and dining space, Materials for all buildings came from ten abandoned houses we found in neighboring villages. The owners of these house had moved into concrete block boxes with glass covered courtyards.

Traditional Tibetan farmhouses were heated by wood stoves with no chimneys. Smoke exited through cracks between loose wooden roof shakes. Over the years, creosote in the smoke left thick deposits of this extremely flammable chemical on the wood columns, beams, and wood paneling of the farmhouse's interior. Supposedly safer in concrete boxes, the villagers were happy to unload their drafty fire-traps for a pittance.

Shangri-La is 1,300-meters higher in altitude than Lijiang. Flat-and-midlanders visitors who don't follow the recommended protocol for acclimatization can suffer severe side effects from hypoxia. Before the Great Pandemic, I visited Shangri-La four or five times a year. I avoided off-season direct flights via Kunming whenever possible. Better to arrive in northern Yunnan via Lijiang airport. Three good reasons for flying to Lijiang: frequent, all-season flights and the five-plus hour drive north to Shangri-La was a chance to slowly acclimate. Then there are the roadside attractions. Heading the list is lunch at La Shi Hai Trout Farm, or sitting overlooking the Yangtze eating a smorgasbord of stir-fried organic vegetables, air-cured honey glazed pork belly, and smoked ham hocks. Along the way, a potpourri of curio and food markets line the narrow two-lane road. By the time we would arrive in Shangri-La, the back of the SUV is full of green apples, peaches, walnuts, hot peppers, plums, sweet yellow corn, red radishes, yellow squash and peppers, green mint, purple cucumbers, green string beans, giant leeks, spring onions, a myriad of wild mushrooms, sunflower and black sesame seeds, raisins, dried dates, sweet clover honey still in the comb, and jars of wildflower pollen. Calling all northern Yunnan tourists! Please do not pick the wildflowers!

When in season, it is all you can do to keep from to picking the roadside's "low hanging fruit," the wildflowers. At the height of the summer tourist season, traffic can back up for several kilometers when too many people cannot resist the temptation to pluck as many flowers as they can hold in one hand. They spoil it for the rest of us.

When I was still in high school, I heard Peter, Paul, and Mary perform "Where have all the flowers gone." Sadly, the low hanging fruit in this song is not wildflowers. The young men who marched off to fight wars, never to return, are the flowers gone.

In the days following the 2008 conference with Vincent, I enjoyed Shangri-La's sublime August weather and deep blue skies with my daughter Amy and my friends Dwight, Ron, and co-resort owner, Lin Hong. For two days, we spent every daylight hour exploring the countryside. The first day, we traversed on foot the meadows and hillsides of a hidden valley halfway between Zhongdian and Little Zhongdian. We walked for hours among the late summer wildflower meadows in a light rain. Our biggest reward came at the end of our hike when we discovered the ruins of an old Tibetan farmhouse. The mud walls of the roofless house were adorned with folk-art paintings of unusual quality. I have not been back to the ruin. By now the elements surely have destroyed this extraordinary artifact.

The next morning, we enjoyed a big breakfast of scrambled eggs, thin slices of Yunnan, salt cured, country ham, flat bread doused with Red-eye gravy made from reduced trimmings of ham fat, fresh fruit, bowls of wild black berries and goat's milk, and local honey. We brewed a big pot of coffee made with fresh-ground Yunnan beans. Then we loaded several 125cc off-road dirt bikes into the back of my truck. With a packed lunch of leftovers, we headed down the valley towards Little Zhongdian. We had a Google Earth map to guide us to some unexplored territory. When we stopped at the head of a sheepherder's path into the wilderness, several Tibetan women from the local village surrounded us. Several of the women climbed into the truck and took turns sitting on the bikes accompanied by loud laughter from all of us. It never ceases to amaze me how open and friendly the local people in that region can be.

After almost five hours of one of the more grueling rides I can remember, we packed up the bikes and headed back to town. The terrain we covered that afternoon on the bikes was not that rough. The real problem came in the form of deep mud and ruts, slick grass, and some poor navigational decisions. We ended up pushing the bikes for as much time as we rode them.

We got back to town late, but not too late for a quick detour to shop in a large produce and meat market in the middle of New Town. We picked up some smoked duck, roast pork, local mushrooms, Yunnan red wine, fresh lettuce, walnuts, tomatoes, potatoes, cucumbers, and eggplant. A couple of hours later, we were enjoying a feast fit for a king.

BENJAMIN WOOD

When the coast is clear
Turn a course to steer
Light bonfires to burn
Signal a Southerner's return
A New England Island farm
Blue Ridge Mountain resort
Low Country nature preserve
Or Sugar Run high valley ground
For a final stand
Meet an Old Architect's band
playing Dixieland
Sweet Home Sweet Sassafras
Coming for to take me home

Suzhou Creek, Garden Bridge, and Pudong behind

25

Intersections

Paths intersect, people, places, things, and events. Mapping all the possible junctions would fill an infinite number of metaverse clouds. A hitch-hiker's guide to our earth-bound galaxy of constellations would have enough mass to create it's own gravitational field.

I was with Donald Trump and representatives from two large real estate development companies when we saw the spot where Bobby Kennedy died in 1968. This was in the early 1990s. The caretaker of the boarded-up Ambassador Hotel (home of the original Cocoanut Grove Lounge) took us to the basement. In a kitchen service corridor, he rolled back a rubber rug exposing a huge blood stain on the concrete slab.

"He must have been dumb to get shot," Donald muttered, loud enough for everyone to hear.

The Ambassador Hotel had been abandoned after Kennedy's assassination, but finally the family that owned it decided to put it up for sale and the LA School Board started a campaign to have the City Council exercise "eminent domain" to take over the property for use as a public high school campus. Trump had other ideas. He teamed up with one of my clients, a New York real estate developer named Scott Malcolm, and one other partner to enter into a purchase agreement with the owners of the

LA's tallest building in the world that never happened.

Hotel, planning to replace it with a golf course, villas, a restored Cocoanut Grove and a massive office tower.

I had an office in Los Angeles at that point, and Scott Malcolm had brought me in as the architect designing everything but the tower. All the rest was my forte. They were given time to perform due diligence, and during that period, the L.A. School Board gave Trump $50 million in return for an option to purchase the property prior to closing at market value. Having checked out the property, Trump decided to renege on the deal and press head with the big plan, convinced that the people of L.A. would love him for it. He held a big press conference announcing plans to tear down the Hotel and replace it with the tallest building in the world, and ten minutes after he had dropped this bombshell, he got a call from the Mayor of L.A. requesting he leave town quietly. It all resulted in a huge legal battle between him and the L.A. School Board, and in the end, the school got the property. But I spent the entire day beforehand with him. He is the most obnoxious person I have ever met.

I met Steve Jobs at a wedding on Cape Cod in 1984 at the invitation of Ben Thompson. He was with Ben's step-daughter, Sheila M Jane Thompson's daughter by a previous marriage. Steve had already made his first TIME magazine cover buy that time and I was busy working on my MIT thesis using the brand new $2,500 Mac (128K), featuring the world's first GUI. The basic design of the GUI for computers has remained unchanged until this day.

While I was waiting in line for an iced-lemonade refill, I spoke with Mr Jobs briefly. He asked me what I did.

"Architect, designer, I work with Sheila's mother," I said. "I like your Issey Miyake turtleneck."

"Taking a few classes on calligraphy hooked me on the elegance of design simplicity," he replied.

Nan Duffly, the first Asian American woman to serve as a judge on the Massachusetts Court of Appeals, introduced me to Joyce Chen, the first chef in America to popularize Shanghai and Beijing cuisine. She called her pot stickers "Peking Raviolis." Her second restaurant was halfway between Harvard and MIT, her fourth restaurant was near Fresh Pond Circle. Built in an elegantly quirky modernist style around a single tree, it hid behind Fresh Pond Seafood Market, encircled by a "living green wall." When I began commuting from Harvard, Massachusetts to Ben Thompson's office near Harvard Square, Fresh Pond Circle was on my route and I often stopped in for dinner. Nan and her husband Paul lived in the same neighborhood. One evening I was buying live lobsters at the Seafood Market when I recognized a young Kennedy right behind me in line. We spoke briefly. When my time came to pay, he asked the guy bagging my lobsters to give me a dozen lemons and put them on his bill. It was then I noticed the famous name was brown-bagging, drinking from a bottle. Not long afterwards, I crossed that line, too, and was arrested for DUI. My driver's license was suspended for six-months and I had to go to ten AA meetings.

The evening I left a famous name leaning on a chrome-railed counter, I drove home to our hillside slate quarry millhouse and pond near Harvard, and in moonlight, I carefully removed the big claw rubber bands and stuffed eight tasty crustaceans into a door-tripped-shut, grid-wire lobster trap. I paddled to the middle of the mill pond and dropped them, painted cork buoy attached, over the side of my canoe. My Fresh Pond Market salt-water lobsters were left gasping for air in the spring-fed fresh water pond, prehistoric creatures of the sea, destined for a cross-cultural, tongue-in-cheek, drawn and buttered, exchange. Next day, I served "fresh-water" lobster raised in my own pond, to five guests who had flown in from Tokyo.

Ten years ago a man walked into our studio. We have no receptionist and no one in the Studio has a private office. The only doors are the ones that let you in or out. The man paused inside the one at the front near the elevator and asked a nearby colleague if it was possible to see me. The colleague directed him to my drawing table. After a handshake, he told me he wanted me to be his architect. No one else would do. He had a dream. Twenty minutes later, I knew we would be flying togther very soon. My path had crossed with yet another man of great intellect, compassion, courage, and grace. Today I call him "brother."

Why for thousands of years has humankind dreamed of flying? Why, for thousands of years, have we built vernacular courtyards filled with sky? An answer to the first is to see farther, to experience the vastness of space. The second is that we build to understand the future. The meaning of sky-rooms, stone circles, and shadow measuring towers unique to every culture has never changed. Two days a year the longest west and east shadows cast are exactly the same length. On two days a year, the north and south shadows darken planes exactly opposite in direction. Shortest in summer and longest in winter. Two Eqinoxes, two solstices. And every year, the same four days. The sky never changes. The quest to know the unknowable, fathom the unfathomable, never ceases.

At that first meeting, my "brother" said, "I have a building I want you to do for me." I asked for some background on his project. His company, he said, occupied space in a high-rise office building in Pudong but he had just bought a plot of land in the Zhanjiang science and tech park on Shanghai's outskirts, and he wanted to me to design his corporate headquarters. He wanted about 20,000 square meters to be occupied by about forty people. He was a really nice guy, but after about thirty minutes, I shook my head.

"Right now, I am working on Disneytown next to the Shanghai Disney Theme Park and a couple of other major projects and, to be frank, your project is just too small," I said. "But if you come back in six months from now, we can talk again."

So he excused himself and six months almost to the day he came back and he said, "What do you think, Mr. Wood?"

I had many conversations with him, and most wanted to understand his business philosophy. Once I had a sense of it, I came up with a plan.

"The message you convey to clients, as I understand it," I said to him, "is that you and your clients are not in it for the short term. So I suggest we make your company headquarters into something like a campus and have the heart of it be a room, an indoor amphitheater, called the 'Sky Does Not Change' room, or the Sky Room. The room will be perfectly aligned, like an ancient time measurement structure from Egypt or the Song Dynasty, to place a sunbeam at the center of the top step of the curved amphitheater at noon on the summer solstice, and at the center of the last step at noon on the day of the winter equinox. That is what you can tell your clients in that room when the come visit, that they can count on the sky never changing, and that they can be sure they are in good hands."

Five or six years later we had the first event in that room.

About six months after I agreed to do the project with my "brother," I was sitting in my bar when four distinguished gentlemen walked in, speaking with pronounced and cultured English accents. One of them came over, and said, "You're Mr. Wood? We're here to see you."

One of the others was Charles Gordon-Lennox, 11th Duke of Richmond, owner of the Goodwood Estate in southern England, and the host of the largest motor sports racing car event in the world, called the Festival of Speed. He wanted my advice on whether it was prudent to lend his name to the Chinese Festival of Speed given the people involved. Cars are flown in from all over the world for the event, and one of the rules is that if you exhibit a car at the Festival, you have to have personally won a race in it. As he left, His Lordship gave me four tickets to the next event at Goodwood in Sussex.

It happened that one of my regulars at the bar owned an estate with a 15th Century farmhouse overlooking the Festival grounds in Sussex, so I said, "Tim, one of these tickets is for you, if I can get to stay in your house."

I gave one ticket to my son, and for the fourth to my "brother," who was thrilled to be invited, and he came and stayed with us. It was an unusual experience for him, but he handled it with great humility. I discovered he had never so much as fried an egg before, but he helped me make breakfast every morning, and that's how we bonded. We sat in the Duke of Richmond's private box every day and we have been good friends ever since. He is a man of compassion and grace, and he is like a brother to me. "Mi casa es su casa," and his family my family.

The first book of poetry I gave my wife was written on a Greek

Sky Room under costruction October 2014, two steps to go to Winter Solstice

isle by Leonard Cohen. We spent a week on a nude beach near this golden isle. In the summer of 2011, my daughter, son, and friends met me in Rome for four days and five nights. In an open-air tennis arena on the site of the world's first Olympic Games, Cohen gave one of the last concerts of his final world tour. The concert ended just before midnight and we took the long way back to our rooms walking the streets for hours shouting love not hate. "Like a bird on a wire, I will try in my way to be free" was the only song the band would let me sing during the Summer of Love.

This is a story about a guy named Don Gao who made a lot of money producing battery-operated power tools. He once worked for an OEM company in China, making tools for other companies under contract. He was in charge of international sales and he eventually decided to try it himself. With the help of a famous Italian industrial designer, he engineered several exquisite battery-powered power tools and his own custom-built battery which was more powerful and lasted longer than the competitors. The ergonomics of the tools were clearly superior, and he was confident that if consumers could just get their hands on them, they would sell well. He took a case full of them to the United States, went to all the big DIY stores and offered his products to them.

"Here's my brand, the tools are better quality and the prices lower than any other brand of power tools in the world," he said. And the head of Home Depot, and all of rest replied, "Mr. Gao, these are beautiful tools, but no one has ever heard of your brand, so we cannot do a deal with you."

He had been traveling around the States for several weeks, and was getting close to running out of money. So he flew to New York to catch a flight back to China, and he didn't have a deal.

He couldnt sleep, and as he channel surfed all-night television, he saw a telemarketing ad selling a set of knives which ended by saying: "Call this number if you're interested in us making an ad for you."

He called the number next morning, and they were in New York, two blocks from his hotel, so he ran down to the telemarketer's office, and they pitched him a deal. "You have to pay for the ad and warehouse some tools, we take 35%, and we're not guaranteeing anything," they said, and he said, "I'm in." Within 30 days he had made $40 million selling his own power-tools under his own brand, Worx. He couldnt ship the tools fast enough.

He amassed a fortune, bought a big US power tool brand, Rockwell International, If you look at the top ten list of power tools on Amazon today, Don will have at leave four of the spots.

Having made his money in power tools, he bought 700 acres of land about an hour from Shanghai which had been an amusement park and botanical garden and hired me to design 250 super luxury villas, a hotel and a restaurant, all for the super rich.

I said, "Don, the first thing we are going to do is take a trip around the world, and I will show what really wealthy people can do with their money, and how they can leave a legacy that's not just money."

We went to many places in the United States and Europe, and showed what exquisite means in architecture and in living. I took him to Thomas Jefferson's home and to art gardens at the foot of Mount Fuji, but the most amazing was the Garden of Cosmic Speculation on the outskirts of Edinburgh, design by the American architect and author Charles Jencks in honour of his late wife, Maggie Keswick, heiress to the Jardine Matheson fortune, made originally on the China coast. His own home, which is called Maggie's Place is also in Scotland, near Glasgow, is also superb. We went to see both of them, and how I wish I had designed them! The Garden features landscaping, with the land moulded and shaped to represent fundamental features of the universe such as black holes, quarks and DNA. There is the Fractal Terrace and Comet Bridge. It is only open to the public one day a week, but we got a special tour as I knew Charles' son from Shanghai. The point was to show Don how a garden could be transformed using what is a called "land art." In Don's park, we created an alley of trees, two double rows that seemingly go on forever. Looking down that avenue generates thoughts about how humanity and nature can cooperate.

Unfortunately, the local government kept changing the rules regarding the usage of the villas and the park designs every time there was a new party secretary, and the project hasn't yet been completed. But one day is will be. Don's vision deserves to be realised. What impressed me was that he bet his last dollar on the quality of his products by latching onto something he saw on late night television and it paid off. It's an incredible story of courage and conviction.

I once met the god of Gonzo journalism, Hunter S. Thompson, over flamed-grilled T-bones, and a bottle of Jack Daniels at the Woody Creek Tavern under elk antlers at his corner table. The Mayor of Aspen Colorado and a local architect were my hosts. Hunter announced that if George Bush Junior got re-elected, he would kill himself. Two years later, George was in for another and Hunter, a man of his word, put a shotgun in his mouth and joined Hemingway.

I went to a Rolling Stones concert on their first US tour in 1964. For my second Stones blow-out in 2005, I bought front row seats at the Shanghai Mercedes Benz Arena. The night before, I was at a table for twelve at M-on-the-Bund hosted by the head of Coca-Cola Asia with Jagger as the special dinner guest. Mick's date was the first Chinese woman to appear on the cover of Playboy. Mick's handshake was that of a professional boxer. Next night, my Benz Area date was Yue-Sai Kan, famous cosmetics brand creator, talk show host, and Queen maker. At that time the owner of the Miss Universe China contest, Yue-Sai sat me between two Miss China's, one current, the other former. My third Stones live performance was in 2019 at my very own New Soldier Field, Bears Stadium. My daughter was with me, and my friend Dwight. Things have slowed down a little since then, but with luck I will live long enough to have Mick's personal attorney, a good friend of mine, get me invited me backstage somewhere on the planet for another handshake between two aging reprobates and relics (one a certified a rock star and the other wannabe me).

Eunoia

The shortest word
In the English language
Containing every vowel
Pronounced *You Noy Ya*
Rhymes with Sequoia
A majestic conifer
Tallest in the world
This gentle giant of the Pacific North-West
Structures countless towering buttresses
For North America's largest living cathedrals
The Redwood Forests
Expressions of Nature's Beautiful Thinking

If pigs could fly
And Scarecrows count
diamonds in the sky
Preachers could lie down,
In green pastures
In hallowed halls
ex-potentates hallucinate
Crash trust dummies
bounce off dumb
And dumber walls
Politicians unwind
Forced to resign
Their absolute
Ivory Tower power

Dimu Shangrila Construction Team

26

Far Away Eyes

A long weekend of golf with friends in 2006 took me to Yunnan Province in southwest China and the Lijiang Spa and Golf Resort. I arrived late evening, a day earlier than my golfing buddies who were coming from Hong Kong. Next morning, I awoke to a northern Yunnan sun rising over a large, man-made lake. A view of Jade Dragon Snow Mountain, a major tourist attraction, was framed by a skyline of snowy, ice capped sawtooth ridges of rock, and deeply carved glacial basins. A few fishermen standing in dugout canoes were casting nets. The surface of the lake mirrored the lifting morning fog. I entered the Resort's main lodge to have my breakfast, asking the maître d' for a lake view, outdoor table. I was led onto an alfresco deck, fifty feet above the lake. To my right, the fairway and green of the 18th hole hugged the edge of the lake. A benevolent, sub-alpine, agrarian landscape surrounded the links. Behind me were the foothills that form Yunnan's gateway to the southern Himalayas, the Rooftop of the World.

Li Yun Li waited on my table. She explained she would serve me all my meals during my stay. Yun Li's family were of the Naxi culture, the indigenous people of the area of northern Yunnan which included Lijiang. Li Yun Li grew up in a small village built on a mountainside high above a stretch of the Yangtze River to the north of Lijiang. A few kilometers downstream from her village is Tiger Leaping Gorge, the deepest canyon in China. Yun Li had not gone beyond high school. Instead, she worked in her father's cement and tile small batch manufacturing company after graduation. She helped her father, doing simple accounting tasks for his company on a desktop computer. In the evenings, Yun Li studied English on the internet because she knew that English would give her an advantage over her peers. When she graduated from high school, her father encouraged her to leave the village and find employment in Lijiang. The waitress job included room and board.

Yun Li served me a lovely breakfast of fresh croissants, fresh grapefruit juice, scrambled eggs, and cured ham. After breakfast, I hit a couple of buckets at the Resort's Driving Range. My buddies were not due to arrive until after lunch, so I dropped off my clubs at a caddie station near the first tee. Next door was a temporary building which housed a sales office and showroom for private villas, under under construction, on a hillside overlooking the Resort. The Resort's developer was taking down-payments for fifty-year villa leases. I filled out some paperwork, called my Shanghai lawyer, and had a salesperson scan the lease documents and e-mail them to him.

For lunch Yun Li suggested a plate of trout sashimi with a side dish of Yunnan mushroom fried rice. I told her I would absolutely love some sashimi. "You are very lucky, my dear American. A native fisherman delivered a half-dozen trout this morning. They are still alive and in the kitchen." The fisherman collected the trout from a gill net strung across the upstream edge of a nearby glacial melt creek. He brought them to the Resort's chef in a portable, waterproof, canvas "live" well.

What an unexpected treat, fresh trout sashimi. When I asked about the mushrooms with fried rice, she went to the kitchen and

and came back with a plate of three different choices. I opted for all three.

Saltwater sashimi raw materials have a longer shelf life than freshwater choices. Trout, native or raised in a hatchery, need cold, continually oxygenated, super clean water to survive. Gourmet quality trout sashimi comes from a fish pulled from a stream or holding tank literally minutes before it is served. If the fish is any less fresh the meat will lose its "body." An unpleasant "mealy" texture replaces the firmness and flavor that makes sashimi a delicacy. It is rare for restaurants in Tokyo to offer trout sashimi. The last time I enjoyed trout sashimi was in a small restaurant on the slopes of Mount Fuji. During the three years I spent working with Japan's largest architecture firm, Nikkei Seikei, I often went trout fishing with one of our Japanese clients, Hamano-San. There was an express train from Tokyo's Central Station to the base of "Fuji San." Several concessionaires within Mt. Fuji's National Park offered "by the hour," white water creek fishing for stocked rainbow. I had trout sashimi there after fishing with a beautifully crafted, handmade antique bamboo fly rod. The bamboo rod was a gift from Hamano-San. I caught several trout using artificial flies, hand tied by Hamano-San. As soon as we had landed our limit, we rushed our catch to the concessionaire's creek-side café where they prepared sushi served with shredded white radish, fermented ginger root, light soy, and homemade wasabi.

If you go to Lijiang and want trout sashimi, you need not take a chance that the Lijiang Spa and Golf Resort will have live trout in the kitchen. You can hire a car to take you to the La Shi Hai Trout Farm, twenty kilometers north of Shangri-La. The Trout Farm is operated by a local entrepreneur who packs most of his production in dry ice for air-freight delivery to fancy restaurants in China's big cities. The trout he ships are served whole, and they never arrive fresh enough to make sashimi. Although he does not advertise it as a restaurant, the Trout Farm has four round, outdoor picnic tables under large umbrellas, on a stone paved deck next to several long, narrow concrete holding ponds. The Trout Farm is happy to accommodate the occasional drop-in diners who have somehow stumbled across the Trout Farm, usually through word-of-mouth.

You can walk over to one of the holding ponds and select from Golden or Rainbows. You can also decide on the size of the fish. Someone from the prep-and-pack room will come out and net the fish of your choice, weigh it, and then hit it on the head with a rock before taking it back inside for final preparation. The sashimi is served on a bed of shaved ice with soy sauce and wasabi. If you want to accompany it with a bottle of sake, then you better BYOB. On our trip around China in 2011, I treated Jeffrey Katzenberg, DreamWorks CEO, and members of his entourage, to a lunch of sashimi at the Trout Farm.

Shangri-La is 150 kilometers north of Lijiang. At an altitude of 3,300 meters, Shangri-La is 1,300-meters higher in altitude than Lijiang. Flat-landers visiting Shangri-La can suffer altitude sickness if they do not follow the recommended protocol for acclimatisation.

At my urging, in 2007, Vincent Lo brought several members of his company to the Lijiang and Shangri-La area to explore the possibility of developing a "second home" planned community, resort town. I knew that no one in Vincent's company, apart from Albert Chan, had any experience with PUD's (planned unit developments), but the idea of an indigenous culture-infused, eco-tourist resort was just starting to take hold in China. "The first in China" resort of this type was developed by my design partner Delphine and her husband, Grant. Their naked Stable and Reserve in Moganshan is two hours by car from downtown Shanghai. I assisted Delphine with the conceptual planning of this phenomenally successful venture.

Before involving his company, Vincent had already made several trips to Lijiang to look for personal real estate investment opportunities with an Austrian developer and good friend. I had drawn up plans for them for a large resort near an old Flying Tigers landing strip and emergency refueling stop on land owned by a local village. My Uncle Jack, on my father's side, had flown the "Hump" for the Flying Tigers. I was probably the first American to stand in the middle of this abandoned landing strip since the 1940s. On the main highway that passed within 350 meters of the airstrip, there was no historical marker. But I did discover, in a local villager's courtyard, a few pre-war Jerry cans and some smudge pots for marking the runway in daylight.

Vincent and his Austrian partner tried for over a year to strike a deal with the government and the local village leaders. They worked with a couple of neighboring villages to piece together enough contiguous property to make a second home resort financially viable, but the scheme ran aground largely because the land was owned by aboriginal natives and before land could be transferred to private land-use, the local government had to acquire the land by negotiating a sale price with the aboriginals. Only then could the government create "land use rights" for sale to private developers.

Vincent and a couple of his most trusted associates arrived in Lijiang ahead of a three-day company conference on Northern Yunnan Resort Development. I took them to lunch at the La Shi Hai Trout Farm. After sashimi, we drove around the lake, stopping at several key vantage points for panoramic views of the freshwater lake and the extraordinarily scenic environs.

The La Shi Hai-Lijiang local government hosted a lunch for us on the last day of the conference. Lunch was one of those rare occasions when I witnessed a Party Secretary, faced with the realization that his tough negotiating tactics were close to scuttling a major real estate development deal, change his tone and tune. With so many people around the table wanting a Vincent Lo project to stimulate an emerging northern Yunnan tourist economy, he was in a bind. The Secretary scrambled trying to find common ground with Chairman Lo. "Art of the deal" Donald "the Trump" can only wish he could be in Vincent's league.

Late that same day Vincent stood with the Secretary on the edge of the vast expanse of the La Shi Hai Wetland and Wildlife Sanctuary. The Secretary placed his hand on Vincent's shoulder: "If this is not one of the most beautiful places in China, then you do not know China," he said. The Secretary's comment centered on an important principle: great resorts rely on intrinsic, site-specific, attractions not found anywhere else in the world.

That night, I asked Vincent and friends to join me for an alfresco dinner on the deck of the Golf Resort Main Lodge. Stars filled the soft air of a summer night sky. Crickets, frogs, and night owls kept us entertained. Yi Lun Yi was there. As we were leaving, Vincent was greeted by the Resort's GM who asked about his dinner. He singled out Lun Yi for her excellent service and charming demeanor. Soon thereafter, Lun Yi was promoted to the job of restaurant manager. Last I heard, she is working in the Lijiang Department of Tourism.

The next morning the Resort Development Team set off for Shangri-La, a five-hour drive north. Most of the group went with Vincent in the tour bus. I took three of Vincent's colleagues with me. All three insisted on riding in the back of the SUV/truck. All flat landers from Hong Kong, they stood up the entire trip holding tight to a cab top grab rail. Our route north to Shangri-La passed by La Shi Hai. At the far end of the lake, the main highway begins a gradual ascent to the top of the long western ridge of Jade Dragon Snow Mountain. After passing through a narrow mountain pass, we started down a steep, nail-biting, switch-backing, 800-meter descent to the ground floor of the great Yangtze River Valley.

By the early 2000s, construction of several new highways and bridges had sparked a dramatic increase in northern Yunnan tourism. Zhongdian, northern Yunnan's largest city, changed its name to Shangri-La. The Zhongdian County Tourism Board hoped to capitalize on the lure of a utopian community made famous by the book and movie versions of *Lost Horizon.*

From the top of Jade Dragon Snow Mountain to the floor of the Yangtze is almost 9,000-feet. This riparian depression is one of the deepest in the world. The inhabitants of the upper Yangtze's stepped-slope valley enjoy sub-tropical Lost Horizon weather. The birthplace of Yun Li, this valley is my Shangri-La. The big city farther north is a name-dropping impersonator.

Just before entering Tiger Leaping Gorge, the main road crosses a bridge over the Yangtze River and heads north towards Shangri-La. We left Yun Li's hometown in the rearview mirror and started up a long and winding road, eventually climbing over 2,000 vertical meters. This dangerously narrow mountain road, carved into the side of rock cliffs, was temporary, serving as a detour around the construction work on a new, divided highway. After an hour of nerve-racking, nail-biting driving, we went through a gentle mountain pass to enter the flatter lands of Zhongdian and Deqing counties, high, alpine grasslands.

We traveled faster than the tour bus, so we had time to take a slight detour. At the south end of the Zhongdian plateau there is a perfectly round pond, surrounded by a circle of dead, or almost dead, walnut trees. No locals recall any history concerning the pond's origins. They say it is the work of the gods.

I was driving my SUV, scouting the back roads for new places to explore, when I discovered this perfect circle pond. The locals had told me that in the old days, before the revolution, a small group of Tibetan monks lived in seclusion in a nearby temple. The temple had long ago disappeared, only a few mud walls remained. Initially I thought the round pond was a hand-dug stock pond. But that didn't explain the perfect geometry. Next, I imagined the twenty-meter diameter circle of reflected sky to be the work of the monks who had lived in the nearby temple.

A few yards uphill from the round pond, a Buddhist stupa stands guard in the middle of a single-track dirt road. Standing at the base of this ancient burial marker, the view north is across a vast wildflower and native grassland meadow. In the foreground is the pond's circle, and inside this circle is a smaller circle, a thin ring within a ring. There are two dead walnut trees next to the pond. A few meters east of the pond are two lines of walnut trees. The rows intersect and deadend at a perfect right angle.

One hundred kilometers in the distance, on the other side of Tiger Leaping Gorge, you can see the top of Snow Mountain. The sweeping expanse of prairie foreshortens and enlarges the Mountain of the Gods. To the people living in northern Yunnan, Snow Mountain is sacred, an eternal sun, setting forever over an endless horizon. Local villagers call the land beyond the round pond the "field of spirits." American land conservationists would call this extraordinarily scenic landscape a "Last Great Place."

I showed a picture of the pond to a friend who had never been to Yunnan. She is all science and does not know it is against divine law to a walk clockwise around a Buddhist Stupa. My "monk's work" theory left her non-plussed. She took a deep breath: "Something from space made that round pond."

My god, I thought, she is right. The proximity of the Stupa and the geometric relationship between perfectly aligned rows of walnuts had stupefied me. Myopia and the promise of perfect

The meteor lake near the temple.

utopias are the burning bushes of mental and physical foreplay. Foreplay can mean different things to different people, but getting caught with your science pants down by an intelligent woman sucks.

A quick look at a "ground level" Google Earth Pro view will confirm that only the rooftops of the nearest inhabited village can be seen from the pond. See coordinates: 27-deg.30-min.38.17-sec.N. 99-deg.47-min.29.22-sec.E. Today, the Meteorite Pond Stupa is visible from a new highway. As you start the final descent into Little Zhongdian Valley's southern end, the lone Stupa's white base is easy to spot. The strike causing the impact crater could have occurred in the middle of the night. No one awake to be blinded by the light. Until the recent advent of modern infrastructure, villagers got up at first light and went to bed at last light. Yaks, who sleep largely standing up, might have been the only witnesses. And judging by the dead walnut trees, the strike was not that long ago. Dead trees are hard to date. Walnuts, valued for both the nut and the deeply grained hardwood, can live for hundreds of years, and stand dead for decades. One day, probably in the last half of the 20th Century, there was only prairie grass and a grove of walnuts downhill from the Stupa. The next day, there was a perfect circle filling with ground water. And walnut trees smoldered and dropped limb embers on a bed of scorched earth.

No bona-fide Zhongdian native believes their round pond is the work of NATURE. Buddhist deities, like all Gods, work in mysterious ways. The farmer who is the closest abutter has put up a fence and blocked the only vehicle access. For a fee, he will unlock the gate. A guard is posted on weekends to charge walk-ins. A lucky draw windfall for a local farm land owner. My mistake for taking friends for a close encounter with the Universe. My own picnics among the walnuts, wildflowers, and round petticoat fringes of a microscopic Big Bang space warp allemande left, circle right, Do Si Do, are lost in time. All evidence carried away by winter winds and drifting snow.

The true origins of the round pond were the result of the explosive nature of a micro-meteorite hitting the earth. My amateur theory compares a micro-meteorite strike with the two-stage munition design of vacuum bombs. Thermobaric weapons, vacuum bombs, set off a first explosive charge at the bomb's point of impact. The explosive charge, packed in a watertight canister, is delivered by a rocket launcher, or dropped from an aircraft. The force of this first blast spreads an aerosol of highly flammable fuel akin to vaporized gasoline. The powerful pressure wave generated by the blast sucks all the oxygen from the surrounding air. This mix of oxygen and superheated fuel auto-ignites progressively, and a huge fireball erupts. I believe a micro-meteor strike behaves the same way, except there is no deafening blast noise.

After this detour, we rushed to join Vincent's group at the Shangri-La resort site. Missing the turn-off just before the tollbooth, we were forced to turn around after a few kilometers of bewilderment. I had been to the resort site before but even after leaving the main highway I missed another turn and ended up facing a locked gate. No sign of life except for a "no trespassing" sign and a score of huge, round stacks of firewood in a large clearing on the other side of the gate. Northern Europeans call them stove wood beehives. This was the first and only time I saw firewood stacked this way in China.

We were the last arrivals at the corporate BBQ. The scene resembled the set of a Fredricho Fellini movie. Spread out on long wooden tables was an outdoor feast fit for a king. Colorful tents, Tibetan cooks in tall white chef's hats, smoke rising from charcoal fires, fresh farm vegetable and grilled lamb kabobs, spit-roasted Yak tenderloins, salads made from wild greens, roasted yams, and many very happy faces.

Next day, the Conference was reconvened at the Paradise Hotel in the New Town. I did not bunk with the group that night but went to the Old Town to stay in a renovated ancient house I had purchased in 2005 with my daughter Amy. There were still a couple of hours of sunlight left, so I made a gin and tonic and retired to my roof deck. Life is good when you can relax, bathed in fresh mountain air, in the fading light of a high-altitude Himalayan sunset. A day of close encounters was ending. Thoughts of a mystical pond, a field of wooden beehives, and a Camelot circus of food and people from all walks of life, conjured up visions of Salvador Dali's paintings. Sitting on my deck, watching the giant, Old Town, golden prayer wheel turn under human power, made the real surreal and the surreal real.

Darkness came late to my deck that evening. And it was not because of the "Single Time Zone" that is China. The poetry of life is inevitably and thankfully more powerful than the politics of even the most sovereign of nations, more meaningful that the hymns and prayers of the most sacred religions.

Next morning, I was on the road again with three conferees,

Mike, Manuel, and Jeremy, and we arrived at the lake and exited the truck to the sound of thunder. We spent the next couple of hours in a drenching rainstorm. Unprepared, we walked through La Shi Hai's Wetland Park without rain gear or umbrellas. Although the Party Secretary bragged that the La Shi Hai site was Shui On Land's for the taking, I had my doubts. The site we walked was "wet, wet, wet" and not just because of the steady rain. Most of the site is below the rainy season's high-water mark. The Park food and souvenir concession lease holder had built a few buildings atop some artificially created islands. The perimeter walkway/dam surrounding the concessions was meant to prevent flooding. Constructed of sod squares removed by hand from the immediately adjacent grassland, this dam was decidedly temporary in nature and rather dubious in value. The same could be said about the entire Wetland Park. Badly planned access roads and parking lots, overfishing of the Park's ponds, and pollution from nearby livestock corrals had badly damaged the original environment. Shui On would have to convince the government to return the Wetland to nature before it was too late and would have to impose environmental conservation restrictions before putting in place the permanent infrastructure necessary for limited development on La Shi Hai's higher ground. A great deal of patience, negotiating skill, and inspired leadership would be required. Nothing less would do.

In the end, it didn't happen. The La Shi Hai site was rendered unfeasible as a resort location after railroad engineers received Central Government approval for plans to extend the Lijiang bullet train to Zhongdian and beyond, connecting with the high-altitude train from Chengdu to Lhasa, Tibet. The route chosen bifurcated the La Shi Hai site and would ruin any views second homeowners might have of the Lake.

Actually, by the early 2000s, construction of several new

highways and bridges had sparked a dramatic increase in northern Yunnan tourism. Zhongdian, northern Yunnan's largest city changed its name to Shangri-La, with the Zhongdian County Tourism Board hoping to capitalize on the lore and lure of a utopian community made famous by the book and movie versions of *Lost Horizon,* the fantasy novel by writer James Hilton. Readers of the book know the main protagonists are survivors of a hijacked airplane forced to land on glacial icefield at an altitude of 6,000-meters deep in the Himalayas. In the distance, thousands of meters below the glacier, the survivors can see Shangri-La, a lamasery shrouded in mystery, nestled in a lush green broad river valley.

In my own fantasized version of Hilton's cult classic, I have often led the forced landing survivors down from the mountain top. An experienced mountaineer, I know the drill. Forging icy streams, climbing over snow drifts, crossing treacherous avalanche paths, we make our way to the bottom of the snow line. From there we slip, stumble, and slide down rock-strewn erosion gullies bisecting glacial outwash alluvial mud. At the bottom of the mud, the slopes go nude. At the lower limit of this tundra zone, we enter the darkness of a climaxed, evergreen, alpine forest. Emerging from this innocent, soporific cathedral we lay down in gently sloping green pastures. A local Sheppard appears and beckons us onward. Christian soldiers, marching as to war, we wade our way through palmetto meadows bordered by coconut and century palms. We walk under waterfalls cascading down from towering rock ledges, carving pools full of crystal-clear water. We follow the shepherd beside the still waters of abandoned meanders in the great river valley. We see people, in straw hats wearing light denim blue overalls and long sleeve white linen shirts, tilling the rich topsoil of the river's bottom lands. We see a horn of plenty pushing up through the furrowed rows. An early, sub-tropical, spring, sunshine illuminates cherubic faces. We discover what we believe is heaven on earth. None of us, heathen or God-fearing, knew we had walked down 3,000-meters from an icy tomb into the valley of the shadow of death. Ice cave to soul cage. None of us, were prepared for the mind-bending, unbelievably twisted, bizarre journey that awaited us.

I can no longer remember how the book ends. And if you have read the book then you know my details of the descent from a sheet of ice thousands of feet thick into Venus Nirvana's F-trap are redacted facts recast as fiction. *Lost Horizon's* many turns, tangled in science and religious fiction, disfigured by horrific tragedy and insanity, are now lost in translation. I suffer from post, long-haul Covid nerve damage. At age seventy-four, I am CPAP weary. For me to hold my clothes and shoes over my head, while fording barefoot a near frozen glacial artery, would be more angst in my pants than I could take. But the quicksand of Hilton's literary genius and his story of a Lucy in the sky, hallucinogenic, alternate, reality remains very powerful. Saddle up, millions of Paperback riders.

Modern China's first diva, Yang Erche Namu, grew up a Musuo tribal native in a village on the western shore of northern Yunnan's Lugu Lake. While barely a teenager, she was awarded a full scholarship to the Shanghai Conservatory of Music. She trained as a singer but eventually had to quit after losing hearing in one ear. She turned to dancing and acting and became famous. Briefly married to an American, she lived for a while in San Francisco. Following the Lijiang Earthquake in 2008, intent on helping rebuild the town, Namu left her husband and returned to China. She got "Shanghai-ed" in Beijing, married a Norwegian, and in 1997, co-authored, with a foreign anthropologist, her first book in English, *Leaving the Kingdom of Daughters*. Her lifelong career as a socialite, actress, and writer is the subject of eight autobiographical "tell all" exposés. China's first modern female author to include the intimate details of sexual conquests, Namu was crowned the premier China Doll of the Middle Kingdom, Yunnan's Queen Cleopatra.

In 2004, I invited Vincent and a couple of his colleagues to visit Namu's Old Town café. I am a little foggy on the exact details of this visit but I do remember her invitation to give Vincent a private tour of her upstairs boudoir. When Vincent politely declined, she made the same offer to me and the other two gentlemen. One by one, we declined. Embarrassed, shocked, or scared? None are the right words. We were all virile men. If alone, each of us might have been more than willing to be devoured by her anther.

In her book, *Leaving Mother Lake,* she complained she did not like Musuo men because they smelled bad. News from America, Namu. All men smell bad. Namu did not need a female anthropologist to co-author this revelation. Ask any woman, straight or otherwise. Pity Namu could not pull the last floorboard from underneath any one of four smelly men.

Critics accuse Namu of self-injected, morphemic Yellow Fever. They condemn her motives, claiming she deliberately and selfishly, transfigured and transgendered into a "cannot be divided or conquered" Silk Road diva. A dedicated maverick and self-proclaimed bitch, Namu once boasted that she could make any Chinese man "feel like nothing" and bring any white man "to his knees."

Namu is no China Doll. Namu is the truth. No woman should ever be subordinate to any man, ever.

27

The Flash of Creativity

I sometimes idly wonder where ideas come from, the contrarian, unexpected concepts that change everything. It can happen to anyone but over the years, but I'd say it happens to me more than to most. Human progress is created more by flashes of enlightenment than by ten years of hard work. There is a lot of value to ten years of hard work, but the one instantaneous flash can push things forward so far and fast. It comes somehow from thinking beyond the obvious, looking for connections between basic elements of a situation and highlighting them, acting upon them.

A case in point is Disney World in Orlando, Florida. During the construction of Shanghai Disneyworld in 2013, I was also invited to pitch a design concept for the commercial area just outside the Orlando Disney World they called Downtown Disney, and instead of just providing a standard design, I did some digging and found a small item in an issue of the Orlando Sentinal from long ago, saying that a guy named Disney had been the postmaster in a town in the very area of the Disneyworld theme park, and I suspected it must be Walt's Dad. Someone I know was a friend of Walt's daughter Diane, and at my behest she called Diane and asked her if it was true that her grandfather had been a postmaster in a town near Orlando, and she was amazed. "How did you know?" She said. "Even the people at Disney don't know that." Choosing that location for the park, it turns out, wasn't random.

So I made up a story about where the name "Disney Springs" came from, half real, half fantasy, and pitched it to their board of directors as the name for reboot of the Downtown Disney area, and they loved it. "You're the only one who can do this," they said. "All the others just do architecture, but you wrote a story." I won the competition to do the project, but then looked at my workload, and thought about having to fly from Shanghai to Orlando once a month, and turned it down. But they now use the name Disney Springs, although you won't see me referred to in any of the materials. They like to make it look like they have all the ideas. Anyway I wrote this story, called "A Small Town Growing Up—The Story of Disney Florida," and it went like this (try and spot what's real and what's not):

Around 1840, Kissimmee River Road was first cut through the palmetto and pine forests of Central Florida. Built for horses and wagons, this road linked the rail line in Orlando to the citrus farms in the southwest. Soon after the road was completed, a young immigrant named Disney bought land on the road twenty-three miles south of Orlando. He built a small hotel next to a fresh water spring that fed into a large swamp, and travelers came to identify his log hotel at the springs as the "Inn at Disney Springs."

Soon a small settlement began to grow up around the Springs as Disney sold off parcels of land to new residents. There was a marketplace with a grocery and produce stalls, several shops including a blacksmith, cabinetmaker, barbershop, and a general store with a lunch and fountain counter. To get local pine logs to make lumber for these new buildings, Mr Disney had the nearby swamp dug out to make a lake. Logs were felled upland of the new lake and then towed by boat to the new Disney sawmill. By the time the Civil War began, this small town became known as Disney, Florida.

Two decades after the War, Mr Disney died. Mr Disney's son Elias ran the sawmill and the inn, taking a wife in 1888. A year later, the Disney's sold out their rural Florida holdings and moved to Chicago to raise a family. They would later move again to a rural community, this time a small town in Missouri.

Throught the last century, Disney, Florida grows and prospers, supplying lumber, goods, labor, and services to the citrus groves and packinghouses. In the 1920s, a steam train replaces the wagon trains. Disney, Florida is the first station south of Orlando. Walt's father set up a hotel there called Disney Springs. In the 1940s, trucks replaced the steam trains. New highways were built across central Florida bypassing the small town of Disney. By the time the Federal interstate highway system connected Florida with the rest of the nation in the 1960s, the town was all but abandoned.

In 1965, two entrepreneurs from California, Walt and Roy, came to town looking for a site for an ambitious new project. Today Disney, Florida is part of the 27,443-acre Walt Disney World Resort they developed. The town of Disney has continued to grow even though there are no full-time residents. Instead, there are tens of millions of visitors every year. People come from all over the world to experience the magic of Disney. And it all began in a small town somewhere in America. What's in a name? Everything. Disney, Florida, a town, a story, mostly true, always imagined.

If you want to ask what is different about me, there are probably a bunch of things, but I learned story telling from two or three of the best story-tellers in the world, including my Dad, my grandfather on my mother's side and my Uncle Ben. I grew up sitting around a fireplace with these guys listening to stories. I learned that when you start a project, you should imagine what the future could be like if you totally ignored all the conventional thinking of what you should do. So the story of Times Square was imagining what the future was like and writing a story about it. When I start a project, the last thing I think about is architecture. When I was growing up, and like me you lived in the middle of nowhere, you spent all day imagining what the world would be like if it was different, and you make up stories.

Another thought on this topic of inspiration. When I was young, I used to go out squirrel hunting. If you're after squirrels and you're looking where you think they are, you will never see them. You can only detect the motion of a squirrel with your peripheral vision. You have to learn to look at everything from the edges of vision and not focus on anything. It's the same flying a jet fighter, you have to use your peripheral vision, because if you just stare ahead all kinds fo bad things can happen to you. By the age of sixteen or seventeen, your life has already been determined, what you're going to be good at or not good at, what's going to interest you or not interest you, and if you haven't learned by then that your imagination is your most valuable tool you have ... you can go to the best law school, MIT and Harvard, but being able to imagine the future is something that very few people can do. And many of them are architects, because they have to imagine what is not there. I just stood in Times Square one night and looked up and thought, "My god. Why isn't this Shibuya?" Of course, if I had never been to Shibuya I wouldn't have had the idea. That's what the whole cultivated serendipity thing is about. If someone calls you up tomorrow and gives you a chance to do something you have never done before, do it. Don't even think, just jump off the cliff. But most people won't do that, they need all kinds of assurances first.

I take photos all the time of anything that looks interesting to me, and it all feeds into the creative process. I have around 350,000 images, photos I have taken over the years, mostly vernacular architecture, that I think perhaps can in some way suggest or inspire or provide a parallel to something else. When I start a project, I go through every single one of them, which takes about three days. I don't necessarily choose any particular image to use as a reference, it's the process of allowing all the images to wash over me. So I was standing in Times Square, and the image of Shibuya came to me, and I said, why not? Then I used the laser disk technology, which was revolutionary for its time to drive them through Times Square and freeze frame on the giant billboards I was proposing. It blew them away.

The next step in my creative process, after rambling through the images, is that I write myself a letter, a long essay about the project, and I list out all the words that occur to me in association with the project. Treehouse, firefly, things from my childhood... By association, I relate pictures and words and then put them in the essay. Then I often do a video for the client, with a narration by me, and the choice of the accompanying music is important. Every sensory button must be pushed. The point I make over and over again, is that the future is to some extent what you imagine it to be, and if you imagine it, it can come true.

I was asked by one China property management company a few years ago to come with a design for the shopping and residential areas that surround the Yu Garden in central Shanghai, an old Chinese-style garden surrounded by a ring of shops and then delapidated old tenement housing. When people built these gardens in China, they were thinking about ways to connect with something that was greater than themselves, and Yu Garden works fine. But the surrounding neighborhood did not give me a good impression. Most of the shops are not unique,

Evangelizing with Albert.

and there was a lot more emphasis on selling things than on creating things. I constantly remind people that culture is about creating things, not consuming things.

Gardens are places where people experience happiness, and the challenge is to create an experience that is entertaining and reminds you that a healthy and happy life is a good life by providing people with places to eat, to shop, to sit down and take a break. The goal is to create a specially unique environment, a collection of spaces, each of which has its own characteristics.

I don't talk much about architecture styles in terms of my professional practice because if you focus on the style you miss out on the underlying life of a project. I focus on the meaning, and in the case of Yu Garden, that would be best reflected in a collection of different architectural styles including references to historical architecture but also elements that were futuristic. I design places I would want to go to, I design for myself. If I see a big building that is all glass and grayness, I don't want to go there. I want to go to a place with flowers and space to breathe and trees and the blue sky above, the sound of birds singing, somewhere that at night looks and feels romantic. It starts in the morning as one kind of place, and by the afternoon it's another kind of place, and by late evening, it's changed again. You need to create a place that makes people feel welcome, that makes them want to come back again and again and again. People go to places that make them feel good, and it takes a lot of work to create that experience.

Everyone on the property management team voted for my design, but it was rejected basically because it was too ambitious, and they went with a Japanese firm's design of a standard shopping mall. The irony is that it didn't get built because the city government declined to put any money into it, and it was too big a risk for the management company to take without the government taking some of the risk.

For a time, I had an exhibition space on the floor under my office in Xintiandi. At the heart of the first exhibition we staged were images by a photographer in Xi'an named Yu Ping, who had taken photos of dozens of villages in Shaanxi province, all now disappeared. The exhibition also included random examples of "design by non-designers," items such as brooms, pastry-making utensils and stainless steel squat toilet bowls designed and made in China, but so ordinary and a part of the fabric of life that no one noticed them. Virtually all the "hardware" came from a gigantic building materials market in Shanghai now, alas, closed and earmarked for redevelopment. You could find everything there from assembly line robots to straw brooms for 5 RMB.

From the exhibition curation and installation, I learned a great deal about light, both natural and artificial. I literally created "photographs" with real objects and it was often difficult to distinguish the two. I have a green wall in my apartment made of house number plates from a nearby neighborhood which was razed to make way for luxury apartment buildings. Some of the items in the exhibition ended up in the Little Shop of Curios, a storefront I have maintained in XTD for years containing an improbable menagerie of unlikely artifacts whose origins can be traced back to the Great Urbanization of China.

Navigate the space of this Little Shop of Curios and enjoy this intimate space filled with unlikely artifacts. All were made in China during the Great Urbanization: all were made by people who still think people should be loved and things should be used. The desire for a new apartment and a BMW, a luxury handbag, a vacation abroad should not change that. Discover the power of your own imagination so you too can beat the odds and make life worth living. Life is life, fun is fun, but it all goes quiet when the last goldfish dies. Enjoy our goldfish, not sure how long they or we will be around, so come again soon. And lay off the selfies.

Lingnan Tiandi – the start of urban renewal.

28

Southern Dragons

The urban rebirth project I did in Shanghai, the Xintiandi entertainment district, is well-known, but the most important work I have done in terms of recognizing the cultural fabric of old urban China and re-imaging it for the future is the Lingnan Tiandi district of Foshan, a city way down south in Guangdong Province. Lingnan TD is recognized as southern China's first successful effort to re-make, adapt and conserve a neighborhood rather than just raze it. It is a visible and tangible transformation that turned a rundown district of Foshan into an extraordinary cultural destination and entertainment attraction. Lingnan TD changed the entire city's identity overnight, and as soon as it opened, every city in southern China wanted to have their own home-grown version. Daily visitor numbers were, and remain, huge and mayors, planning directors, and tourism and cultural bureaus from dozens of other Chinese cities visited to check it out and consider how to repeat the trick back home. My studio, Studio Shanghai, has worked on multiple projects in various cities including Enning Street in Guangzhou, which Chinese leader Xi Jinping visited, commenting that it was a stellar example of the social benefits of a "people-centric, culturally-focused" urban re-development.

In early 2006, the City of Foshan announced that a large,

multi-block area surrounding its most famous landmark, the Ju Miao temple, would be made available for private, for-profit re-development. In the official brief, the city placed special emphasis on the conservation of a large historic neighborhood immediately west of the Temple containing eight historic landmark sites. Shui On Land, led by Vincent Lo, was invited to submit an overall masterplan for the entire multi-block project.

Back then, you could count on one hand the number of developers in China who had experience of heritage conservation projects, and thanks to Xintiandi, in the Foshan invitational, Shui On was in pole position, but navigating government restrictions and rules, and discretionary interpretation of unwritten policies, would be a challenge.

Lingnan Tiandi was considered a financial "long shot" by many people advising Vincent Lo. The biggest concern was the economic level of Foshan itself. Foshan was a third-tier Pearl River Delta city with average household incomes substantially lower than first-tier Shanghai. The neighborhood west of the temple was also in the throes of a downward social and economic spiral. Every aspect of life was under siege. Once home to some of Guangdong's wealthiest merchants and families, in 2006 the neighborhood was considered a slum. The city government worried that if something was not done, the Provincial and Central governments would intervene. Heads would roll.

When I first visited Ju Miao Temple, renowned as one of the birthplaces of martial arts, I found large crowds lined up to pay admission. Visitor had to first traverse a plaza lined with dozens of tacky souvenir, incense, and noodle shops. The West Gate neighborhood had once been home to Foshan's wealthy aristocracy, but in the wake of the communist revolution, they had fled the city, many ending up in Hong Kong. The historic West Gate had been walled up for decades.

Valuable artifacts of the neighborhood's golden era were hidden under layer upon layer of ad hoc, ill-conceived social and civil interventions. Decades of economic decline, infrastructure decay, and civil neglect had taken their toll. Poverty was desperately inescapable. A smattering of small shops survived, most peddling sugar drinks, cigarettes, candy, and a few cutting hair, doing nails, altering garments, selling cheap shoes and clothes, and flimsy pots and pans. Small "speak-easy" massage parlors had a front room and a back room, one legit, one not. There were piles of rotting refuse everywhere, and back alleys that smelled of urine.

All but one of the neighborhood's "listed" sites were in poor or very poor condition. Several the residents interviewed by the development and design team were unaware of the significance of the "listed" sites. Altered beyond recognition, all but one were identifiable only by a special plaque.

A few weeks after starting work, our design team had decided the challenges of reviving the neighbourhood were not comparable with anything we had previously confronted. Reconnecting the people of Foshan with the dignity, beauty, and joy, the very heart and soul of this historic neighborhood, was vital. Lingnan TD would not be a small job. Meeting the practical and psychological demands of a rapidly expanding, contemporary middle-class in a Guangdong city was big, big work.

Devising a strategy for the conservation and preservation of the eight "listed" historic sites topped the list of essential tasks for my on-site team. Beyond these eight sites, the conservation of existing buildings, historic or otherwise, was ruled out. Too much ground, not enough figure. Except for the space under and around a few mature trees, and a few small courtyards, the neighborhood was devoid of any community open space. There were no places where children could play safely. There was one lane-and-alley intersection that afforded an area large enough for a few Mahjong tables. A lone billiard table, which had seen better days, was parked under a building overhang. But you had to bring your own cue stick, chalk, and balls.

The solution to the open space issue was obvious. More than a score of three-to-five story, walk-up apartment blocks, hastily constructed in the 1980s and 1990s dotted the site. They did not conform to even the most basic of habitable building standards. They had to go and their elimination paved the way for more public open space.

My team spent thousands of hours discovering, understanding, and documenting the character intrinsic to the remaining urban fabric. "In living color," a woven tapestry of shade, shadow, and patina, painted the walls of the lanes and alleys. Conserving this spatial framework was of crucial importance, both commercially and culturally. For the buildings that were to remain, we mixed a design vocabulary derived from local vernacular shops, houses, courtyard compounds, and market buildings.

Construction proved to be more costly and time consuming than anyone had anticipated. Five years of blood, sweat, tears, interrupted by moments of joy and wonderment, took me and my colleagues to the brink of exhaustion.

The design team found only a limited number of historical documents pertaining to the listed buildings. The few they found had been collected by local, amateur historians. Tucked away during the Cultural Revolution, these documents did not always concur with the information available from the Foshan Cultural Bureau. In 1998, the year all eight Municipal and Provincial sites were "listed," a professional historian put together two volumes of information. The best information available describing the urban fabric were Tax Bureau lot-line maps. The design team embarked on the laborious task of documenting through photographs and drawings every square meter of both pedigree and non-pedigree, built forms.

We studied the ratio of the existing building height to lane width. We monitored the day and nighttime temperature of different surfaces. The areas with the most pleasant microclimates were carefully studied in terms of building materials and spatial proportions and later used as a reference to maximize natural comfort zones in the design of new outdoor public spaces.

On one field trip, Dwight Law and I visited an orchid house with thousands of orchids growing in pots on long tables under a single span, glass-roof conservatory. At one end of the conservatory were several through-wall exhaust fans while at the other end, there were honeycombed walls dripping water from top to bottom. You could feel a gentle breeze as the powerful fans pulled outside air through the glistening wet honeycombs and across the pots of delicate, pungent beauties. The temperature outside was 35 degrees centigrade, but inside, the orchids enjoyed a pleasant 27-degree bubble.

Following this discovery, I requested our mechanical engineering team investigate the latest innovations in evaporative cooling technology, and we began working with a Canadian engineer living in Foshan, employed by the company that had made and installed the orchid house system. Before we could proceed, we had to test the orchid house system in a full-scale, on-site, installation, but Shui On declined to fund the development so I decided to go ahead anyway, using my own "nickel" to build the first of what we had started to call "cool walls." I offered to pay the Canadian engineer to build my prototype in the Foshan factory. He called his owner in Canada who volunteered to build the prototype for free. When the hot weather arrived, the Project Architect, Matt White, reported the results of the on-site test in a letter to Shui On: "On a very hot day, 36-degrees-C, and very humid, we were able to achieve a temperature drop of 8 degrees C in an outdoor alley with a cooling wall. Fan air exit speeds were within the limits of comfort. We consider this a big success."

Using a locally produced, inexpensive and effective greenhouse cooling system, "cool walls" became part of the architecture and landscape of Lingnan TD. Custom-designed fiberglass "nacelles" permitted both horizontal and vertical installations of the "cool wall" and the factory prefabricated package was concealed behind traditional, clay tile, vertical latticework and horizontal decorative iron grates. The same clay tile lattice screens were used to ventilate dozens of new semi-detached stair wells. Energy consumption for "cooling walls" was several times lower than that of conventional air-conditioning. Recycled rainwater, supplemented with tap water, irrigated the cardboard evaporative "medium." Chalk one up for climate change mitigation.

In the lanes and alleys, one built form stood out: the Boundary Stones. Laid end-to-end, long lengths of thick granite slabs ran longitudinally down both sides of the lanes and wider alleys. Survey monuments, the boundary stones, had been used to mark private-versus-public ownership. Through two dynasties, an industrial revolution, a wartime occupation, and a People's Republic makeover, they shouted, "you stay on your side, and I will stay on mine." Many Boundary Stones had family names carved on them. It is hard to imagine a more prescient cultural artifact. The design team marked each stone with a number corresponding to an exact location. Construction workers surgically removed the stones and transported them to an off-site storage yard.

When not busy with site walks and design tasks, team members took field trips to historic gardens, clay pottery, tile, and brick kilns, and local artist studios. We brought back hollow and solid cast samples from foundries, stones from quarries, wooden windows, doors, furniture from workshops, metalwork from blacksmiths, and pottery in dozens of shape and sizes. This treasure trove of local booty inspired the design of countless Lingnan TD architectural and landscape elements.

Some of the eight "listed" sites contained more than one building. Some, like Jian's Family Mansion, the Japanese Commander's House, and the Poets' Society were walled compounds with large courtyards and gardens. Others, like the Wine Guild, fronted onto neighborhood lanes with stately entrances framed by two posts and a lintel beam made of granite. These three-stone entry gates featured an elegant entry system comprised of three types of doors: a pair of tall in-swinging solid wood black lacquer doors with keyed lock, an outer pair of "cafe" doors, half the height of the main doors, and a third pair of sliding doors, Yi Men, with round horizontal bars. The keyed entry doors were closed when the family was away. When left open on hot days and nights, the Yi Men provided security and natural ventilation, especially at night when the family was sleeping. When the other two types of doors were left open, it was a signal that someone was home and visitors were welcome to knock. Unique to Ling Nan culture, this door system and variations was used throughout the project on traditional buildings of brick and stone with distinctive gable-end "Guo'er" (Dragon) style firewalls. Steel doors with bars in front had often replaced the Guo'er's far more elegant traditional door system.

One serious, practical issue was how to bring the brick-bearing wall, wood beam, floor joist, and roof rafter structural system into compliance with seismic standards. Our structural engineers were used to working with steel and reinforced concrete structures. They referred to the existing shophouses as "shanty shacks," insisting it was cheaper to tear down and rebuild. Making a brick bearing wall and wood structure code-compliant was, for them, problematic. They were adamant that the shophouses be re-constructed using reinforced concrete, column and beam grids, filled with cinder block and wrapped in brick veneer. Brick fucking veneer? I went ballistic. I went on Amazon and ordered several technical journals. The architectural team, after much research into case studies of successful conservation of old brick buildings, was finally able to convince the structural engineers that a tried-and-true, minimally invasive, non-destructive, cost-effective, seismic code compliant, solution existed and could be implemented. We saved the walls.

In China, we were often in touch with local historic preservation "experts," venerable scholars whose input often seemed to be more motivated by the politics of power than the pre-requisite process of intellectual inquiry that one would presume should be part of a preservation debate. Requiring a wrought iron fence (with gates to prevent entry) to be put up around Jian's Villa was a case-in-point. Why would you want to keep the public out, especially during normal hours of operation? What use would take precedence over public access to a Nationally Protected Landmark? It seemed that discretionary access to the Villa by local officials might be the real reason.

Working on preservation projects in China, as with anywhere in the world, usually involves preservation "experts" who always have an answer. They never tell you what they do not know, that they might not have a definitive answer. I have never heard one say that maybe we do not know what is the best approach. My own opinion is that old buildings are artifacts of a culture and every new generation should create their own artifacts to be found by future generations. Create new things based on the past. Only in rare cases should artifacts be isolated and protected. Adapt, change, re-use is almost always the better model for paying our respect to history, rather than embalming the cadaver.

Surprisingly, the main obstacle was often the Cultural Bureau. One case in point was Jian's Villa. A third floor, which bore no resemblance to the architectural style of the first two floors, was declared original by the Bureau's "experts." They were the same "experts" who had helped prepare the documentation accompanying the official "Listed Site" application. We pleaded with these "experts" to visit the Villa with us. Led by the Design Team to a ceiling hatch door in the corner a second-floor bedroom, the "experts" climbed a ladder to investigate a small interstitial space between the intersection of the third floor a slightly larger second floor. They discovered what we had already found: the stub ends of what used to be the rafters of a symmetrical, hip-roof. These stubs were supported by the Villa's second floor exterior walls.

Prior to the "attic visit" we had the good fortune to meet a local, unofficial historian and a retired architect. The retired architect told them he believed strongly that the third floor was a relatively recent addition and suggested a thorough inspection of the Villa's second floor ceilings. A home for un-wed mothers and their infant children, the Villa had originally been off-limits. Following up on the advice given by the retired architect, our team got special permission to go inside the Villa and discovered the rafter stubs. After their Villa visit, the "experts" pushed back and recommended approval of the removal the Villa's third floor.

There were many other incidents similar in nature to the Villa third floor controversy. All were resolved "peacefully". Support from our client for the necessary resources, both financial and intellectual, to properly "save as original" was never in doubt.

Recognizing the value to society of heritage conservation

through adaptive re-use starts with an understanding of the human condition. The manifestations of the human condition are on parade every day in every city across the world. Like Foshan, China, most of the people living in cities are ordinary, middle-class citizens. They want to live in a neighborhood here they can "Shout in the Street" and someone will hear them. Lingnan Tiandi was, and is now again, that kind of place.

A "Shout" on a street in China is the audible equivalent of Jane Jacob's "eyes in the street." How many shouts and how many eyes does it take to look beyond conventional urban planning guidelines and unearth the meaning inherent in people-centric, culturally focused heritage conservation. The answer: as many human encounters with that cultural heritage as possible. Vigorously rummaging through a curated museum filled with artifacts and drawings of cosmetic details or months spent surfing the internet is of no use when one is trying to discover the sense of a place.

Foshan's new landmark, Lingnan Tiandi, invites the visitor to abandon homogenized guided tours in favor of self-discovery. Promenade slowly and proudly through a sea of ordinary people. See other people while they see you. Today, tens of thousands of visitors a day are welcomed with open arms. None face social or economic barriers. Freelance flaneur or hopeless romantic, young or old, everyone comes to Lingnan Tiandi to make choices: alone or with friends or lovers, dressed-up or dressed down, café, bar, or restaurant, early or late, erotic or simply curious eye contact with a stranger, drinking coffee, tea, or wine, standing, leaning, or sitting as the world passes by in front of them. The choices they make create, not consume, culture.

There is no reason to treat heritage sites "as ancient relatives to whom we felt close as children only to grow up and find that as adults we have nothing in common," as Alain de Botton described it in his book *Architecture of Happiness.* The future is what we imagine it to be. Finding common ground for a discourse with these ancient relatives can only serve to enrich our visions. A hundred years ago, everyone in China lived in a house they built, or their ancestors built. Now over 600 million middle class people do not. They now inhabit mass-produced, ready-mix concrete "commodities" known as "apartments." The conservation and preservation of eight "listed" buildings are the coloratura ornamenting extemporaneous expressions of an architecture of humanity. Beauty, dignity, and the art of living is alive and well in Foshan.

Sadly, today the West Gate of Temple remains closed. The Temple, despite the canons of the religion it represents, continues to overtly promote the consumption of culture every time a turnstile turns. The Temple does not like people who shout in the street. They want quiet people, people who pay admission. People who look but do not touch. The Temple is now less a place of worship and more a maximum-security repository for dead artifacts and a stage for choreographed re-enactments of history. Opening a gate to a neighborhood vibrant with life is an existential threat for a Temple with an identity crisis. I hope that the culture self-evident in Lingnan Tiandi never faces a similar crisis and remains, for generations to come, Foshan's unmistaken common ground.

In 2011, the final phase, the western third of Lingnan TD, was nearing completion. I invited the Creative Director of Disney's Imagineering Department Bob Weiss to visit Lingnan Tiandi. During a roof-top dinner of spit-roasted pig he asked, "How was this done? Even we cannot do this. Who paid you to direct this movie?" He was most impressed by the sense of hospitality that Lingnan TD offered visitors. I believe Bob left Foshan with a much clearer idea of why the new Shanghai Disney Resort needed to be unlike any other Disney World: they knew and I knew that it had to have Chinese characteristics if he and his team were going to produce the high fidelity, high-definition visitor experience for which Disney is famous, and Lingnan TD was a living example of how to do it.

A year after the Disney visit, the Chairman of DreamWorks, SKG, Jeffrey Katzenberg, came with his entourage to Lingnan TD. He had a similar reaction. On his return to Los Angeles, Dreamworks announced that there would be two versions of their newest animated blockbuster, the feature film Kung Fu Panda. They would both be produced in China: one would be in Chinese, the other in English. Neither would be "dubbed" copies. They would be complete originals.

What does it mean to be Chinese? Katzenberg, like I did in 1998, knew this question would demand a new answer every day. If Dreamworks was going to succeed in China, he and his colleagues would have discover, just as we had, what they did not know.

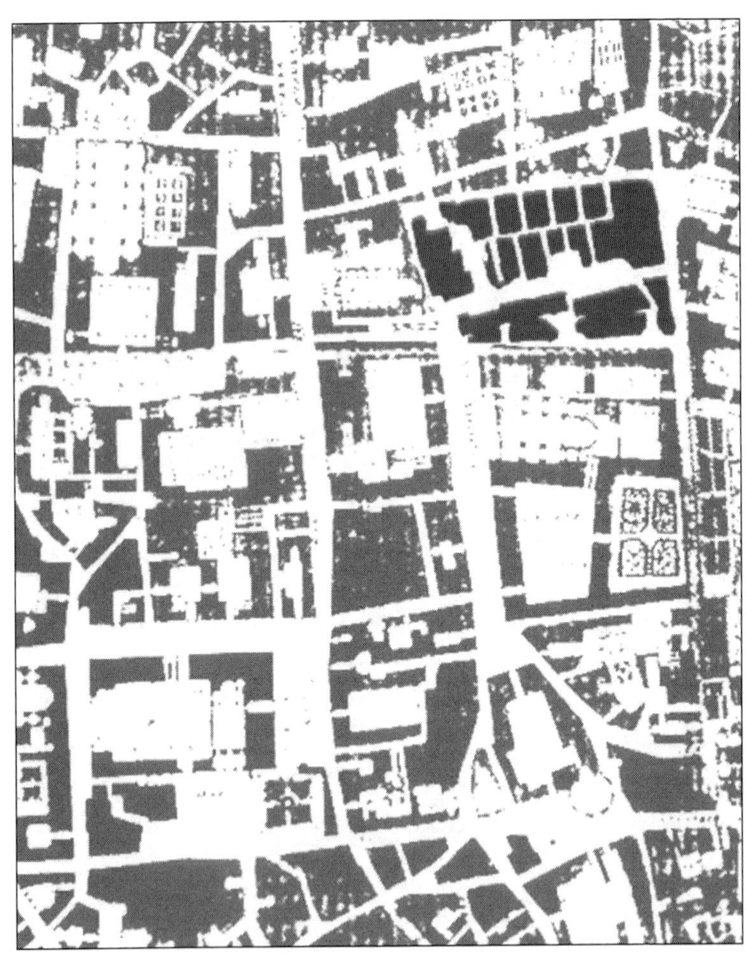

North Block XTD inlay on Nolli Map of Rome.

29

Designing what is Unbuilt

I was once asked by a Jewish philanthropist and art gallery owner to design a memorial monument for the European and Russian Jewish immigrants who, after the Bolshevik Revolution and rise of Nazism, started to come to live and work in Shanghai. They numbered perhaps 20,000 and many of them lived in the Hongkou district, close by the old Ward Road prison. Peace Park was originally a cemetery, and after the communist takeover, the tombstones were hauled away to be sold at local stone yards. The Jewish philanthropist had for years been searching for the lost tombstones and he had discovered hundreds, in alleyway pavings and walls in small villages on the outskirts of Shanghai. He wanted to retrieve as many tombstones as possible and use them to build a "Monument to the Stateless Refugees."

Before beginning work on the "Monument," I visited Peace Park and found it to be a run-down amusement park and children's petting zoo. Very little of the old cemetary remained. We talked to the park manager who showed us a grave monument recently discovered by his staff in a small bamboo grove, dedicated to Mary Pomeroy Ford (1874-1938), her family, and several descendants, including granddaughter Maude, who died at age 26. I implored the philanthropist not to try and recover the lost tombstones. For me, the cemetary's scattered memorial, represented the diaspora, the dispersion, the seeds of a foreign culture, formerly concentrated in one place. Let them be. Unlike Mary, allow the others to remain nameless, proud voices. "In situ," in Peace Park, Mary's monument alone will speak for all, bringing dignity to all the foreigners, who died because they were unable or unwilling to leave Shanghai. He agreed, and I did nothing.

The lesson, for architecture and for life, was that what you don't do is often as important as what you do.

While at college studying civil engineering, I often visited the student workspaces at the Architecture School. I remember thinking, after seeing students' beautiful hand sketches pinned up on the walls, "I can never be an architect—I can't draw like that."

Years later, at MIT, my first semester courses included a not-for-credit night-class in life drawing. After completing the first semesters of life drawing, the head of the Architecture Department offered me a TA position which included a sketch and drawing class for undergraduate students. I've always wondered what prompted MIT to offer a class in life drawing—MIT had no art department. The nude models, both women and men, came from the general student body. They earned some extra money and people like me learned to draw the human figure. Maybe that was reason enough.

The hand-drawn sketch is now an endangered species in architecture. If one of my colleagues shows me a computer-generated elevation or 3-D model of a building, without at least one human figure depicted, I always ask: "How do you expect me to help you design this elevation when there's no human scale reference?"

An architectural drawing is an abstract construct of what

may one day be real. Without at least one average-height human included as a direct visual reference, I'm forced to reach for another abstraction: a measured ruler. The first one, in my mind, is quicker, better, and faster. My mind's eye is enhanced with the space and time recorded by hundreds of thousands of photographs I keep backed-up on an orange hard drive.

In the history of architecture, no one knew the difference between style and substance better than Leonardo Da Vinci. Substance, not style, defined everything he did. Da Vinci spent his life asking questions, and drew on his remarkable skills of observation, his insatiable curiosity, and his tireless imagination to find answers. Unlike many of his contemporaries, Da Vinci did not paint in the style that was fashionable. Da Vinci found inspiration in exploring the infinite and fascinating world of physical phenomena. He sought to understand the meaning—the substance, not the style—of everything in our universe. "Why are things the way they are?" is the central question of his work. Da Vinci, the Renaissance Man, drew his answers from life.

In Walter Isaacson's book on Da Vinci, there is a chapter on water, which Da Vinci considered the most fundamental force in nature. His journey into the substance of water led him to ponder the question of why the sky is blue. Although Da Vinci's contemporaries considered this question mundane, for Da Vinci the answer was rooted in the study of fundamental—natural—phenomena.

Just as Da Vinci had a fondness for staging theatrical productions, I have devoted much of my career to creating urban entertainment destinations, performing arts venues, and related cultural attractions. Disney selected my Studio Shanghai as design architect for the Disneytown retail, dining and entertainment district next to their Shanghai theme park, choosing us over their usual suspects. Disney would have normally selected an architect from their regular stable of West Coast, New York, and Boston design firms, but their majority partner, the City of Shanghai, made it clear when they signed on with Disney: We want a design made in China, for the people of China. Disney did their homework. An advance Disney Imagineering team visited Xintiandi on days when the sun was shining and days and nights when rain was falling. They could see that each of our Tiandi projects told a different, but always culturally focused, story. They also knew that all shared the same business model as Disney, aiming to give China's exploding population of middle-class urban dwellers a place to see and be seen. We did one in Hangzhou, then Chongqing and Wuhan, then we did Lingnan Tiandi in Foshan, which was a huge and significant project. Each one possesses a sense of ubiety, and each one is uniquely driven by references to local vernacular architecture, indigenous culture, and local traditions. Each one aims to be both familiar and modern for the people who visit.

Clients that employ style-biased market studies to validate their own preference for a particular architectural genre are ignorant of the commercial and cultural value inherent in a more open-ended discussion with their architect or urban planner. Creating a livable community starts by recognizing where we live, work, and play—strongly influencing who we are. Substance, not style, makes one place better than another. A client who says they do not like the style of a building with one or more flat roofs has never spent a summer's evening on a rooftop deck gazing at the stars.

My mentor Ben Thompson believed that the primary purpose of architecture was to create a more humane environment for the pursuit of happiness by all people, and all of our projects began with research into the vernacular origins of the local architecture. An architecture of humanity can transcend cultural barriers, and can excel at promoting social discourse, making is possible for people to be better able to deal with the psychological and practical demands of society. The onus is on architects and urban planners to connect the places they design. Crafting three-dimensional, physical space, built or unbuilt, begins with the recognition that people and the places they prefer to inhabit are expressions of an innate desire for a better life. The value of these artifacts cannot be measured or defined by a one-to-ten scale, or a sponsored online survey. Buildings and places stand their ground by embracing patterns of well-being in everyday life. We care about the people and places that care about us. We go back, again and again, to the places that help us appreciate life.

Architects who tell their clients that they can make a tall building sustainable are full of shit. Their portfolios showcase LEED-rated buildings which are actually on life support. LEED is a private monopoly whose ratings are routinely awarded to buildings with typological birth defects, such as mega-tall high-rises. They vary only in their height and the corresponding size of the life support systems that force air into the lungs of the people inside. Developers can earn award "points" for installing the most energy-efficient, intensive care equipment on the market. Manufacturers who sell this equipment advertise: "We are your best source for "LEED endorsable" heating, ventilation and air-conditioning equipment." This is like asking a Covid patient if they know anybody who could provide a "better" incubator. But a higher-tech ventilator only prolongs the agony.

The ecstasy for new owners of LEED Platinum status buildings is short-lived. One of my clients bragged about his company's LEED-rated consumer palace (I was not the architect) until he got his first round of utility bills. LEED should really be meting out warnings, not awards, to dealers, proponents, advocates, and addicts of the uncontrollable, unsustainable, environmentally destructive, direct and side-effects of ubiquitous, indoor, hermitically sealed, multi-level shopping malls, hotel, and office with expansive atriums. The spoils of the wars raging between the world's tallest building and largest mall competitor, should be confiscated by UN-backed Blue Helmets and turned over to the World Wildlife Fund. A LEED Award banquet invitation should headline with a menu of boiled fish heads and rice laced with MSG. Abalone and tiramisu should be reserved for disqualified, ineligible losers. The open-air promenades and al fresco dining rooms of places like Xintiandi are ineligible for LEED award "points." Reducing a carbon footprint requires that you have one to reduce.

Considered trendy, smoking is on the rise among China's youth. Lung cancer kills by robbing the heart of oxygen. Oxygen supply for ubiquitous skyscrapers is supplied mechanically. A warning, "This building can kill you," should be prominently displayed in elevator lobbies of multi-storied structures without operable windows. An alarm should go off every time you push a number that will take you to a floor whose sole source of "fresh" air is "forced" air. A voice should come over the intercom: "You are about to enter an environment on life support. If this building experiences loss of electricity, the back-up generator may not be able to supply enough air-conditioning to keep you alive, much less in an acceptable zone of comfort. Do not waste valuable time looking for a fresh air rescue hatch, there are none."

But this is not the whole truth. If the elevators fail in a super-high rise, a walk down the fire stairs from a floor 600 meters off the ground will take hours, not minutes. On a summer's day, in one of China's "furnace cities," you will die from heat stroke, brought on by extreme hydration, before reaching the exit-to-the-street level.

Covid and a ban on "weird architecture" has sent all but a few of the Damned Yankees, and other sovereign carpetbaggers, packing. Good riddance and goodbye to this mostly male, highly educated, Ayn Rand-ish, dressed in all black, bunch of elites. In 2014, the Communist Party's Central Committee issued a directive that "oversized, egocentric, and weird" architecture, devoid of cultural tradition, should be rejected in favor of buildings that are more "suitable, economic, green, and pleasing to the eye."

Over the last past two decades based in Shanghai, I have developed a lot of techniques and a lot of solutions as to how to take an older district and create new opportunities not only for existing businesses but also for start-up businesses people who want to open a restaurant or a small shop. A truly successful neighborhood has to be unique, a vibrant place which will also attract people from other neighborhoods. Landlords and tenants of the buildings can contribute their own ideas on what will help bring people into the shops and restaurants. Beyond the facade of the buildings is the core of how people live, and in my world that means social equality.

When you're designing buildings, there are different kinds of building personalities that determine how the buildings are used. The role of the architect is to create architecture of joy. I like to think of my work as the architecture of humanity, with everything project feeding somehow off my experience in life.

In architecture, knowing "how" builds a sustainable, environment, "who" doesn't matter and "why" is a given. I was once a part of an expert panel discussion on the topic of Urbanization before an audience of a thousand Tongji University students in Shanghai, and my talk was entitled "Pick a Rule and Break It." I was referring to government urban development regulations, but did include the caveat, "Make sure the rule is not ideological in origin." I have won major competitions for clients and held on to my sanity by following this rule, and kept my Work Visa by following the caveat. My two co-panelists were Tongji University Executive Vice President Wu Jiang and real estate company Vanke's founder Wang Shi, two of China's most famous city shapers, one a lifelong public servant and academic, the other a powerful Chinese real estate developer. Both got the job done because they knew that inventions, not interventions, would lead to better cities. One helped make the rules, and if you had a better idea, he let you break the rules. The other knew that helping, by example, was critical to financial success. People do not bite the hand that feeds them. So, students, take a sad song and make it better. Let the city into your heart. And ideas that may seem a little crazy will keep you from being afraid, too afraid to change the world.

Ubiety is the opposite of Ubiquity. Ubiety in Latin is "loci locus," two fancy words for "hooked on place." Creating ubiety requires a deep understanding of a project's cultural, geophysical, and environmental context. Ubiety reflects the specificity and authenticity of a community's cultural evolution.

Ubiety is a site-specific reality. A non-transferable, non-virtual, non-fractious asset, ubiety is not a "one-size fits all" proposition. No two sites are the same. Devoid of any sense of belonging, "signature" buildings differ only in degrees of ubiquity, relying on academic theory, or metaphor-based, machinations to attract attention. Here today, gone tomorrow.

Architectural firms lose their ability to create ubiety in direct proportion to the number of professionals they employ. The bigger the firm, the more they copy, cheat, or steal designs from other architects. Any hope of achieving ubiety is problematic when plagiarism's fog lifts over the wrong valley. The websites of many large firms are rife with claims of authorship for exemplar projects in which they were only peripherally, or sometimes not at all, involved. Unethical conduct from bulimic firms with too many mouths to feed. When an English Pointer bitch has more pups than teats, she must turn a blind eye to litter equality.

Arriving at a design philosophy based on "an architecture of humanity" was my deliverance, my source of eunoia. Humane architecture has set me and my Shanghai colleagues free to explore phenomena, not abstract ideas. For visitors to one of our finished projects, the experience begins before they go inside a building. We must spend more time than any other architecture firm in the world designing the space between our buildings. Our outdoor spaces are pregnant with ever-changing natural light and ventilation. A full canopy of trees covers all but the narrowest of alleys. We want our visitors' field of vision to be filled with an orchestral landscape of motionless sound and moving color. We want their eyes wide shut, waiting for a lover's embrace, or an erotic glance from a stranger.

Built form that fosters social diversity and equality never shouts, "look at me." Signature styles and formal, abstract, machinations may bring architects fame and fortune, but they do not make the world a better place. Shouts should come from the people in the streets, not from the buildings that line them. Rare is the architect who can put aside their own ego to join their clients in the street, on the "other side," shouting.

Exploring a Tuscany hill town, a nomadic encampment in Inner Mongolia, a remote village perched high on a terraced stone Himalayan mountainside, or wandering through a ghost town on the edge of the Gobi Desert, is sublime. I have visited all but one of China's provinces. Countless trips on foot, horseback, jeep, mountain bike, off-road motorcycle, and white-water raft have transported me across five continents. I take photographs of everything and the best images are of non-pedigree architecture and humanitarian infrastructure taken early in the morning or just before sunset. At first light, when only a few people are outside their homes, the shadows are longer, the colors brighter, and the textures more legible.

Experiencing the eunoia inherent in vernacular forms is like discovering the trick behind a master of illusion's magic. Basking under an event horizon of sun, shade, and shadow, the "other side" of architecture is for ordinary people leading ordinary lives. People centric champions and their benefactors give the world idiosyncratic, individual expressions of truth and beauty. A few of this genre's primo gender form-givers: Bernard Rudofsky, Frank Lloyd Wright, Luigi Nervi, Renzo Piano, Frank Gehry, Carlos Scarpa, and Herzog and de Meuron.

Sadly, many of my fellow practitioners, never take this "other side" seriously. They believe ordinary is ordinary. Nothing more, nothing less. Their work is a life-long pursuit of signature styles lifted from preciously fashionable, encrypted lexicons. Bespoke infatuations with formal manipulations define their individual, self-referential pedigrees. They deride the "other side" as the arch enemy of style. Their enemy has always been my most fertile ground for new ideas, new inspiration. Next time you are in one of those beautifully ordinary places pick up a small stone or a bit of loose dirt. It's not theory, it's not ideology. In your hand is the spirit of the world around you. Ask any farmer. Or any potter. Or any carpenter, stone, or brick mason. Or any naked woman covered in earth.

Making places for people of all ages and flavors to meet other people both indoors and out involves a host of professional disciplines including interior design, landscape and streetscape design, and graphic design. Thirty-five years experience in venue design has taught me one very important principal: the individual subjectivity inherent in design aesthetics can be a source of great energy.

Aesthetics are defined by the choices an architect makes. I do not believe less is more. I believe more is more. The more choices you are able to give people, the more people you will attract. Human scale must be evident everywhere: in the color and texture of materials, in the way form and space inform movement, and in the way our senses are engaged by things they can see and touch and feel.

The diversity of site and culturally specific experiences play an important role in defining the intrinsic character of a particular building or place.

My graduate studies at MIT were focused on architecture, not urban planning. But I have been studying life my whole life. It doesn't matter how often it happens but, when a complete stranger says "hello" to me in a public place it always "makes my day" a better one. I have noticed that the "hello" comes most often when I am on a busy shopping street and have paused to look into the same window at the same time as the stranger. The frequency of phenomena goes up almost exponentially with an increase in the number of window and doors that open onto the street. This notion is backed up by numerous books and articles deal with different types of public spaces and their corresponding quantity and quality of social discourse. You are at least a hundred times more likely to chance an encounter with a stranger and exchange words on a busy shopping street that you are when walking alone on a block with no doors or windows facing the street. A stranger sharing the sidewalk but going in the opposite direction will almost always avoid eye contact with you. People are attracted to people. They walk slower when there are other people stopping to look into windows or entering shops. In my studio we have a rule of thumb when designing active streets: a mimimum of ten entry doors flanked by large windows for every 300 feet of sidewalk. Double that number if there are shops on both sides of the street.

In our studio there is a large city map. It is the Nolli Map of Rome which dates back to the 16th Century. Space inside the buildings of Rome which can be rendered private is depicted in solid dark grey. Publicly accessible space, both inside and outside buildings, is blank white. As you all know, the Noli Map is a "figure-ground" map. The "connectivity" of an urban fabric is measured by how often and in what ways is the unbuilt "ground," the public space, defined by the built-form, the "figure" of private space. We always begin a project involving public space by doing scale comparisons between the figure-ground of our conceptual design with different places on the Noli Map. Reference to this wonderful and often poetic experiential matrix of squares and streets helps keep us "in scale."

Many people who study social relationships consider Rome one of the world's greatest places for understanding public space. We are, as a species, an average of 5 foot 8 or 9 inches high. Our view of a place is "horizontal" in nature. We can detect human movement at a distance of 300 feet. But we can only begin to interact socially and use facial expressions at much closer distances. That is why blocks that are not interrupted by lively activities at least every 300 feet become virtual "deserts" devoid of life. Monumental public squares like the famous Tiananmen in Beijing can only be made lively by forced participation or the machinations of social unrest.

Better to build softly with the right architect, carry a big stick when fording mountain streams, and pick mushrooms, not fights, with your neighbors.

BENJAMIN WOOD

Naked All in White with Delphine 2018

30

Naked with Delphine

In 1983, I went to Los Angeles for the second time. The first time was during my first (and last) year of Law School at the University of Colorado in Boulder. While in Law School, I earned money playing bass guitar in a rock band. One weekend, I ended up in Durango and met a gorgeous girl from LA at the party where our band played. Next day, after finally waking up sometime after lunch, I offered to drive her home. Twelve hours later we drove up to her apartment. I do not remember the next few days at all, but I know it must have involved a great deal of sex, drugs, and rock-n-roll.

By the time I got back to LA, the Vietnam War was over and I was an architect. I had a client who had bought a large chunk of land in Westwood Village. He was a young man from Japan who had inherited several hundred million dollars. He picked me up at the airport in a new Ferrari convertible. We drove around Westwood for a couple of hours and he said he would put me up at the Bel-Air Hotel.

We drove up to the Hotel's entrance on Stone Canyon Road in the yellow Ferrari convertible. The "entrance" was a young woman standing under a large outdoor umbrella, in her hand a black notebook. The Bel-Air's flack catcher was a very attractive young woman. Undoubtably an actress wanna-be. Who crossed the bridge to Stone Canyon's paradise was solely up to her.

She asked my name and then told me she could not find my reservation. I guess driving a yellow Ferrari, my client thought we could just do a walk-in. Not going to happen. She said she was willing to try and get us in. The hotel was not full, but that was not the issue. She then escorted us to her office just on the other side of a footbridge across a pond full of swans. She asked me questions like had I ever stayed there before? What did I do for a living? Who was this Japanese kid? Did I have any references who were regular Bel-air customers? Bottom line, if you cannot come up with something better than arriving in a Crazy Rich Asian's supercar, you're not getting in.

I had met an Indy 500 winner through a Boulder, Colorado developer at a party in Aspen a few months earlier. I remembered he had a house in Brentwood. He was not movie star level but close enough. I still had his card in my wallet. I called him and got his wife on the phone who agreed to talk to the Bel-air lady. She got me in, and a few minutes later, I was ensconced in my very first super luxury boutique hotel room (a garden suite with private entrance, patio, and outdoor Jacuzzi). Later that night, she called me and said she would leave her backyard pool gate open and invited me to come over and join her for Jacuzzi and drinks.

The world's best hotels are more than a collection of well-appointed rooms, gourmet restaurants, sumptuous spas, champagne, and candlelight. Great hotels are places where some of the most extraordinary events in the lives of some of this planet's most interesting people begin and sometimes end. John Carradine died in a hotel room in Bangkok, and John Belushi died of an overdose in my favorite LA digs, the Chateau Marmont on Sunset Boulevard. Bobby Kennedy died of gunshot wounds in the service corridor of the Ambassador Hotel, home of the original Cocoanut Grove Lounge. Couples in much of the world usually spend their first night married in a hotel, but of course illicit affairs far outnumber these legally licensed intercourses. What happens in hotel rooms can make or unmake lives. Martin Luther King was shot on a balcony of his hotel room in Montgomery Alabama and designer Coco Channel made the Hotel Ritz in Paris her home for more than thirty years until the day of her death at 87. Many of the most creative writers, actors, and singers of the 20th Century spent years living at the Chelsea in New York, Bob Dylan, Leonard Cohen, and Robert Di Niro among them. Chelsea-based writers include Mark Twain, O. Henry, Dylan Thomas, Arthur C. Clarke, William S. Burroughs, Arthur Miller, Jack Kerouac, Jean-Paul Sartre, and Thomas Wolfe. The caliber and character of this cast is self-evident and if you stay at the Chelsea, the Chelsea stays with you, part of your life story.

My original design partner in Studio Shanghai was Delphine Yip, a native of Hong Kong. Her parents sacrificed everything so that she and her sister could attend private Catholic schools. Delphine went to Harvard University on an academic scholarship and then went on to earn a Master's in Architecture from Harvard's Graduate School of Design, the GSD. Her first job was with Carlos and I in our Boston studio.

Delphine is an amazing woman, blessed with natural beauty and an extraordinary mind. When she asked if we could design a resort for her husband, I told her about my Stone Canyon experience. Her husband Grant Horschfeld is a native of South Africa, a former male model and semi-pro-golf player, he is a blue-blooded, out-of-Africa thoroughbred stud who looks and thinks like a young Richard Branson.

As an architect, urban planner, and collaborator in the Studio, she became a pre-eminent role model for colleagues. Quite apart from my own, she earned her own reputation for excellence in design. I am reminded of a comment made by the famous war correspondent Martha Geller, for ten years a collaborator with Ernest Hemingway: "I have not the intention of being a footnote in someone else's life." This is quintessential Delphine. Take note, Grant.

Delphine is my heroine. She is my Beryl Markham. Beryl was the first person, man, or woman, to fly across the Atlantic solo east to west. Her book, *Westward with the Night*, puts you in the single seat cockpit with her piloting a tiny, single-engine plane west in darkness over open ocean for seventeen hours. Hemingway said Beryl was the only person in the world who could write better than him. He called her a first-class bitch. I am not a betting man, but this slur can only be in reference to her unwillingness to bed him. Delphine was surely not an easy catch.

Grant and Delphine built Naked Stables and Reserve, a whole shit-and-caboodle world-class, back-to-nature resort in a Moganshan valley three hours from Shanghai. Naked's centerpiece is a ménage, a horse-riding outdoor arena with thatched roof, rammed earth, roundels, and glass-sliding Miesian cottages wearing stilts, and a bridge over-water "frikaans" dining room and wine bar. A walk beside the Valley's brook, flanked by slopes of tea plants and bamboo jungle, serves nature's breakfast, lunch, and dinner, naked.

For the first two years, Naked's patrons were predominately expats escaping Shanghai for a weekend of intrigue, suspense, betrayal, mystery, madness, and requited love. But soon Chinese discovered that "back to nature" was a novel experience and came in droves bringing along parents, grandparents, children, and friends.

After Naked Stables, Delphine gave Grant a Scottish castle high on a mountain top in Moganshan. Delphine knows well another castle in China. A famous fairy, Tinker Bell, lives in Shanghai Disney World's version of Neuschwenstein. Studio Shanghai, under Delphine's superb direction, designed the majority of non-gated attractions outside the Theme Park's turnstiles.

Last I heard, Delphine and Grant were sailing around the world, home schooling three wonderful daughters. I hope these young women grow up remembering their Uncle Ben, who loved making them blueberry buttermilk pancakes, smothered in butter, swimming in maple syrup.

But by then, my design partner Delphine and her husband Grant had offered China's resort industry a Magna Carta for transformative change. The NAKED Resort is the cause célèbre for cultural climate conservation activists and for advocates of non-destructive, semi-orchestrated, outdoor adventure. Local culture and natural wildlife habitat are priceless. Spell it NAKED, NATURE, or EUNOIA, and it is the birds that are singing in the sky and the people shouting in the village streets who deliver us all a sense of well being.

31

A Message in a Bottle

In 2016, I created a series of collages entitled Visible Transformations. The concept was that the Human City is imperfect, defined by dreams, shaped by time, measured by the improbable. We live in these dystopias and they live in us. Though technology changes dramatically and continuously, human beings do not. For thousands of years people lived in homes they built for themselves. Today they do not. Designed by professionals, built by real estate developers, approved by governance, a roof over your head is today marketed and sold like a commodity, not a home.

People were created to be loved. Things were created to be used. Why is the world engulfed by chaos? Because things are being loved and people are being used. The future of the Human City is what we imagine it to be. Will it be a city of Despair or of Love? The answer is blowing somewhere in the wind of a modern life.

Visible Transformations was a collection of 3-dimensional "city" collages of discarded and "found" objects. None were objects of art, or at least not intended as such, dominated by an elephant's head which was a life size, a 3D, animatronic, sculpture made of latex. Lighting effects included various professional photography studio lights, a ground fog machine, a sky fog machine, various LED disco lights, a semi-spherical ceiling mirror, and a compressed-air confetti machine. The installation was enclosed by a black box "tent" measuring 4m x 4m x 3m.

Today, a portion of the the Visible Transformation 3-D collage survives as part of The Little Shop of Curios, a shopfront just a few doors away from my office entrance in Xintiandi. It's not open because the space is not registered for retail operations, but everything inside is visible from the street, and it is a wild mixtures of unlikely artifacts. The Elephant is there in the company of a very cool motorbike, and two of the best-made axes made in the United States. The axes are perhaps a veiled reference to the pioneering spirit that built America, and a reminder to the Chinese government that they should not forget that it was agriculture and the hard work of peasants that provided China with a way out of the age of feudalism. The axes were part of my exhibition entitled "Design Without Designers" featuring items made during the Great Urbanization, all made by people who still think people should be loved and things should be used. The desire for a new apartment and a BMW, a luxury handbag, a vacation abroad should not change that. Discover the power of your own imagination so you too can beat the odds and make life worth living—that was the message. Life is life, fun is fun, but it all goes quiet when the last goldfish dies. And lay off the selfies.

You are welcome to look around. Sorry if it is a bit of a mess. It is hard to throw anything away. Where is my mother when I need her? Without asking, she went and died on me a few years back. But not before she taught me that life, against all odds, is worth living.

A war baby from the Deep South and who flew a spy plane in the

Cold War, I am cursed and blessed with life for life: Cursed with a life of trying to explain the unexplainable and finding answers to the unanswerable, blessed with a life of cultivated serendipity which led me to architecture and mastery of the tools to create my own deliverance. And to avail myself of the goodwill and determination of extraordinary patrons to make this planet better than I found it.

Before America was rocked by the anti-war and civil rights movements of the mid-1960's, a Beat generation of writers, filmmakers, artists, musicians, and poets had already opened the door for a war-baby generation of hippies, activists, and heroes and heroines of social equality—to help Congress bring an end to the War in Vietnam and pass the first Civil Rights Act since Emancipation. Three generations later, America is more divided than it has ever been since the Civil War. On a radically different heading than the American mainstream, both the far left and the far right between them appear to be ripping America apart. Despite it all, America remains the Shining City on a Hill, but at the same time, our social safety net and the constitutional rights guaranteed every citizen need a major overhaul.

The US Constitution has been amended only once in the last fifty years. The 27th Amendment, ratified in 1992, dealt with the timely payment of salaries for congressional representatives. Over the last century, only two amendments providing additional guarantees of fundamental democratic values have made it past Congress. The oldest gave women the right to vote, and the other, in 1971, prohibits denying the right to vote to anyone eighteen or older. The rest of the Amendments in this hundred-year span read like a pilot's aircraft emergency check list: if shit happens, don't panic, just clean it up, step-by-step. For the world's largest democracy, this is an impressively dismal, pathetic and appalling score card. The low-hanging fruit of systemic gerrymandering, the Electoral College, needs to be addressed with a 28th Amendment. Responsible parents do not let kids play with matches.

I have been dealing with the consequences of ignorance and inequality from the day I was born. I will never understand why there were no Black children aboard the Yellow School Bus. Pride and prejudice are strange bedfellows in every society's struggle for human dignity. Black, white, brown, yellow, naked-in, naked-out, in the Dragon's Mouth or the Deep South, we all face the same end.

Respect others, but also respect yourself. I beg you: find ways to outrun the void-of-personality, nihilistic, social media rat race to distribute falsified, photo-shopped images in a vain effort to provide proof of your individual identity. Before it is too late, re-capture the social currency of eye-to-eye dialogue and bilateral discourse and governance. Do not fall victim to selfish, hedonistic behavioral models. Kick the habit of one-way vicarious experiences with money-grubbing, vacuous opinion leaders. Encourage corporate movers and shakers around the world to drop out of contention for branding a record number of unsustainable tall buildings. Ask architects, desperate for fame, to take time to reflect on what is more important, style or substance? Symbolic forms or architectural well-being? Romance the beauty and the joy of living. Slow dance with an architecture of humanity.

Look into the "Selfie Dish." Nothing is sacred. Voyeuristically correct and suitable for social media distribution, take-away selfies are like fake silicone breasts and vodka martinis: three is too many and one is never enough. When I was growing up, my mother told me that taking your own picture was something reserved for the vain, superficial, and self-indulgent.

Today, the young women and men, single or married, visiting

the bar devote almost all their attention to the surrogate realities in the palm of their hands. The women drag rollercases with extra outfits to ensure all their selfies don't look like they were taken on the same day. Young men brighten their selfies with lipstick bought from Tom Ford or Valentino. But a bit of news for all young dudes and dudettes: you cannot pick flowers while riding a horse. Technologically advanced media shod with networked, transplanted, prosthetic, cosmetic, silicone hooves—it's still a galloping horse. On the flip side of 24/7 social networking, a whole world of au-natural, sensually erotic adventures await you.

Climate change is here, not coming across the rye. Driverless cars, impossible beef, carbon credit markets, block chains, crypto currencies, and other scarecrows of technology are not going to keep the varmints out of the henhouse. Genetically modified corn-raised livestock is not going to keep polar ice from melting or stop the waters from rising. Only people, by changing the way we live, can arrest the deadly, entropic demise of our sun-screened blue and green earth.

The need for social and racial equality, like climate change and pandemics, is not subject to cultural or geo-political boundaries. Nor is the need for humane architecture. No one should ever be made to feel unequal or humbled by monumental works of architecture. Absolute power corrupts absolutely. When used as a symbol of power, architecture corrupts. And, in turn, the architecture itself is corrupted. Free of corruption, architecture can be beautiful: the kind of beauty that comes not from style but from substance. Form should follow function. Any good building must first serve the purpose for which it was built. Rarely is any single form perfect. A simple black dress can take many forms and still be a simple black dress. Gloria Vanderbilt and Princess Grace Kelly were elegant even in the most basic of black dresses.

These two women chose substance over style for each and every occasion.

Campaigns for public office focus on group-grope base appeal. Cheered on by dogmatic, incompetent replicants, political candidates sling hash-tagged, branded anthologies at town hall meetings of undecided voters, neoliberals and ultra-right storm troopers alike. Mix this dog's breakfast of bull with the rants of fogged-in, life-coached, myopic, head-spaced evangelists living in a Zuckerberg-controlled metaverse and you get "eyes in the headlight" candidates fixated by teleprompters on an indigestible, unchecked, mumbled, jingle jungle of jargon and jism. The danger of a complete moral meltdown by the un-decided and stillborn is clear and present.

The optics alluded to in the previous paragraph are meant to be vivid, vulgar, and repulsive. Deliberately coarse, this diatribe is my "Lest we forget" remembrance of the dark gravitas of a system which is in danger of takeover by the unjust and the inhumane, murderous sycophants and those consciously complicit in spreading the Big Lie.

China, a much older country and culture, has its strengths and its weaknesses, just like America. The country is now in a foundational period, and everyday decisions are being made that will shape the future of the world's most populous country, for this century and beyond. For China's city builders, architects, and urban planners, the challenge and the opportunity is there, and to a remarkable extent it is being grasped and humane architecture is gradually replacing cosmetic magazine-cover designs. An architecture of humanity has begun to transform the landscape of the Middle Kingdom's urban environs visibly, materially, and spiritually. From a people-centric, culturally focused approach to architecture come the building blocks of China's Yellow Brick Road to prosperity and social equality.

Whenever I see another block of Shanghai's historic, human scale, human-friendly, urban fabric vanish into thin air, I am reminded of another stark contrast, that between Sherman's Civil War March through the South and the Long March of China's Communists. Sherman's campaign was a "to the victor goes the spoils" progress. It was meant as an apocalyptic, self-righteous round-up. On their way across the Mason-Dixon Line to Savannah, Sherman's troops pillaged and burned everything that could be used to rebuild the South. Sherman's "leave nothing behind," scorched-earth victory march led to extreme poverty in a post-Civil War, defeated South. Left with nothing, far too many white farm owners, attorneys, doctors, bankers, accountants, schoolteachers, gin-millers, masons, grocers, pharmacists, morticians, livery owners, and innkeepers descended into an ugly abyss of racial prejudice that persists to this day.

The Long March marked the beginning of an ideological revolution. Post-Cultural Revolution, block-by-block wholesale relocation, and redevelopment of China's blighted urban neighborhoods did not lead to extreme economic disparity. It led to severe social dislocation, and the collapse of the neighborhood support systems that were the heart of Chinese life in villages and cities. But the money raised by selling "land use" permits to real estate developers has funded trillions upon trillions of dollars worth of infrastructure improvements. The fastest urbanization in the history of civilization has led the most populous country in the world to the brink of having the world's largest economy. In less than forty years, China has gone from a predominantly agrarian society to an urban and urbane giant industrial complex and consumer machine, both supplying cheap goods for the rest of the world and producing first-world technologically advanced products.

Today China's economy has slowed. But this downturn has not stopped potential clients, often with more money than intellect, from approaching us. I have a few rules. One is to listen politely, even if a potential client lacks any semblance of intellectual sophistication. You have to first want to make a place better than you found it. Only then can you begin to understand the value that humane, human-scaled architecture brings to the table. For about an hour, I extend them the benefit of the doubt. When they have made it perfectly clear they prefer to stick with a tried and true, relentless pursuit of idiosyncratic, Pavlov's dog, wow-factor, one-liners, I bid them adieu.

To my astonishment, one came back years later. He asked if we could work together, confessing he had ended up with a project that was neither beautiful nor practical. Both he and his "signature" architect made money. The visually arresting podium and twin tower design proved easy to market, and sold out almost overnight. He had reserved the two penthouses for his family and the family of a close friend. His friend paid in cash and never moved in. Most of his apartment buyers were speculators. Turned out his friend fell into this category. His wife decided she preferred their old neighborhood and friends over status. He sold his penthouse to an eager speculator.

The commercial podium enjoyed a couple of years of success but then went downhill when a bigger mall opened next door. Today, both malls are virtually uninhabited. And we are working together on an open-air, people-centric, culturally-focused, mixed-used community next to a new bullet train station in Nanjing.

Being first, being perfect, spells the end for change. I want to live in a city that is in second place, a city that never stops changing, a city on the move to a better place. All of us in Shanghai deserve to live enraptured with a richly diverse, evolving urban fabric of old and new neighborhoods. We deserve a Shanghai where every urban community is a city within a city, every block a town within a town, and every building a place to live, work, and play. This rape of Shanghai must end. Ban super-block development, take down the walls, and open the gates.

Ironically, insular residential compounds, have received a new lease on life. China's Zero-Covid policies are infinitely easier to police in a city of 27 million people when the largest demographic, the middle class, resides inside gated urban communities surrounded by walls topped with four strands of electrified barbed wire.

In architecture, humane invention should never be confused with human intervention. A humane building envelops, nurtures, and shelters the spirit. My story of the trip to the bottom of a Colorado canyon, with three friends, is about human deliverance. The choices and actions made that hot summer evening, by a naked woman covered in earth, belonged to her. She chose from a world of phenomena, not abstract ideas. She chose innocence over guilt. She did not shout out in fear and loathing. She did not look away. Instead, she but raised her head and embraced humanity. She wanted me to understand her, not stare at her. In the moments I watched the naked woman in Colorado, we were two people crossing a bridge to meet on the "other side." We put our trust in each other. Driving to the milk truck, she said her husband was a third-generation rancher. He was in Denver for a few days and left her with a loaded shotgun. The gun was in the same shed where she had left her jeans. The heightened receptivity we felt in those few moments set us both free.

The noble servants in architecture are the designers who care more about people and less about fame and fortune. Being good at the former does not preclude the latter. But reversing the order has bitten many a young architect in the ass. Pedigree architecture is a primrose path. Any meanings inherent in the work of a signature designer become superficial stylistic differences when subjected to cross-cultural translations.

One of the first things an apprentice carpenter learns is how not to end up with a board too short. "Cut once, measure twice" are words to live by. To see far, fly higher. Situational awareness, and creative responses, are the mothers of a prime mover's invention. Necessary intervention can be achieved using grace and compassion. Make your success look easy. And if, after reading this book, you are not convinced that serendipity can be cultivated, ask Vincent Lo, Dan Gao and Michelle Garnaut. Or ask my sister, my brother, my daughter, my son, or any of my other hero-heroines. I can count on one hand the people who have truly changed my life. It doesn't take hundreds or dozens of clients to make or break a creative pursuit, and it only takes a few people to change the world. It is people who change the world, not politics, not religion, not ideology, not legislation, but individuals with inspiration and a will to make the world a better place.

Our survival as a species is irreconcilably linked to the human condition. Our ability to reason is unique to humankind. We are not born good or evil—neither is a given, neither *a priori*. Our earliest experiences can tip the scale in either direction, and so can the built environments in which we are born, live, procreate, and die.

My daughter

In Edgartown, Massachusetts, on the island of Martha's Vineyard, the On Time Ferry takes drive-ons and walk-ons back-and-forth to neighboring Chappaquiddick Island. During the peak tourist season, dozens of drive-on's wait their turn for a twenty-minute maritime trek on On Time: ten minutes to fill a one-lane belly, walk-on's last, then ten minutes to cross over to the other side. On Time is always on time. No schedule is posted. For propulsion, a mechanical arm latches onto an underwater slow-moving cable that propels the boat across a narrow Lagoon to Chappy and back. Simple and low tech, On Time is like being pulled up a baby ski slope by a slip-slidin' away tow rope. What's the point? The point is we are all on our own On Time magic sleigh no matter where we are. Ride it for all its worth. Use your intellect and curiosity to weave a thick carpet of cultivated serendipity. In the words of the Summer of Love gang, take it easy, go greasy.

Jane Lipton-Cafritz and her daughter in Shanghai

My daughter helped me host a trip to Shanghai by Jane Lipton-Cafritz and her daughter, Today Jane has joined that small group of clients who are champions of the art of living and creators of living art.

In first world countries, where very few people design and build their own houses, real estate developers and their consultants, are, by default, the sole source of new human habitat. In this closed loop, decisions are seldom based on the real needs of a healthy society. I implore them to add extra weight to the scale in favor of a humane environment and to insist on a designer who has learned through observation and experience. The architect who espouses formal theory as the fundamental building block of design should not be hired. Seek an architect who has an in-depth understanding of the genius loci of local vernacular architecture, and bone up on historical precedent before entering the ring of modernity and advanced technology.

I urge China and all the world's urban planners and architects to make zero-carbon, environmentally friendly infrastructure ubiquitous. Invite governance to use an easy touch when ushering in the future. Board an "On Time Future" ferry loaded with healthy doses of cautious optimism. Put a love letter in a bottle for the survivors of humankind. Pray a mutant free, human comber, finds the bottle half-buried in the sand of an active tidal beach at the back end of this century.

Today we are living in a world preoccupied with grossly premature self-destruction. China is at the center of that world. The water is rising. No need to spend a fortune to go to space to see further. Wherever we are, we are here. We all arrived about the same time. When you shut your door, please leave **Now** better than you found it.

The future is what we imagine it to be. Imagine a future that brings us all back together. Imagine a time when all of humankind is again free to roam the planet in search of life's adventures.

Acknowledgements

My path has crossed with Movers, Shakers, Misfits, and Miscreants. Cultivating serendipity is made easier by crossing paths with people who see the world differently. Famous celebrities, infamous enemies, old and new friends, two obnoxious geniuses and one psychopath, in no particular order:

From the world community: Sister Mary Jo, Brother Jere, his wife Claudia, Eddie and Jeanette Chapman, Shirley Young, Jane Lipton-Cafritz and her husband Calvin, Carlos Zapata, Ben and Jane Thompson, Kurt Vonnegut, Norman Mailer, Studs Terkel, Don Gao, Han Feng, Sin Sin Man, Mick Jagger, Anthony Montalto, Stanton Englehart, Dennis Hopper, Lord March the Earl of Goodwood, Charlies and Kiera Morgan, Adam Clayton, Nancy Pelosi, Martin and Corabel Shofner, Peter Oldsberg, Simon Oldsberg, Scott Malkin, Brian Garrison, Jesse Jackson, Lois Conner, Ric and Jane Fulop, Steve Jobs, Herbert Muschamp, Blair Kamin, Annie Morita, Laurent Broda, Jean Pierre Heim, Melisa Koff, Tony Montalto, Craig Robbins, Patrick Lyons, Pete Burkheimer, Daryl Johnson, John and Megan Rosenthal, Les Otten, Maurice, Ben, and Maggie Smith, Stanford and Nancy Anderson, Brian Kesner, Stanton Englehart, Shun and Keiko Kanda, Bonnie Fogel, George Spano, Gerald and Nancy van Wessup, Harvey and Mary Finestein, Terrance Meehan, Tony Pritzker, Johann Rupert, Vivienne Tam, Graham Earnshaw, Bob Weiss, Bob Hagen, Carol Abreu Gassiert, Pamela Tang, Norman Foster, Evan Osnos, June and Andrew Flake, Colin Flavin, Fifi Kao, Steve Lovell, Scott Wilson, Sonja and Tom Hout, Andy and

Barbara Senchak, Mera and Don Rubell, Frank Gehry, Fredrick Balfour, Gerald Chan, Benoit Lesmonde, Sylvie Levy, Jiang (Zurich), Robert A.M. Stern, Miles White, Bill Faschon.

And from my dear Shanghai and greater Asia community: Francis Yum, Tim Addison, Christopher Shallis, Justin Jencks, Michelle Garnaut, Lorentz Heibling, William Wang, Tao Zhang, Emma Zhang, Edward Cai, Emma Gao, Eliza Wong, Ann Nui, Handel Lee, Walter Zahner, Harold, Eric and Chuk Wear, Wu Jiang, Dr Luo Xiao Wei, Wang Ling, Dave Barboza, Albert Winnington, Steve and Melissa, Dr Kathy Shi, Dr Qiu, Evelyn Zhang, Kay Kuo, Doctor Penguin, Christian Zentz, Harry and Mae Pang, Doris Woodward, Ben Snagler, Paul Pariet, Didi Pei, Malcom and Vicki Au, Jim Morrison, Mark Mobius, chef António, Dr Sun Jiwei, Wu Jiang, Mr Zhou, Guangzhou's Ms Sun Yue, Wuhan's Ms Tian Yan, CRRC's Ms Liao and Ms Nui, Jeffery Lehman, Xiao Ting, Robert Ching, Allan Zeman, Christian Rohmberg, Janet Yang, Chu Man Wong, Claude Wong, Frank Wu, and the beat goes on.........

And a very special thanks to six of the finest woman professionals in China: Dr Kathy Shi, Dr Qiu, Guangzhou's Ms Sun Yue, Wuhan's Ms Tian Yan, and CRRC's Ms Liao and Ms Nui.

And A Few More Words...

Dwight Law is a great friend, soulmate, and my collaborator on over a hundred stellar projects. Dwight, you deserve a great deal of credit for creating what I believe is an urban scape that has no equal on China's expanding, people-centric, culturally focused stage. Our mutual client, Shui On Land, has won five Urban Land Institute Awards of Excellence, and you and I designed four of these award winners. One of the most memorable events of my life was the honor of being the only non-family member present when you married an extraordinary Chinese-American woman. Forever young, I hope you both decide to stay in China. There is still a lot of important, big work to do here.

Career journalist Russell Flannery is another good friend and currently an "editor-at-large" for Forbes. Russell interviewed many of the people who helped me change China, and a plan to include these interviews in a book co-authored by Russell was abandoned after I decided to go the course alone. But it was Russell's unwavering support and encouragement that led to this book.

A Sort of Bibliography

To stay on point and remain motivated in writing this book, I drew on a host of literary, cinematic, artistic, musical, and governance Joshua Trees. And one Judas from an Ivy League Law School:

A Shout in the Street: The Modern City, Peter Jukes

Architecture of Happiness, Alain de Botton

Architecture Without Architects, Bernard Rudofsky

Animal Farm, George Orwell

Beauty and the Beast, Walt Disney

Cat's Cradle, Kurt Vonnegut

Deliverance, James Dickey

Don't Look Back, a 1967 Bob Dylan documentary, by D.A. Pennebaker

"Easy Like Sunday Morning," Lionel Ritchie

Every song he sang in our rental car on our two-week tour of Italy, Michael McCaskey

Flight of the Phoenix, 2004 remake starring Dennis Quaid

Field of Dreams, starring Kevin Costner

Genius Loci: Towards a Phenomenology of Architecture, Christian Norberg-Schultz

"Gettysburg Address," Abraham Lincoln

Gorbachev *Time Magazine* interview, Henry Grunwald

Goodwood Festival of Speed, Lord Goodwood the Earl of March

Governance in China, Volumes I, II, III, Xi Jinping

Hillbilly Elegy, J.D. Vance

"Imagine," John Lennon

Jericho the South Behold, Herbert Shuptrine and James Dickey

Jonathan Livingston Seagull and *Above the Clouds,* Richard Bach

Let Us Now Praise Famous Men, James Agee with Walker Evans

"Bird on the Wire," Leonard Cohen

"Like a Rolling Stone," Bob Dylan

Lost Horizon, James Hilton

Man In Full, Tom Wolfe

Maggie's Place, Scotland, a tribute of love, by land art sculptor, artist, and author Charles Jencks

"M.T.A.," Kingston Trio

Naked Lunch, William S. Burroughs

On the Road, Jack Kerouac

Out of Africa, a Sydney Pollack film, starring Meryl Streep and Robert Redford

Perfect Storm, the search for 72-foot Andrea Gailmy"Sending Out an SOS," Phoenix James

Silent Spring, Racheal Carson

"Slip Slidin' Away," Simon and Garfunkel

Stick and Rudder, Wolfgang Langewiesche

"Swing Low, Sweet Chariot," American South gospel song

"Take My Breath Away," from *Top Gun,* performed by new wave band Berlin

"The Beat Goes On," Sonny and Cher

The complete works of artist and sculptor James Turrell

The World Without Us, Alan Weismann

Trout Fishing in America, Richard Brautigan

The Death and Life of American Cities, Jane Jacobs

To Kill a Mockingbird, Harper Lee

To Kill a City, Robert Moskowitz

West with the Night, Beryl Markham

Que sera, sera.

About the Author

Benjamin Wood is an American architect born on a farm in Georgia in the country's Deep South. He flew F-4 Phantom fighter jets for five years in Europe during the Cold War before earning a Master of Architecture degree at MIT, since when he has designed a myriad projects, both in the United States and China. These include the Xintiandi area of Shanghai, completed in 2003, which in the words of one critic "reinvented the urban entertainment venue" by preserving and re-imagining Shanghai's old houses and alleyways with a "radical quaintness" which changed the city and China beyond. Since then, he and his team have completed over 200 projects in China, and an estimated 450 million people visit a Ben Wood-designed venue every year. At the end of 2022, he received the prestigious Magnolia Award from the Shanghai City Government in recognition of his contributions to enhancing the city's vitality. He believes the future can be what we imagine it to be.